'Right-wing extremism is taking [illegible] [illegible] [illegible] forms across the globe. *CasaPound Italia* is a brilliant [illegible] [illegible] how extremists can penetrate into the practices of daily life. A must-read for scholars, activists, and all those concerned about the spread of far-right ideas into contemporary politics'.

— *Kathleen Blee, University of Pittsburgh, USA*

'While scholars of contentious politics have mainly focused on progressive social movements, this in-depth analysis brilliantly applies the main concepts and hypotheses developed in that field of studies to the mobilization and communication of the extreme right in Italy. Based on very rich empirical material, the research points at how the adoption of a hybridization strategy allowed the ideas of CasaPound Italia into the political'.

— *Donatella Della Porta, Scuola Normale Superiore, Italy*

'How does a relatively small far right group, with little electoral support, attract international media attention and influence national politics? This book does not only provide the first systematic analysis of a prime example of such a group, CasaPound Italia, it also introduces a theoretical framework that can help us understand disproportionate successes of other (far right) groups'.

— *Cas Mudde, University of Georgia*

'Based on a historical and ethnographic approach, this book captures the essence of CasaPound Italia: hybridization. A unique mix of party politics and street protest, ideology and pop culture, left-progressiveness and nativism, CPI makes fascism entertaining and attractive, way beyond the traditional extreme right circles. A must-read'.

— *Nonna Mayer, Sciences Po,* CEE, CNRS, *France*

CASAPOUND ITALIA

In 2003, the occupation of a state-owned building in Rome led to the emergence of a new extreme-right youth movement: CasaPound Italia (CPI). Its members described themselves as 'Fascists of the Third Millennium', and were unabashed about their admiration for Benito Mussolini. Over the next 15 years, they would take to the street, contest national elections, open over a hundred centres across Italy, and capture the attention of the Italian public. While CPI can count only on a few thousand votes, it enjoys disproportionate attention in public debates from the media. So what exactly is CasaPound? How can we explain the high profile achieved by such a nostalgic group with no electoral support?

In this book, Caterina Froio, Pietro Castelli Gattinara, Giorgia Bulli and Matteo Albanese explore CasaPound Italia and its particular political strategy combining the organization and style of both political parties and social movements and bringing together extreme-right ideas and pop-culture symbols. They contend that this strategy of *hybridization* allowed a fringe organization like CasaPound to consolidate its position within the Italian far-right milieu, but also, crucially, to make extreme-right ideas routine in public debates. The authors illustrate this argument drawing on unique empirical material gathered during five years of research, including several months of overt observation at concerts and events, face-to-face interviews, and the qualitative and quantitative analysis of online and offline campaigns.

By describing how hybridization grants extremist groups the leeway to expand their reach and penetrate mainstream political debates, this book is core reading for anyone concerned about the nature and growth of far-right politics in contemporary democracies. Providing a fresh insight as to how contemporary extreme-right groups organize to capture public attention, this study will also be of interest to students, scholars and activists interested in the complex relationship between party competition and street protest more generally.

Caterina Froio is Assistant Professor in Political Science at Sciences Po (Centre for European Studies and Comparative Politics), and research associate at the C-Rex (University of Oslo, Norway). Her research and teaching interests are in political parties and their transformations as agents of representative government and as organizations, the relations between extremism and democracy, and e-politics. Since 2016, she is joint convenor of the European Consortium for Political Research (ECPR) Standing Group on Extremism and Democracy. Her research has appeared in peer-reviewed journals in various languages including *Party Politics*, *Perspectives on Politics* and the *Revue Française de Science Politique* and in several edited volumes, policy reports and media outlets.

Pietro Castelli Gattinara is Assistant Professor at the Centre for Research on Extremism, University of Oslo, Norway, and research associate at the Centre on Social Movement Studies, Scuola Normale Superiore, Florence, Italy. His research focuses on comparative politics, the far right and migration in Western Europe. He is currently leading a comparative research project on collective action against migration during the refugee crisis. He recently published *The Politics of Migration in Italy* (Routledge, 2016). His work related to public debate on the Charlie Hebdo attacks appeared on international peer-reviewed journals including *South European Societies and Politics* and the *British Journal of Politics and International Relations*.

Giorgia Bulli is Senior Research Fellow in Political Science at the University of Florence, Italy, where she teaches Political Communication, and Discourse Analysis. Her main research interests include the transformation of political parties and political movements in Europe in an organizational, political, cultural and communication strategy perspective. She has conducted extensive research in Germany, where she has held seminars on political communication and radical right parties and movements at the Humboldt University, Berlin.

Matteo Albanese is a post-doctoral fellow in contemporary history at the University of Padua, Italy. He works on transnational relationships between far-right organizations in Europe. His last book, *Transnational Fascism* (Bloomsbury, 2016) was awarded the ERICS prize by ICS and has been welcomed by the academic community as a cutting-edge text in the field of fascist studies. He has also published several articles in different top journals.

Routledge Studies in Fascism and the Far Right

Series editors: Nigel Copsey, *Teesside University*, and **Graham Macklin**, *Center for Research on Extremism (C-REX), University of Oslo.*

This new book series focuses upon fascist, far right and right-wing politics primarily within a historical context but also drawing on insights from other disciplinary perspectives. Its scope also includes radical-right populism, cultural manifestations of the far right and points of convergence and exchange with the mainstream and traditional right.

Titles include:

Trumping Democracy
From Ronald Reagan to Alt-Right
Edited by Chip Berlet

A.K. Chesterton and the Evolution of Britain's Extreme Right, 1933–1973
Luke LeCras

Cumulative Extremism
A Comparative Historical Analysis
Alexander J. Carter

CasaPound Italia
Contemporary Extreme-Right Politics
Caterina Froio, Pietro Castelli Gattinara, Giorgia Bulli and Matteo Albanese

The International Alt-Right
Fascism for the 21st Century?
Patrik Hermansson, David Lawrence, Joe Mulhall and Simon Murdoch

CASAPOUND ITALIA

Contemporary Extreme-Right Politics

Caterina Froio, Pietro Castelli Gattinara, Giorgia Bulli and Matteo Albanese

Routledge
Taylor & Francis Group
LONDON AND NEW YORK

First published 2020
by Routledge
2 Park Square, Milton Park, Abingdon, Oxon OX14 4RN

and by Routledge
52 Vanderbilt Avenue, New York, NY 10017

Routledge is an imprint of the Taylor & Francis Group, an informa business

British Library Cataloguing-in-Publication Data
A catalogue record for this book is available from the British Library

Library of Congress Cataloging-in-Publication Data
A catalog record has been requested for this book

ISBN: 978-0-367-43547-9 (hbk)
ISBN: 978-0-367-43549-3 (pbk)
ISBN: 978-1-003-00551-3 (ebk)

Typeset in Bembo
by Integra Software Services Pvt. Ltd.

CONTENTS

ILLUSTRATIONS

Maps

Figures

Tables

ABBREVIATIONS

Abbreviation	*Name*	*Translation*
AN	Alleanza Nazionale	National Alliance (Italy)
AvNa	Avanguardia Nazionale	National Vanguard (Italy)
BLU	Blocco Lavoratori Unitario	United Workers' Bloc (Italy)
BS	Blocco Studentesco	Student Bloc (Italy)
CPI	CasaPound/CasaPound Italia	The House of Pound (Italy)
CM	CasaMontag	The House of Montag (Italy)
DSA	Direct Social Actions	
ECB	European Central Bank	European Central Bank
EDL	English Defence League	English Defence League (United Kingdom)
EU	European Union	European Union
FdI	Fratelli d'Italia	Brothers of Italy (Italy)
FI	Forza Italia	Go Italy (Italy)
FN/RN	Front National/Rassemblement National	National Front/National Rally (France)
FzNv	Forza Nuova	New Force (Italy)
FT	Fiamma Tricolore	Tricolour Flame (Italy)
GD	Χρυσή Αυγή/Chrysí Avgí	Golden Dawn (Greece)
GRE	Gruppi di Ricerca Ecologica	Groups of Environmental Research (Italy)
GRECE	Groupement de Recherche et d'Études pour la Civilisation Européenne	Research and Study Group for European Civilization (France)
IPN	Il Primato Nazionale	The National Primacy (Italy)
LI	Les Identitaires	The Identitarians (France)
ISIL	Islamic State of Iraq and the Levant	Islamic State of Iraq and the Levant
LN	Lega Nord/Lega	Northern League/League (Italy)

(*Continued*)

(Cont.)

Abbreviation	*Name*	*Translation*
MSI	Movimento Sociale Italiano	Italian Social Movement (Italy)
MS-FT	Movimento Sociale-Fiamma Tricolore	Social Movement – Tricolour Flame (Italy)
M5S	Movimento 5 Stelle	Five Star Movement (Italy)
NA	National Action	National Action (United Kingdom)
NAR	Nuclei Armati Rivoluzionari	Armed Revolutionary Cores (Italy)
ND	Nouvelle Droite	New Right (France)
NDE	Nuova Destra	New Right (Italy)
ON	Ordine Nuovo	New Order (Italy)
PD	Partito Democratico	Democratic Party (Italy)
PDL	Il Popolo delle Libertà	The People of Freedom (Italy)
PEGIDA	Patriotische Europäer gegen die Islamisierung des Abendlandes	Patriotic Europeans Against the Islamisation of the Occident (Germany)
PNF	Partito Nazionale Fascista	National Fascist Party (Italy)
RRPP	Radical right populist party	
RSI	Repubblica Sociale Italiana/ Repubblica di Salò	Italian Social Republic
Sol.Id.	Solidarité Identités	Solidarity Identity (Italy)
TP	Terza Posizione	Third Position (Italy)
ZZA	ZetaZeroAlfa	Zed Zero Alpha (Italy)

ACKNOWLEDGEMENTS

This book is the result of a research project that started on the morning of 13 December 2011, when Gianluca Casseri, a 50-year-old accountant and sympathizer of CasaPound, drove to a crowded street market in Florence. There, he shot at a group of Senegalese market traders, killing Samb Modou and Diop Mor, before turning the gun on himself. Five days later, we joined twenty thousand people in the streets of the city to say no to racism. At that time, all of us lived in Florence, and all of us studied far-right politics and right-wing extremism, albeit from different angles. But none of us knew much about CasaPound. We knew it was a fringe group. We knew it claimed inspiration from historical Fascism. And we knew it operated by borrowing left-wing clothes. But none of us had an idea about what CasaPound really was on the 'inside'.

One of the first persons with whom we discussed this project was Hanspeter Kriesi, whose comments the theory of this book owes much: 'Why do you do this? They are *irrelevant*.' This pushed us to scratch our heads and start thinking what 'irrelevance' meant. The reason we studied CasaPound was not because we thought that Fascism was about to win elections or to come back. Rather, we wanted to explore how a group with no electoral support and inspired by 'old' ideas does politics at a time when the role of ideologies and conventional forms of political activism are dissolving. This took us on a long journey of over five years, during which we travelled across Italy, from north to south, and got to know places, people and ideas distant from our usual political horizons. We hung out at the headquarters, parking lots, concerts, bookstores, squats and demonstrations to study CPI and its activists: their ideas, fantasies, activities, clothing and music tastes. In this respect, we are thankful to the members of CPI who accepted to participate in our study, agreed to talk with us and let us enter their world. This work owes a lot to the insights provided by the interviewees (those who accepted being recorded and those who refused), but it has also benefited from the many exchanges with colleagues and friends who supported us during the writing.

In an increasingly profit-oriented academic world, this study on a small extreme-right group would simply not have come into being without the intellectual curiosity and support of Craig Fowlie and of the series editors Nigel Copsey and Graham Macklin. We are thankful to all of them and to Routledge for their trust. We are also indebted to many colleagues who helped us rethink our impressions and challenge our own assumptions, and notably to Marco Tarchi who never spared bold but constructive feedback on the project. This work owes much to Pauline Picco, Andrea Pirro, Anath Ariel de Vidas, Samuel Bouron, Marc Lazar, Nonna Mayer, Nicolas Sauger, Benedetta Voltolini, Hugo Meijer and Emilien Houard-Vial because they always found the time to discuss and comment on the manuscript. During these years, we were also able to present and discuss our work in various research environments; our colleagues at the C-Rex in Oslo, the European Consortium for Political Research (ECPR) Standing Group on Extremism and Democracy, the *Groupe d'études pluridisciplinaires sur l'Italie contemporaine* (GREPIC) Italian politics group and the *Centre d'études européennes et de politique comparée* (CEE) at Sciences Po, believed in the project even more than we did, and allowed us to present early and incomplete versions of this manuscript. If we had been able to take into account all the comments we received from our colleagues over the past years, this book would be more interesting, challenging and complete than it currently is. We are also grateful to our semiologist Alberto Caselli for the design of the paperback cover of the book. He always found a clear image for our (less clear!) ideas and intuitions. We also thank those who will find the time to read this book and will not spare us their comments. As authors, we are solely responsible for any mistakes in the volume.

1

CASAPOUND ITALIA: HYBRIDIZATION IN THE CONTEMPORARY EXTREME RIGHT[1]

> The reference to Fascism is fundamental. We do not put fasces everywhere and we will not always quote Mussolini but if you have not read *The Doctrine of Fascism* and you come here [*to CPI*], you are out of place. You can go around and put up CPI's posters, but you are doing it wrong. The link with Fascism is total.
>
> *Simone di Stefano, deputy president of CPI, Rome 2012*

As shown by the above quote, CasaPound Italia (CPI) makes no secret of its appreciation of Benito Mussolini's regime. Since its birth on 26 December 2003 with the occupation of a state-owned building in Rome, this fringe group rapidly expanded to other parts of Italy acquiring national relevance and eventually running for general elections. In the last five years alone, the CPI opened 94 new local chapters. While it still constitutes a marginal electoral force in Italy, it has been successful in penetrating mainstream public debates, receiving disproportionate attention by mass media and commentators, surfing on the journalist-invented nickname of its members: the 'Fascists of the Third Millennium'.[2] The visibility of CPI in the media, the recognizability of its symbols, campaigns, and brand among large audiences are unprecedented for a fringe group so openly inspired by historical Fascism.

This is at odds with the findings of most literature on the far right, according to which contemporary far-right organizations had to dissociate themselves from historical Fascism and Nazism to avoid marginalization in post-World War II democracies. Open nostalgia for non-democratic regimes and outmoded forms of activism, in fact, usually relegates far-right groups to the margins of political systems and to (few) extreme supporters. This is why most of these groups chose to move beyond inter-war ideologies and extremist codes in search of credibility and broader support (Mudde 2016a; Von Beyme 1988). How to explain, then, the high profile achieved by the openly nostalgic CasaPound?

This study contends that CPI gained high-profile public attention through *hybridization*, resulting from the strategic combination of organizational features and activities inspired by different political cultures, institutional party politics, and non-institutional contentious politics. At first sight, in fact, CPI looks no different from other post-war extremist 'groupuscules' in Europe (Griffin 2003). But a closer look at its internal workings and external mobilization shows that several crucial elements set it apart from classic models of extreme-right organization and activism. Since its origin, CPI has exhibited references to Mussolini, but also to Gramsci, Marx, and Che Guevara. It mobilized the iconography of historical Fascism but did not use traditional symbols like the fasces or the tricoloured flame. It has called for law and order policies, but also resorted to the practice of squatting to promote an agenda of housing rights. It has campaigned against Islam but refused theories of a 'Clash of Civilizations'. It praised Vladimir Putin and the Russian philosopher Aleksandr Dugin but criticized Donald Trump and Steve Bannon. It has heavily invested in the youth subcultural milieu, but renovated the aesthetic stereotype of the male skinhead with combat boots and swastikas (Fielitz and Laloire 2016; Koch 2017). In short, several features, references, and activities of CPI are hybrid in nature. They build on the tradition of inter-war and post-war Italian Fascism but aim at renewing the style of extreme-right politics to make it more acceptable in public debates.

Specifically, *hybridization* refers to the strategy by which a group combines references drawn from different political cultures, as well as organizational structures and repertoires inspired by different types of collective actors. For CPI, hybridization stems from the juxtaposition of left-wing themes, extreme-right ideas, and pop-culture symbols, as well as from the combination of the internal structures, repertoires of action, and communication of both political parties and social movements.

As we shall show, two main logics drive this hybridization strategy: the *need to find resources* and the *need for recognizability*. On the one hand, hybridization means that resources can be supplied from multiple venues, which is fundamental for fringe groups that cannot rely on state funding alone. Specifically, the double investment in electoral campaigning and extra-institutional mobilization responds to the need to gather money, staff, and members, which are necessary for survival and to sustain its internal structure and everyday activities. On the other hand, hybridization ensures the recognizability of a group amongst its competitors, which is crucial as the nativist scene becomes more and more crowded. In a context of media-centred politics, fringe organizations thus use hybrid imagery and communication styles to build their own 'brand' of stylized ideas, idioms, and practices.

For CPI, therefore, hybridization represents a double strategic asset, which allowed the group to gather the resources necessary to strengthen its organization and achieve special recognizability in the crowded milieu of the Italian far right. Hybrid symbols and unconventional repertoires of mobilization and communication (often synthesized in CPI's notion of 'non-compliant' politics, *politica non conforme*) contributed to create a CasaPound political 'brand' which was necessary to reach beyond the restricted public of nostalgic fans of Mussolini and extremist activists.

Our analysis will show that the outcomes of hybridization are more complex than the simple achievement of electoral 'success' or 'failure'. In fact, at the time of writing (April 2019), hybridization has granted CasaPound a high-profile position in Italian public debates, but very little electoral support. If CPI has been successful in attaining public recognizability and in attracting the attention of the media, it has failed to transform this visibility into votes. Because of its hybrid strategy, CPI risks appearing too moderate for extremist supporters, and too extremist for radical and moderate right-wing audiences.

The broader implication of our findings is that hybridization has an impact on how democratic societies relate to the extreme right. In fact, the combination of activities, resources, and protest tactics mediated from different political cultures, and from both political parties and social movements, may help to expand the reach of these groups and the diffusion of their ideas beyond fringe milieus. The changes brought by hybridization have an impact on the reasons why people (and especially youth) develop sympathy for or engage in extreme-right organizations but also on the ways in which extreme-right ideas become accepted among non-extremist audiences. The notion of hybridization advanced in this volume helps to make sense of some of these important changes in contemporary extreme-right politics.

By focusing on the notion of hybridization we do not wish to suggest that this phenomenon represents a novelty for far-right politics. Previous studies have suggested that both historical and post-war Fascism have been shaped by dynamic forms of cross-fertilization, or by the subsequent re-contextualization and the re-adaptation of a wide spectrum of ideas, discourses, and political experiments (see for a discussion Costa Pinto and Kallis 2014). In this respect, the notion of hybridization allows exploring how contemporary extreme-right actors perceive and operationalize different mass ideologies, organizational paradigms, and mobilization practices in their everyday political action.

This book provides the first comprehensive study of the politics of CasaPound in Italy. The approach is entirely multidisciplinary, bringing together expertise from the academic fields of political science, sociology, and contemporary history. In so doing, the volume intends to contribute to existing knowledge on extremism and democracy in two main ways. First, the book provides a theoretical framework to tackle the 'complex heterogeneity' of far-right politics at large (Mudde 2016b: 618). While there is a vast literature explaining how far-right parties succeed in elections and how right-wing movements mobilize on the street, the interconnections between these two phenomena have remained largely unexplored. The need to combine insights from party politics and social movement studies seems rather compelling in this field of research, as most far-right actors engage simultaneously in the protest and electoral arena (Castelli Gattinara and Pirro 2019; Pirro 2019). Second, the book offers a time-sensitive account of the changes and challenges of contemporary extreme-right politics. It shows that, today, the extreme right does not necessarily coincide with marginalized old-style ideals and stereotyped violent practices. Rather, extremist groups increasingly try to 'drift into the mainstream', their ideas becoming routine in national public debates (Bail 2015: 10). Overall, therefore, the volume could provide a blueprint for future research on hybrid strategies of nativist collective actors and their impact on democracy, further contributing to the study of the complex relationship between party competition and street protest, and thus the interconnections between fringe groups and mainstream politics.

1.1 Studying CasaPound in the European far-right context

Writing yet another book on the far right can be risky as there is no shortage of literature on the topic. A quick look at Kai Arzheimer's bibliography on the *Extreme/Radical Right in Western Europe*[3] reveals that this is one of the most prolific fields in political science and sociology, counting more than 170 peer-reviewed articles in just the last three years (for an overview see Hainsworth 2016). In related disciplines, such as history (Mammone 2015; Mammone et al. 2013), political communication (Aalberg et al. 2016; Ellinas 2010), and more recently international relations (Liang 2016), the situation is not much different.

This impressive scholarly attention, however, has overwhelmingly concerned certain aspects of far-right politics, whereas others attracted less interest. While much is known about the ideology and electoral fortunes of far-right parties, non-electoral aspects of right-wing activity are, overall, still under-studied (Virchow 2016; Pirro and Castelli Gattinara 2018). Similarly, despite much scholarly knowledge on contextual and individual factors driving electoral support for the far right, little is known about the internal workings and developments of these organizations, especially the less established and extremist ones. By studying the 'internal supply side' of CasaPound Italia and its external mobilization, this book aims to redress some of these theoretical and empirical lacunae. To this end, we start by presenting the ideology of CPI and its organizational configuration in the context of the multiple variants of contemporary far-right politics in Europe.

In this respect, it is hard to classify CPI due to its unconventional way of doing politics. Indeed, while journalists picked on the aesthetic side and addressed CPI militants as 'hipsters' (The Guardian 2018) and its ideology as 'glamorous fascism' (Torrisi 2018), scholars are divided about the nature of CPI politics. Some have claimed that CPI represents a genuine transformation (if not an evolution) of traditional extreme-right politics (Di Nunzio and Toscano 2011; Rosati 2018). Others, instead, suggest that the new image is only deceptive, a façade used strategically to increase the attractiveness of historical Fascism for broader audiences and youth (Cammelli 2017; Koch 2013, 2017). Besides ideological factors, however, very little attention has been paid to the way in which the group organizes to sustain mobilization, and communicates with the external world. To contribute to this debate, the next sections justify the authors' choice to consider CPI as an extreme-right organization engaging simultaneously in the social movement and electoral arena.

1.1.1 How to distinguish extreme and radical variants of far-right politics

Several designations are used to qualify different types of far-right actors. Acknowledging these differences is necessary not only to recognize that the far right is more heterogeneous than usually assumed, but also to define specific collective actors, in the present case CasaPound, with respect to the vast ideological and organizational spectrum of far-right politics. Actors located at the 'right' end of the political spectrum have in fact been alternatively labelled as extreme right, populist right, neo-fascist right, post-fascist right, and radical right (Mudde 1996). While these different labels have been pinned to groups displaying substantially different worldviews, scholars have also recognized a set of common ideological traits. In this respect, the umbrella concept of 'far-right politics' is used to recognize standing differences within the political right while also including several of its ideological and organizational variants.

Varieties of far-right politics are thus defined by three core ideological features: the relationships with (representative) democracy, nativism, and authoritarianism. The democratic element informs the distinction between so-called 'radical' and 'extreme' variants of the far right, as we discuss below. Nativism and authoritarianism refer to two core far-right beliefs: respectively, that nation states shall be inhabited only by native people; and that societies must be strictly ordered and any infringement severely sanctioned (Mudde 2007: 18–23).

The differentiation between 'radical' and 'extreme' right-wing organizations ultimately rests on their hostile or oppositional attitude towards constitutional democratic principles. Extreme-right organizations, in fact, reject even the minimum core features of democracy: popular sovereignty and majority rule (Mudde 2007: 138–56). On the contrary, radical right organizations oppose liberal democracy but accept popular sovereignty and the minimal procedural rules of parliamentary democracy. The most important ideology for the extreme right is fascism, a patchwork of ideas that took different forms (Mudde 2000; Costa Pinto and Kallis 2014). Defining fascism across its subsequent historical variations and contextual re-adaptations certainly goes beyond the scope of this volume. For the purposes of this study, instead, we are only interested in pinning down some of the core characteristics of Italian Fascism (which we refer to as historical Fascism or Fascism with a capital 'F') that we deem important to understand contemporary CPI's politics.

In the vast literature dealing with this subject, classic Italian Fascism is addressed as a nationalist ideology rooted on the glorification of the figure of the leader as the embodiment of the nation and of the state (see Payne 1996; Griffin and Feldman 2004). In historical Fascism, the state was not just a formal legal institution, but an ethical and mystic entity that requires devotion and full submission (see Gentile 2008). Accordingly, historical Fascism rejected democracy and party politics and it aimed at creating a new man who would be free from class struggle (Paxton 2004; Mudde 2019). Fascism calls for a 'third way' beyond socialism and liberalism and it believes in violence as a regenerating force for the nation and the state, and on the prominence of actions over words (Eatwell 2011).

Another important variant of fascism is German fascism that is better known as Nazism or National Socialism. It shares some characteristics with Italian Fascism but also crucial differences (see for an overview Kallis 2000). If Fascism is characterized by vitalism, Nazism is driven by Nihilism. Furthermore, if Fascists believe that the state is the main entity, Nazis believe that it is race. Nazis believe that there are different races and that the Aryan race is superior. As such, they consider that the superior race (*Übermenschen*, superhumans) has the right to dominate and exterminate the inferior one (*Untermenschen*, subhumans). Nazism sees Jews as physically and morally inferior but economically powerful and politically influent and it claims that Jews infect the Aryan race. While Fascism does not give to race the same relevance as Nazism does, in 1938 Mussolini openly supported racism by endorsing the 'Manifesto of Race' and passing the 'racial laws'. (Neo-)fascist, (neo-)Nazi, fundamentalist, or supremacist extreme-right groups thus openly refer to these variants of fascism and they advocate for the instauration of non-democratic regimes. They believe in a system ruled by individuals who possess special leadership characteristics and are thus naturally different from the rest of the 'people'. In this sense, the *Duce* and the *Führer* are a direct embodiment, rather than the representatives, of the will of the people (Eatwell 2002, 2018).

Radical right groups, instead, seek to obtain the support of (a majority of) the people by criticizing crucial aspects of liberal democracy. Notably, they target pluralism and minority rights and defend a 'monist' vision of society (Rydgren 2007: 243). In this respect, as we shall see, CPI's ideology cannot be located completely outside the legal boundary of democratic electoral competition in Italy, despite being strongly indebted to the ideas of historical Fascism.

The second core ideological feature of the far right is nativism. Just like democratic values, nativism too can be articulated in multiple ways (Bar-On 2018; Brubaker 2017). Some organizations privilege biological interpretations positing that specific ethnic groups are genetically superior to others (e.g. white supremacism or racial nationalism). Most radical right parties, instead, reject racial hierarchies, but posit that the mixing of ethnic groups creates insurmountable cultural problems. These positions, often referred to as 'ethnocentric nationalism' (Rydgren 2008; Taguieff 1985), draw on cultural racism and on distortions of dominant conceptions of citizenship and liberal values (Froio 2018; Halikiopoulou et al. 2013). With respect to nativism, as we shall see, CPI takes inspiration from both strands, advocating a predominantly cultural interpretation of the native people that is not immune to biological understandings of race.

The third feature of far-right ideology is authoritarianism. Some organizations believe that a strictly ordered society can be achieved only within a non-democratic regime, either authoritarian or totalitarian (see Linz 1985). Others simply display authoritarian attitudes: this includes the uncritical glorification of authority figures of the in-group, and the predisposition towards punishing any behaviour considered 'deviant' from the far right's moral standards (Adorno et al. 1969: 228; Ignazi 1992). Both interpretations however see order and punishment as the crucial conditions to keep society together. As we shall discuss, CPI's authoritarianism combines both elements. On the one hand, the group is openly nostalgic for the Italian fascist regime. On the other, it advocates 'law and order' measures punishing deviant behaviour within the democratic constitutional and legal system.

Overall, we contend that CPI ought to be considered as an ideologically 'extreme'-right group (Cammelli 2017; Koch, 2013). In fact, its political campaigns focus on specific features of liberal democracy such as pluralism and the protection of minorities, and thus articulate authoritarian and nativist values within the legal boundaries of the Italian constitution. At the same time, however, the importance of Mussolini's Fascism for the group's ideology makes it barely compatible at all with liberal democratic principles in general.

1.1.2 How to identify the organizational variants of the far right

These various breeds of the far right often differ also in terms of their internal organization and main political goals. Still, there is no one-to-one correspondence between a group's ideological profile and its preferred mode of doing politics. While most of the established far-right parties belong to the populist radical right category, there are also examples of electorally successful extreme-right actors, such as the Greek *Χρυσή Αυγή* (Golden Dawn, GD). Conversely, while most street activism pertains to extremist right-wing groups, there is no shortage of radical right social movements, as illustrated by the cases of *Les Identitaires* (the Identitarians, LI) in France and PEGIDA in Germany.

Organizational configurations of the far right thus notably include political parties that run for elections and that are primarily oriented towards office and policy seeking. Many of these parties were 'new' to their party systems when they first emerged in the 1980s and 1990s, but are now established in terms of electoral support and (increasingly) access to office. In addition, scholars identified far-right social movements, social movement organizations, and grassroots groups aiming at influencing politics and policy with informal means, protest actions, the mobilization of citizens and/or intellectual activities. In between these two organizational configurations, some researchers have also looked at far-right 'movement parties' (Castelli Gattinara and Pirro 2019). Movement parties are able to transpose contentious politics into the electoral arena by upholding the structures, procedures, and practices of both parties and social movements to influence policy-making (Kitschelt 2006). Movement parties engage in both contentious and electoral politics. As we shall illustrate, CPI can be considered as a movement-party organization, since it opted to engage in electoral politics only in recent times and approached electoral campaigns as part of a broader political and cultural project implying unconventional tactics and non-institutional mobilization.

In addition to the above varieties of organizational configurations, far-right collective actors also pursue different, and at times complementary, goals. Specifically, the literature distinguishes between electoral and cultural goals (Bar-On 2012; Hirsch-Hoefler and Mudde 2013). While these two aims are not mutually exclusive, far-right organizations often have to choose between the one and the other as a primary venue of their action. In general, the more established groups tend to be oriented towards election-related rewards: policies and political offices but also acquiring financial resources and personnel from participation in electoral campaigns and state institutions. Conversely, fringe groups pay little attention to electoral competition and election-related payoffs and aim at creating political consensus mostly through contentious actions, or cultural and intellectual activities. While many right-wing movements are quite action-oriented, a specific breed of so-called 'Gramscians of the Right' believes in the power of ideas over action (Hirsch-Hoefler and Mudde 2013: 5). These actors mobilize mostly outside any electoral process, engaging in agitprop campaigns through magazines and newspapers, promoting music and cultural events and campaigning extensively on the internet. CPI takes inspiration from influential far-right movements like the French *Nouvelle Droite* (New Right, ND),[4] and engages extensively in creating consensus through cultural and intellectual activities, but it also sustains action-oriented politics and occasional participation in the electoral arena. Indeed, previous studies suggested that this hybrid model of political action operates through a mix of 'social movement imaginaries and repertoires' and 'ventures in electoral politics' (Zúquete 2018: 62).

1.2 The argument

The principal contribution of this book is to explain how CPI achieved such a high profile in Italian public debates despite no electoral support and its explicit extremist references. In the volume public debate is defined as the open debate about ideas relevant to politics (Bennett and Entman 2001: 3). One of the most important spaces in which the debate is carried out is the media (Roggeband and Vliegenthart, 2007: 525; Rooduijn 2014: 727).

We contend that the specific, hybrid, way, in which the group organizes internally and mobilizes externally, has been crucial for its fortunes. Hybrid features, in fact, represent a strategic asset for CPI to exploit the emotional bias of the mass media and its appetite for sensational, simplified, and controversial news stories (Bail 2015; Ellinas 2010; Vliegenthart and Walgrave 2012). Media coverage, in turn, gives a fringe organization like CPI the visibility necessary to consolidate its position within the far-right milieu, but also to routinize its extreme-right ideas in the public sphere, thus contributing to radicalizing mainstream debates.

As noted earlier, we refrain from making a simplistic distinction between the 'success' and 'failure' of CPI (Amenta et al. 2010; Bosi et al. 2015; Bosi and Uba 2009). While most party politics' literature focuses only on electoral performances (see Eatwell 2016; Mudde 2007), analyses of social movements consider the various outcomes that protest activities may have on the political and cultural domains (Giugni 2008). Separately, we argue, these two approaches are unable to account for how a group like CPI could acquire prominence in the public sphere despite its poor electoral scores and fringe extremist ideas. In this study, therefore, we combine party politics and social movement perspectives to look at the high profile of CPI in terms of both the electoral and non-electoral outcomes of hybridization.

To do so, we examine the internal workings and external mobilization of CasaPound Italia. Notably, we look at how CPI organizes, recruits personnel and activists to sustain mobilization and reach a wider public without downplaying extreme ideas and practices. This is in line with internal supply-side interpretations of far-right success, suggesting that the internal workings of a group critically shape its external mobilization and impact (Mudde 2007).[5] Specifically, factors such as a group's ideology, its leadership, the way in which it defines internal democracy, and the way in which it organizes locally, are deemed crucial in determining the nature and intensity of its street mobilization, and the extent of its success in the polls (Carter 2005; Heinisch and Mazzoleni 2016; Taggart 1995). This does not imply that *agency* is considered more important than, or disconnected from, *context*. Rather, it implies recognizing that a group's organizational choices and mobilization strategies also depend on political and discursive opportunities at the contextual level (Kriesi 1989; McAdam et al. 1996; Mudde 2007: 256–76; Tarrow 1996).

Our central claim is that the high profile of CPI stems, at least to a certain extent, from the specific way in which the group organizes, mobilizes, and communicates – which we analyse in terms of the notion of *hybridization*. We defined hybridization as the strategy by which a group combines: a) ideas and symbols inspired by different political cultures, and b) the organizational features and forms of mobilization of political parties and social movements. More specifically, this study considers five crucial aspects of CasaPound's politics: the group's ideology, its internal structure, activism, mobilization, and communication.

A first, crucial dimension of hybridization concerns the *ideology* of extreme-right groups. As we shall show, CasaPound adopts from historical Fascism a set of normative ideas about the nature of man and the organization of society (Sainsbury 1980: 8), and then articulates these selectively to address themes borrowed from other political cultures or emerging from topical events. In this respect, CPI differs from electorally successful radical right parties, who have (at least openly) detached themselves from inter-war ideologies (Mudde 2007: 32–60) and endorsed more liberal (yet always restrictive) positions on the cultural issues that they 'own' (Petrocik 1996), notably immigration and integration (Halikiopoulou et al. 2013). On the contrary, CPI has not moved away from traditional ideologies. Rather, it uses elements from historical Fascism and post-war right-wing extremism to interpret contemporary events and advance new demands that might resonate with, and radicalize, the political mainstream (Bail 2015). Notably, *ethnopluralism* allows the group to attain a coherent worldview across different themes, while also avoiding appearing anachronistic (and explicitly racist or anti-democratic). Hybridization thus helps extreme-right actors like CPI to cope with the public stigmatization of historical Fascism and Nazism, and the decreasing importance of ideological conflict in contemporary politics (Mair 2008).

The *internal structure* refers to a group's organizational configuration (Art 2011; Carter 2005; Heinisch and Mazzoleni 2016) – the machinery, procedures, and mechanisms driving its internal working. As we shall show, the hybrid internal structure of CPI combines the organizational aspects of institutionalized political parties (Scarrow et al. 2017), and those helping to sustain the collective action of social movements (McCarthy and Zald 1977; Olson 1965). Political parties are normally configured as hierarchically and territorially structured organizations resting on a set of intermediate bodies that regulate decision-making, and on a body of formal rules that determine selection of the leadership, access to membership, and political engagement (Panebianco 1988; Poguntke et al. 2016). Social movements, instead, are organized horizontally and feature predominantly informal rules concerning recruitment, decision-making, and activism (Della Porta and Diani 2009). By looking at the internal structure of CPI, our study argues that these two organizational configurations can coexist and contribute to the high profile of the group. Hybridization enables CasaPound to uphold specific features of the party model alongside the seemingly looser structures and procedures of social movements (Pirro and Castelli Gattinara 2018), facilitating the drawing of financial resources and personnel from different venues.

Activism refers to the participation of individuals within a political group, or the enduring investment in a collective struggle that goes beyond the simple act of casting a vote (Polletta and Jasper 2001). In this context, the hybrid strategy of CPI implies various ways to promote activism. This includes conventional and unconventional modes of participation and hybrid imageries aimed at crafting a collective identity and influencing politics. The formal political participation that is normally associated with political parties includes lobbying, electing representatives, and contacting the news media (see Norris et al. 2005). Alternative and informal participation, instead, includes social movements promoting protest, online networking, and subcultural or counter-cultural activities (Fantasia 1988). Our study shows that the high profile achieved by CasaPound partly rests on a blurring of the distinction between party and social movement models of participation, and the styles of extreme-right, left-progressive and pop culture. Combining conventional and unconventional modes of activism, symbols and imageries, in fact, hybridization contributed to supporting the engagement of individuals in CPI and to consolidating the group's identity.

Another crucial dimension of hybridization is *external mobilization*, consisting of a repertoire used by collective actors to advance their demands in public arenas (Tilly 1978). Notably, the CasaPound strategy of mobilization implies engagement in both the electoral and the grassroots arena. On the one hand, CPI is similar to political parties that normally participate in the democratic process by fielding their candidates, and is therefore geared towards elections (Kitschelt 2006: 279); on the other hand, CPI is similar to social movements, as it uses protest and disruption to pursue its collective goals (Della Porta and Diani 2009: 13–16). In this respect, CasaPound's external mobilization shows that the repertoires of collective action adopted from social movements, and of electoral participation usually associated with political parties, may be complementary rather than alternatives to one another. This unconventional mix of agitprop actions, campaigning, and contentious demonstrations contributes to ensure a high-profile media coverage in both the protest and electoral arenas.

Finally, by *political communication* we refer to the way in which a group interacts with its members and the outside world, including public officials and the media, as well as other individuals. CPI's political communication is intended to convey the idea of continuity with the most iconic features of historical Fascism, alongside a renewal of extreme-right symbolism and imagery. Due to the growing importance of the media in electoral competition, political parties have professionalized their strategies, adopting 'media codes' of personalization and dramatization (Altheide and Snow 1979; Ellinas 2010; Mazzoleni and Schulz 1999). Studies on the visibility of social movements, moreover, suggested that media coverage is linked to the organization of highly spectacular events (Castelli Gattinara and Froio 2018; Wouters 2013), the diffusion of information through old and new media (Bouron 2017; Froio and Ganesh 2019), and the creation of alternative platforms (Mattoni 2016). In this respect, CasaPound has developed a semi-professional communication apparatus to seize the attention of the mainstream media, but has also broken away from the usual communication style of political parties, through agitprop operations, sensationalistic actions, and sustained activism in the digital environment.

Building on these five crucial aspects of CPI's politics, this volume focuses on hybridization as a strategy deployed by extreme-right actors to avoid marginalization and achieve a high profile in the public sphere. We argue that CPI sets out hybrid strategies to trigger the interest of external observers and the media, with the goal of reaching beyond the restricted political space that is generally available to fringe political groups. In other words, CPI seeks to diffuse its messages among mainstream audiences through the strategic combination of left-wing issues, extreme-right ideas, and pop culture. At the same time, it seeks to make extremist politics mainstream by juxtaposing the communication activities and repertoires of institutional parties and protest movements.

1.3 Research design

Studying how extreme-right groups achieve attention in public debates presents formidable methodological challenges. Whereas the Appendices offer more details about the data and methods used to study hybridization in CPI's politics, this section focuses on three crucial elements in the research design of the volume. First, we describe the case selection strategy; then, we present how we gauge CPI's profile in public debates, internal supply-side and external mobilization factors, presenting data sources and methods. Taken together, these choices allowed us to observe CasaPound's politics over a time span ranging from the foundation of the group in December 2003 until the latest Italian general election in March 2018.

1.3.1 Case selection: why CasaPound Italia?

We focus on CPI as a deviant case study (Seawright and Gerring 2008). The group's extreme-right political beliefs and poor electoral support are at odds with the high profile that CPI currently enjoys in Italian public debates. Unlike CPI, in fact, most far-right organizations in Europe either gave up their direct links with inter-war ideologies (to get legitimation), or stuck to these while accepting that they would then be viewed as an outcast and play a minimal role. Even the extreme-right Golden Dawn, which is often described as neo-Nazi by pundits and political opponents, has repeatedly denied any official connection to National Socialism. On the contrary, groups that have failed to take a distance from either Fascism or Nazism have generally been relegated to underground roles, often incurring legal sanctions or proscription as with National Action (NA) in the United Kingdom.

In this respect, we consider that CasaPound represents a deviation from the norm, as one would expect similar groups to be either more cautious in claiming inspiration from historical Fascism or enjoy less political leeway in accessing public debates. By focusing on CasaPound's politics over the past 15 years, this study sets out to uncover the hybridization strategies that allowed it to succeed where others had failed. The volume builds on a broad empirical base, which allows us to address how CPI's profile in public debates relates to internal supply-side and external mobilization factors: ideology, organization, activism, mobilization, and communication strategies. Both are addressed by means of different data types and mixed-methods techniques for analysis (Della Porta and Keating 2008).

1.3.2 Gauging CasaPound's profile in public debates

To gauge CPI's profile in public debates in Italy, we consider two main indicators accounting for the group's visibility. We follow classic approaches and study the content of public debates through articles in quality newspapers (see Rooduijn 2014). Although quality newspapers are not the only media venue where public debates take shape – for instance, there are also TV and radio programmes, magazines and tabloids and sources generated by movements themselves – quality newspapers are designed to be for most people a 'forum for the articulation of multiple ideas in an attempt to promote public debate on salient issues' (Day and Golan 2005: 62).[6] Additionally, quality media sources are of utmost importance because of their wide distribution and status. Furthermore, while newspaper circulation has declined in established democracies mostly to the benefit of new media they still serve as major channel for public debates and act as core agenda-setters (Vliegenthart and Walgrave 2012). This is particularly relevant when observing the relationship between media contents and visibility of collective actors (Koopmans and Statham 1999). To measure the visibility of CasaPound in the media, we use a Political Claims Analysis (PCA) and coded all the claims by CPI that were reported in the quality paper *Il Corriere della Sera* in the period 2004–2015, based on an ad hoc codebook (see Appendix 3). To account for possible media bias, we then applied the same coding scheme to all online press releases published by CPI between 2009 and 2015 and scraped automatically from the official website of the group. As public debates increasingly take shape on the internet and in online fora, we also collected indicators of CPI's online visibility. We use the number of Facebook followers of CPI's official pages and website traffic statistics from *SimilarWeb*.

1.3.3 Studying the internal supply-side and external mobilization

To study how CPI's internal-supply side and external mobilization factors relate to its visibility in public debates, we use data derived from party manifestos and literature, official campaign and online material, books, face-to-face interviews, and fieldwork notes. Data collection started in 2012 and then continued intermittently until April 2019. The dataset was assembled in an archive including fieldwork notes and pictures collected during open participant observation of three core events organized by CPI and at numerous other informal meetings. The archive also features CPI's internal literature (listed in the Appendix 2), the music and lyrics of CPI's official band *ZetaZeroAlfa* (ZZA), campaign material and election manifestos, online press releases and social media content from Facebook, as well as the recording of 17 face-to-face interviews with leaders and activists in six Italian cities.[7] The material collected during interviews and open participant observation was analysed through qualitative text analyses, looking at the presentation and discussion of aspects and issues that we deemed of relevance, and reporting illustrative quotes from interviews and texts. To limit the risk of subjective interpretations in the qualitative data analysis we structured the discussion of this material to be rooted in the five aspects of CPI's politics (related to internal-supply side and external mobilization) illustrated above and discussed in detail in the empirical chapters.

A first set of data facilitated examination of CPI's *ideology*, but also its themes and policy proposals. This material includes 'party literature' (Mudde 2000: 22), such as the books and comment pieces published by CPI leaders, notably in the group's newspaper *Il Primato Nazionale* (The National Primacy, IPN), available online and offline. Furthermore, considering the importance of music in the diffusion of ideas (Eyerman 2002; Kahn-Harris 2007) and in the far-right milieu (Teitelbaum 2017), we also analysed the lyrics of CPI's official band ZZA. We retrieved CasaPound's policy suggestions from official documents, notably party manifestos presented ahead of the 2013 and 2018 Italian general elections (e.g. Budge and McDonald 2006; Laver 2014). We follow a standard content analytical approach (Laver et al. 2003), using the quasi-sentence coding scheme developed by the Comparative Agendas Project (CAP) to study policy attention[8] (see Appendix 4 for further details).[9] We then use descriptive statistics to map the importance of the different policy issues in the group's electoral supply, and to measure change over time.

When needed, we integrated this data with other propaganda material (flyers and advertisements for public events available on CPI's website and Facebook pages). This material provides information about CPI's *internal structure*, such as the territorial distribution of the headquarters, size of membership, and details about decision-making procedures and the administration of group activities. To examine the territorial distribution of CPI's chapters we use official data on the location of headquarters and other offices available on the group's website. Each entry was associated to a geolocation, which enabled the creation of map charts, highlighting the presence of CPI in Italian regional capitals, and changes over the time between a first observation (when data are available) in 2013 and in 2018.[10] We use data from the Ministry of the Interior on CPI's electoral results for the general elections (https://elezionistorico.interno.gov.it).

To study the *collective identity* of the group we mostly used face-to-face interviews, and gathered visual and written material from open participant observation during CPI's public and private events.[11] The fieldwork lasted from January to September 2012; it covered CPI's territorial units in Florence, Milan, Naples, Rome, Turin, and Verona. Access to fieldwork was negotiated in late 2011, when we got in touch with CPI's national leaders. Conscious that our fieldwork would take place in an environment where we would be both the object and the source of suspicion (see Russell Hochschild 2016) and that a rapid internet search would be sufficient to find out who we are and what we do, we decided to present ourselves as researchers and to openly describe the nature of our proposed research. The selection of the venues for fieldwork followed a double logic: on the one hand, we chose territorial chapters in different geographic contexts in the north, in the centre, and in the south of Italy; on the other, we sought variation in their longevity.

In addition, we were also formally invited to attend three public events organized by CasaPound: the national festival *'Direzione Rivoluzione'* (Direction Revolution, September 2012), the demonstration *'Italia in Marcia'* (Italy on the Move, November 2012), and the congress *'Mediterraneo Solidale'* (Mediterranean Solidarity, September 2015). This was complemented by occasional observations at public events organized by CPI between 2013 and 2017, including conferences, art exhibitions, demonstrations, and concerts. While numerous conversations, informal interviews, and exchanges with CPI militants took place during the fieldwork but could not be recorded, we were allowed to hold and register 17 face-to-face interviews. These involved three high-ranking national officials, who formally spoke on behalf of CPI, the local secretaries of the five territorial headquarters that we visited, and a number of other activists who accepted to participate in the study individually. From a sociodemographic perspective, 15 of our interviewees were men and 2 women, aged mostly between 17 and 35. The interaction, even informal, with activists allowed observation of socialization and organizational practices within the group, as well as the processes of formation of collective identities that promote and sustain involvement in CPI through interpersonal relations, shared symbols and codes (Brewer and Gardner 1996; O'Reilly 2005).

We used established techniques in the field of social movement studies to account for the nature and intensity of CPI's *external mobilization*, distinguishing different tactics using Political Claims Analysis (Hutter 2014; Kiousis et al. 2006; Koopmans and Rucht 2002; Koopmans and Statham 1999) as detailed in Appendix 3. Furthermore, we studied CPI's *political communication* combining data from the interviews, from CPI's official website, and the Facebook accounts of CPI and its leaders and candidates. In doing so, we explored the group's activity in media environments, the content of its online campaigns, and style of its communication on social networks. Online interactions with other organizations are addressed by data on mutual reactions on Facebook collected and analysed by the website *Patriaindipendente*.

1.4 Outline of the book

The argument of the book is built through eight chapters. The present chapter presented the puzzle of the study, the main argument, and the design used to address it. Chapter 2 introduces the reader to the history and background of CasaPound, while also locating the group in the context of the Italian far right. Subsequently, five empirical chapters address hybridization in ideology, internal structure, activism, mobilization, and political communication, with the goal of uncovering their impact on the attention and visibility acquired by CPI over the years. The volume then concludes with a chapter where these separate factors are brought together to assess how hybridization relates to the high profile of CPI in the Italian public sphere, thinking about possible implications for research on change and continuity in contemporary extreme-right politics.

Notes

1 The book expands and updates material from Albanese et al. (2014), reproduced with permission. While the volume is the result of the joint work of the four authors, different authors have been in charge of the various chapters: Chapter 1 (Caterina Froio and Pietro Castelli Gattinara); Chapter 2 (Pietro Castelli Gattinara); Chapter 3 (Matteo Albanese, Caterina Froio, Pietro Castelli Gattinara); Chapter 4 (Caterina Froio and Pietro Castelli Gattinara); Chapter 5 (Caterina Froio); Chapter 6 (Pietro Castelli Gattinara); Chapter 7 (Giorgia Bulli, Caterina Froio, Pietro Castelli Gattinara); Chapter 8 (Caterina Froio and Pietro Castelli Gattinara).

2 The expression first appeared in an article titled *Il Fascismo del Terzo Millennio riparte dalla lotta per la Casa* [Third Millennium Fascism restarts from housing], published by the newspaper *Il Giornale* in July 2004.
3 See: Kai Arzheimer, 'The Eclectic, Erratic Bibliography on the Extreme Right in Western Europe', available at: www.kai-arzheimer.com/extreme-right-western-europe-bibliography (accessed 10/09/2018).
4 The *Nouvelle Droite* (New Right) was a neo-conservative French intellectual movement. It was born in the late 1960s around the cultural association GRECE (*Groupement de Recherche et d'Études pour la Civilisation Européenne*) and the writer Alain de Benoist. The *Nouvelle Droite* is known for its 'ethnopluralist' ideological doctrine (see section 3.1) and its attempts to re-elaborate from a right-wing perspective themes considered typical of the left-wing culture (Taguieff 1998; Bar-On 2012; Capra Casadio 2014).
5 Demand-side explanations, in fact, have been used to examine voting behaviour and citizens' attitudes, recognizing the individual characteristics breeding far-right support. External supply-side explanations focus instead on the environment where the far right operates, and single out the contextual drivers of far-right support (Arzheimer 2009).
6 Moreover, we limit the analysis to quality newspapers because these have been found to report more extensively on political matters than other types of outlet (Druckman and Parkin 2005).
7 In addressing this broad wealth of raw data, we were aware that different types of sources convey distinct information. While interviews with activists may not be representative of CasaPound's official stances, information that is representative of formal group positions was provided by party programmes, interviews with high-ranking officials, and the 'party literature'.
8 We integrated the original topic list with the category 'Ideology'. This accounts for quasi-sentences that did not have a specific policy content, but referred to general ideological beliefs and/or commemorations of historic events. We also broadened the scope of the CAP category 'Government operations' to include quasi-sentences focusing on the (dis)functioning of democratic institutions, and political accountability of parties and their leaders.
9 See the codebook of the CAP project (Baumgartner et al. 2019), available at: https://www.comparativeagendas.net/pages/master-codebook (accessed on 14/08/2017).
10 We thank Flavia Albanese (Iuav University of Venice) and Prof. Marco Cremaschi (Sciences Po CEE) for their precious assistance with the maps.
11 By 'open participant observation' we mean the qualitative research method by which the researcher participates overtly for a relatively long time in the group she is observing, in its natural environment. This method has made it possible to establish a relationship of interaction with CPI's groups members, in order to describe their actions, understand their motives as well as the meaning they attribute to their actions and practices. To immerse ourselves in CPI's spaces and locations did not imply the abandonment of our value orientations which in fact were openly communicated to the interviewees upon their request (Avanza 2008; Blee 2007; Brewer 2000).

References

Aalberg, T. et al. (eds). 2016. *Populist Political Communication in Europe*. New York: Routledge.

Adorno, T.W. et al. 1969. *The Authoritarian Personality*. New York: John Wiley.

Albanese, M. et al. 2014. *Fascisti Di Un Altro Millennio? Crisi e Partecipazione in CasaPound Italia*. Roma: Bonanno Editore.

Altheide, D.L., and R.P. Snow. 1979. *Media Logic*. London: Sage.

Amenta, E. et al. 2010. 'The Political Consequences of Social Movements', *Annual Review of Sociology* 36(1): 287–307.

Art, D. 2011. *Inside the Radical Right: The Development of Anti-Immigrant Parties in Western Europe*. Cambridge: Cambridge University Press.

Arzheimer, K. 2009. 'Contextual Factors and the Extreme Right Vote in Western Europe, 1980–2002', *American Journal of Political Science* 53(2): 259–75.

Avanza, M. 2008. 'Comment faire de l'ethnographie quand on n'aime pas « ses indigènes » ?', in A. Bensa (ed.), *Les politiques de l'enquête*. Paris: La Découverte, pp. 41–58.

Bail, C. 2015. *Terrified: How Anti-Muslim Fringe Organizations Became Mainstream*. Princeton, NJ: Princeton University Press.

Bar-On, T. 2012. 'The French New Right's Quest for Alternative Modernity', *Fascism* 1(1): 18–52.

———. 2018. 'The Radical Right and Nationalism', in J. Rydgren (ed.), *The Oxford Handbook of the Radical Right*. Oxford: Oxford University Press, pp. 17–41.

Baumgartner, F.R. et al. (eds). 2019. *Comparative Policy Agendas: Theory, Tools, Data*. Oxford: Oxford University Press.

Bennett, W.L., and R.M. Entman (eds). 2001. *Mediated Politics: Communication in the Future of Democracy*. Cambridge: Cambridge University Press.

Blee, K.M. 2007. 'Ethnographies of the Far Right', *Journal of Contemporary Ethnography* 36(2): 119–28.

Bosi, L. et al. 2015. *The Consequences of Social Movements*. Cambridge, MA: Cambridge University Press.

Bosi, L., and K. Uba. 2009. 'The Outcomes of Social Movement Action: An Introduction', *Mobilization* 14(4): 405–11.

Bouron, S. 2017. 'Des « fachos » dans les rues aux « héros » sur le web', *Réseaux* (202–203): 187–211.

Brewer, J.D. 2000. *Ethnography*. London: Open University Press.

Brewer, M.B., and W. Gardner. 1996. 'Who Is This "We"? Levels of Collective Identities and Self Representations', *Journal of Personality and Social Psychology* 71(1): 83–93.

Brubaker, R. 2017. 'Between Nationalism and Civilizationism: The European Populist Moment in Comparative Perspective', *Ethnic and Racial Studies* 40(2): 1191–226.

Budge, I., and M.D. McDonald. 2006. 'Choices Parties Define Policy Alternatives in Representative Elections, 17 Countries 1945–1998', *Party Politics* 12(4): 451–66.

Cammelli, M.G. 2017. *Fascistes Du Troisième Millénaire*. Milan: Mimesis.

Capra Casadio, M. 2014. 'The New Right and Metapolitics in France and Italy', *Journal for the Study of Radicalism* 8(1): 45–86.

Carter, E.L. 2005. *The Extreme Right in Western Europe: Success or Failure?* Manchester: Manchester University Press.

Castelli Gattinara, P., and C. Froio. 2018. 'Getting "Right" into the News: Grassroots Far-Right Mobilization and Media Coverage in Italy and France', *Comparative European Politics* 1–21.

Castelli Gattinara, P., and A.L.P. Pirro. 2019. 'The Far Right as Social Movement', *European Societies* 21(4): 447–62.

Costa Pinto, A., and A. Kallis. 2014. *Rethink Fascism and Dictatorship in Europe*. London: Palgrave Macmillan.

Day, A.G., and Golan, G. 2005 'Source and Content Diversity in Op-Ed Pages: Assessing Editorial Strategies in the *New York Times* and the *Washington Post*', *Journalism Studies* 6(1): 61–71.

Della Porta, D., and M. Diani. 2009. *Social Movements: An Introduction*. Oxford: Blackwell.

Della Porta, D., and M. Keating. 2008. *Approaches and Methodologies in the Social Sciences: A Pluralist Perspective*. Cambridge, MA: Cambridge University Press.

Di Nunzio, D., and E. Toscano. 2011. *Dentro e Fuori CasaPound: Capire Il Fascismo Del Terzo Millennio*. Rome: Armando Editore.

Druckman, J.N., and M. Parkin. 2005. 'The Impact of Media Bias: How Editorial Slant Affects Voters', *Journal of Politics* 67(4): 1030–49.

Eatwell, R. 2002. 'The Rebirth of Right-Wing Charisma? The Cases of Jean-Marie Le Pen and Vladimir Zhirinovsky', *Totalitarian Movements and Political Religions* 3(3): 1–23.

———.2011. *Fascism. A History*. New York: Random House.

———. 2016. 'Ten Theories of the Extreme Right', in C. Mudde (ed.), *The Radical Right: A Reader*. London: Routledge, pp. 200–25.

———. 2018. 'Charisma and the Radical Right', in J. Rydgren (ed.), *The Oxford Handbook of the Radical Right*. Oxford: Oxford University Press, Chapter 13.

Ellinas, A.A. 2010. *The Media and the Far Right in Western Europe: Playing the Nationalist Card*. Cambridge: Cambridge University Press.

Eyerman, R. 2002. 'Music in Movement: Cultural Politics and Old and New Social Movements', *Qualitative Sociology* 25(3): 443–58.

Fantasia, R. 1988. *Cultures of Solidarity*. Berkeley and Los Angeles: University of California Press.

Fielitz, M., and L.L. Laloire. 2016. *Trouble on the Far Right: Contemporary Right-Wing Strategies and Practices in Europe*. Bielefeld: Transcript.

Froio, C. 2018. 'Race, Religion or Culture? Framing Islam between Racism and Neo-Racism in the Online Network of the French Far Right', *Perspectives on Politics* 16(3): 696–709.

Froio, C., and B. Ganesh. 2019. 'The Transnationalisation of Far-Right Discourse on Twitter: Issues and Actors that Cross Borders in Western European Democracies', *European Societies* 21(4): 513–39.

Gentile, E. 2008. *Modernità Totalitaria. Il Fascismo Italiano*. Roma-Bari: Laterza.

Giugni, M. 2008. 'Political, Biographical, and Cultural Consequences of Social Movements', *Sociology Compass* 2(5): 1582–600.

Griffin, R. 2003. 'From Slime Mould to Rhizome: An Introduction to the Groupuscular Right', *Patterns of Prejudice* 37(1): 27–50.

Griffin, R., and Feldman, M. 2004. *A Fascist Century*. London: Palgrave Macmillan.

Hainsworth, P. (ed.). 2016. *The Extreme Right in Europe and the USA*. London: Bloomsbury Academic.

Halikiopoulou, D. et al. 2013. 'The Civic Zeitgeist: Nationalism and Liberal Values in the European Radical Right', *Nations and Nationalism* 19(1): 107–27.

Heinisch, R., and O. Mazzoleni. 2016. *Understanding Populist Party Organisation: The Radical Right in Western Europe*. New York: Springer.

Hirsch-Hoefler, S., and C. Mudde. 2013. 'Right-Wing Movements', in R.P. Snow (ed.), *The Blackwell Encyclopedia of Social and Political Movements*. Oxford US: Blackwell, pp. 1116–24.

Hutter, S. 2014. 'Protest Event Analysis and Its Offspring', *Methodological Practices in Social Movement Research*. Oxford: Oxford University Press, pp. 335–67.

Ignazi, P. 1992. 'The Silent Counter-Revolution', *European Journal of Political Research* 22(1): 3–34.

Kahn-Harris, K. 2007. *Extreme Metal: Music and Culture on the Edge*. Oxford: Berg.

Kallis, A.L. 2000. *Fascist Ideology: Territory and Expansionism in Italy and Germany, 1922–1945*. London: Routledge.

Kiousis, S. et al. 2006. 'First- and Second-Level Agenda-Building and Agenda-Setting Effects: Exploring the Linkages among Candidate News Releases, Media Coverage, and

Public Opinion during the 2002 Florida Gubernatorial Election', *Journal of Public Relations Research* 18(3): 265–85.

Kitschelt, H. 2006. 'Movement Parties', in R.S. Katz and W. Crotty (eds), *Handbook of Party Politics*. Thousand Oaks, CA: Sage, pp. 278–90.

Koch, H. 2013. *Casa Pound Italia: Mussolinis Erben*. Münster: Unrast.

———. 2017. 'CasaPound Italia: The Fascist Hybrid', in M. Fielitz and L.L. Laloire (eds), *Trouble on the Far Right: Contemporary Right-Wing Strategies and Practices in Europe*. Bielefeld: Transcript.

Koopmans, R., and D. Rucht. 2002. 'Protest Event Analysis', *Methods of Social Movement Research*. Minneapolis: University of Minnesota Press.

Koopmans, R., and P. Statham. 1999. 'Political Claims Analysis: Integrating Protest Event and Political Discourse Approaches', *Mobilization: An International Quarterly* 4(2): 203–21.

Kriesi, H. 1989. 'The Political Opportunity Structure of the Dutch Peace Movement', *West European Politics* 12(3): 295–312.

Laver, M. 2014. 'Measuring Policy Positions in Political Space', *Annual Review of Political Science* 17(1): 207–23.

Laver, M. et al. 2003. 'Extracting Policy Positions from Political Texts Using Words as Data', *American Political Science Review* 97(2): 311–31.

Liang, C.S. 2016. *Europe for the Europeans: The Foreign and Security Policy of the Populist Radical Right*. London: Routledge.

Linz, J.J. 1985. *Totalitarian and Authoritarian Regimes*. Boston: Addison-Wesley.

Mair, P. 2008. 'The Challenge to Party Government', *West European Politics* 31(1–2): 211–34.

Mammone, A. 2015. *Transnational Neofascism in France and Italy*. Cambridge: Cambridge University Press.

Mammone, A. et al. 2013. *Varieties of Right-Wing Extremism in Europe*. London: Routledge.

Mattoni, A. 2016. *Media Practices and Protest Politics: How Precarious Workers Mobilise*. Abingdon: Routledge.

Mazzoleni, G., and W. Schulz. 1999. '"Mediatization" of Politics: A Challenge for Democracy?', *Political Communication* 16(3): 247–61.

McAdam, D. et al. (eds). 1996. *Comparative Perspectives on Social Movements: Political Opportunities, Mobilizing Structures, and Cultural Framings*. New York: Cambridge University Press.

McCarthy, J.D., and M.N. Zald. 1977. 'Resource Mobilization and Social Movements: A Partial Theory', *American Journal of Sociology* 82(6): 1212–41.

Mudde, C. 1996. 'The War of Words Defining the Extreme Right Party Family', *West European Politics* 19(2): 225–48.

———. 2000. *The Ideology of the Extreme Right*. Manchester: Manchester University Press.

———. 2007. *Populist Radical Right Parties in Europe*. Cambridge: Cambridge University Press.

———. 2016a. 'The Study of Populist Radical Right Parties: Towards a Fourth Wave', *C-REX Working Paper Series* 1(1).

———. 2016b. *The Populist Radical Right: A Reader*. London: Routledge.

———. 2019. *The Far Right Today*. Cambridge: Polity.

Norris, P. et al. 2005. 'Who Demonstrates? Antistate Rebels, Conventional Participants, or Everyone?', *Comparative Politics* 37(2): 189–205.

O'Reilly, C. 2005. 'Narrating Backpacker Identity', in A. Jaworski and A. Pritchard (eds), *Discourse, Communication, and Tourism*. Clevedon: Channel View.

Olson, M. 1965. *Logic of Collective Action*. Cambridge, MA: Harvard University Press.

Panebianco, A. 1988. *Political Parties: Organization and Power*. New York: Cambridge University Press.

Paxton, R.O. 2004. *The Anatomy of Fascism*. New York: Alfred A. Knopf.
Payne, S.G. 1996. *A History of Fascism, 1914–1945*. Madison: University of Wisconsin Press.
Petrocik, J.R. 1996. 'Issue Ownership in Presidential Elections, with a 1980 Case Study', *American Journal of Political Science* 40(3): 825–50.
Pirro, A.L.P. 2019. 'Jobbik and the Crafting of a New Hungarian Far-Right", in M. Caiani and O. Císař (eds), *Radical Right Movement Parties in Europe*. London: Routledge.
Pirro, A.L.P., and P. Castelli Gattinara. 2018. 'Movement Parties of the Far Right: Organization and Strategies of Nativist Collective Actors', *Mobilization* 23(3): 367–383.
Poguntke, T. et al. 2016. 'Party Rules, Party Resources and the Politics of Parliamentary Democracies: How Parties Organize in the 21st Century', *Party Politics* 22(6): 661–78.
Polletta, F., and J.M. Jasper. 2001. 'Collective Identity and Social Movements', *Annual Review of Sociology* 27(1): 283–305.
Roggeband, C., and R. Vliegenthart 2007 'Divergent Framing: The Public Debate on Migration in the Dutch Parliament and Media, 1995–2004', *West European Politics* 30(3): 524–48.
Rooduijn, M. 2014 'The Mesmerising Message: The Diffusion of Populism in Public Debates in Western European Media', *Political Studies* 62(4): 726–44.
Rosati, E. 2018. *CasaPound Italia. Fascisti Del Terzo Millennio*. Milan: Mimesis.
Russell Hochschild, A. 2016. *Strangers in Their Own Land*. New York: The New Press.
Rydgren, J. 2007. 'The Sociology of the Radical Right', *Annual Review of Sociology* 33(1): 241–62.
———. 2008. 'Immigration Sceptics, Xenophobes or Racists? Radical Right-Wing Voting in Six West European Countries', *European Journal of Political Research* 47(6): 737–65.
Sainsbury, D. 1980. *Swedish Social Democratic Ideology and Electoral Politics 1944–1948: A Study of the Functions of Party Ideology*. Stockholm: Lmqvist and Wiksell International.
Scarrow, S.E. et al. 2017. *Organizing Political Parties*. Oxford: Oxford University Press.
Seawright, J., and J. Gerring. 2008. 'Case Selection Techniques in Case Study Research: A Menu of Qualitative and Quantitative Options', *Political Research Quarterly* 61(2): 294–308.
Taggart, P. 1995. 'New Populist Parties in Western Europe', *West European Politics* 18(1): 34–51.
Taguieff, P.-A. 1985. 'Les Nouvelles Idéologies de Droite en France (1976–1984)', in J.-Y. Potel (ed.), *L'état de la France et de Ses Habitants*. Paris: La Découverte, pp. 446–50.
———. 1998. *Le Racisme. Un Exposé Pour Comprendre, Un Essai Pour Réfléchir*. Paris: Flammarion.
Tarrow, S. 1996. 'States and Opportunities: The Political Structuring of Social Movements', in D. McAdam et al. (eds), *Comparative Perspectives on Social Movements*. New York: Cambridge University Press, pp. 41–61.
Teitelbaum, B.R. 2017. *Lions of the North: Sounds of the New Nordic Radical Nationalism*. Oxford: Oxford University Press.
The Guardian. 2018. 'The Fascist Movement that Has Brought Mussolini Back to the Mainstream'. URL: https://www.theguardian.com/news/2018/feb/22/casapound-italy-mussolini-fascism-mainstream (consulted February 2018).
Tilly, C. 1978. *From Mobilization to Revolution*. Reading, MA: Addison Wesley.
Torrisi, C. 2018. 'How the Italian Media have helped to Glamourise Fascism', *Open Democracy*. URL: https://www.opendemocracy.net/en/5050/italian-media-casapound-glamourise-fascism/(consulted January 2018).

Virchow, F. 2016. 'PEGIDA: Understanding the Emergence and Essence of Nativist Protest in Dresden', *Journal of Intercultural Studies* 37(6): 541–55.

Vliegenthart, R., and S. Walgrave. 2012. 'The Interdependency of the Mass Media and Social Movements', in H.A. Semetko and M. Scammel (eds), *The SAGE Handbook of Political Communication*. London: Sage.

Von Beyme, K. 1988. 'Right-wing Extremism in Post-war Europe', *West European Politics* 11(2): 1–18.

Wouters, R. 2013. 'From the Street to the Screen: Characteristics of Protest Events as Determinants of Television News Coverage', *Mobilization: An International Quarterly* 18(1): 83–105.

Zúquete, J.P. 2018. *The Identitarians*. Notre Dame, IN: Notre Dame Press.

2

HISTORY AND CONTEXT OF CASAPOUND ITALIA

To understand hybridization in the politics of CasaPound Italia, one must first contextualize the group within the specific Italian scenario. Most scholars, in fact, consider Italy a particularly suitable case for right-wing extremism due to its broadly open political opportunities (Mammone et al. 2013), which facilitate far-right mobilization by modern populist radical-right actors such as the *Lega Nord* (Northern League, LN), as well as extra-parliamentary and grassroots collective actors such as CasaPound (Caldiron 2009; Marchi 1997). In tracing the history of CPI's emergence, this chapter relies on secondary literature to address the historical and institutional factors defining right-wing mobilization in post-World War II Italy. In addition, we use official data from CPI's website and interviews with national leaders to reconstruct the origins of the group. Building on the notion of political opportunity structures (Kriesi 1989; McAdam et al. 1996; Tarrow 1996), we argue that the symbolic legacy of extreme-right politics in post-war Italy informs the internal-supply side and mobilization strategies of CPI. First, the chapter introduces the reader to Italy's far-right milieu in the years post World War II (2.1); then, it discusses recent developments in Italian politics and the turning points that contributed to revitalizing far-right street politics (2.2). Section 2.3 discusses specifically the origins of CPI in the early 2000s and its ambivalent engagement in protest and electoral activities. Section 2.4 examines how the group progressively expanded its political platform and reached national relevance.

2.1 Far-right politics in Italy: from 1945 to Fiuggi

In this section, we address the legacy of historical Fascism as part of the opportunity structure for far-right mobilization in contemporary Italy. We shall devote particular attention to the outspoken mistrust, among the ideologues of

Fascism, towards party politics (Gentile 2013; Payne 1996). A crucial current of Italian Fascism, in fact, has been considered as 'Fascism as a movement', because it featured anti-democratic, revolutionary and secular tendencies, as opposed to the more conservative, institutional features of 'Fascism-as-a-regime' (De Felice 1969). If the conservative current of Fascism-as-a-regime emphasized order and tradition, Fascism-as-a-movement pursued revolutionary ideals based on dynamism, youth activism and the rejection of modernity and democracy (Ignazi 2003). While this tension has characterized historical Fascism since its inception, here we look at its manifestation in post-war activism as a crucial factor explaining the ideological and cultural trajectories of contemporary extreme-right actors in Italy.

Cultural and historical factors are key to understanding the openness of political and discursive opportunity structures for collective action (Giugni 2009; Koopmans and Statham 1999). Unlike Nazi Germany, the Italian Fascist dictatorship was ended by a civil war, which left a profound emotional divide between the pro- and anti-Fascism camps. After the execution of Benito Mussolini, Italy did not experience a genuine process of transition or 'de-fascistization' (Mammone et al. 2013). Consequently, the Italian collective imagination considered inter-war Fascism as a sort of accident of history rather than as the result of Italy's pre-existing political culture, and the resulting massive adhesion to the regime in the 1930s (Gentile 2013). From 1952, with the approval of the so-called *Legge Scelba* (Scelba Act, from the name of its main promoter), the Italian legal and constitutional system prohibits the diffusion of Fascist and Nazi ideologies and the reconstitution of the National Fascist Party (*Partito Nazionale Fascista*, PNF). This certainly limited the activity and propaganda of post-war extreme-right groups, since the presence of such forces was reputed to be anti-democratic in itself (Chiarini 1995).

Nevertheless, the cultural and symbolic legacy of Mussolini's regime, its ideology, policies and organization had a profound influence on the ideas and mobilization potential of extreme-right parties and movements in the post-war years (Cento Bull 2007). Fascist groups were soon able to reorganize themselves, with the foundation of the Italian Social Movement (*Movimento Sociale Italiano*, MSI) in the very first years of the Italian republic. While initially envisaged as a militia-style organization, the MSI rapidly turned towards the structure and organization of a legal political party organized along the mass-party model, contesting elections based on a mix of calls to national pacification and nostalgia for the past regime (Ignazi 1998). From its origins, however, the party was torn between two main factions. A 'movement' or 'radical' faction claimed continuity with the revolutionary and anti-liberal style of the republican Fascism of the mid-1940s and opposed the very principles of the newly established democratic system. The 'moderate' faction, instead, preferred the clerical, corporatist and conservative tendencies of the fascist regime: it was more inclined to access the party system, supported Italy's membership of

NATO and was open to compromise with the ruling parties against the Communist 'threat'.

Although the moderate strategy proved electorally rewarding in the 1950s and early 1960s, the radical faction gained momentum in subsequent years as the MSI found itself progressively isolated in the Italian political system. The electoral strategy of the MSI in fact was met by a rising dissatisfaction among the subcultural and youth components of Italian neo-fascism, frustrated by the post-war ghettoization of the extreme right (Tarchi 1995, 1997). While new groups emerged within and outside the MSI, calling for hard-line clashes with political opponents in the streets, a part of the movement was clearly differentiated by its efforts to renovate extreme-right ideology based on the French *Nouvelle Droite*'s critique of the liberal-capitalist system, individualism and consumerism (Bar-On 2012).

Of considerable impact on younger generations was the organization of a series of summer camps, which aimed at taking the MSI out of the gloomy neo-fascist ghetto, to assume an active role in Italian society. The so-called 'Hobbit Camps' (organized in 1977, 1978, 1980) represented perhaps the last attempt to achieve authentic ideological and cultural renewal in the Italian extreme right (Tarchi 1997, 2010). By introducing concerts, cultural performances and public debates in direct emulation of the model introduced by left-wing parties and movements, the organizers of the festivals intended to re-formulate the cultural roots of post-war Fascism in Italy. The MSI leadership however did not appreciate the efforts of the youth section to renovate, and soon reinforced the hierarchical principle, marking the end of this short-lived season of cultural renewal and experimentation with innovative organization models. While these attempts did not succeed in bringing the MSI out of its isolation, due to the party's enduring nostalgia for the regime and its reluctance to take a distance from street violence and terrorism, the memory of the summer camps is still very much alive in contemporary extreme-right groups in Italy. This renewed worldview was an encouragement to join the MSI for students and younger people who wished to put a halt to the bloody confrontations between fascists and antifascists (Ignazi 2003).

Meanwhile, extra-parliamentary groups had become increasingly active alongside the parliamentary extreme right (Picco 2018). Since the early post-war years, its components had been involved in a multitude of episodes of street violence, attempts at coups d'état and various acts of terror of serious magnitude. Not only, therefore, has neo-fascist violence been prolonged compared to most other European countries, but the acts of aggression have also been more numerous and diverse than elsewhere, including a high number of terrorist attacks during the so-called *anni di piombo* (years of lead) between 1969 and 1982 (Ferraresi 1995; Weinberg 1995). Over these years, activists of *Ordine Nuovo* (New Order, ON) and *Avanguardia Nazionale* (National Vanguard, AvNa) were involved in activities ranging from street corner brawls to widespread urban rioting (such as the protests in Reggio Calabria in 1970), whilst neo-fascist militants were also responsible for bomb massacres intended to sow mass panic and trigger military intervention in Italian politics (Ferraresi 1995). Violence further escalated as the ideologues of *Terza Posizione* (Third Position, TP)[1] and the *Nuclei Armati Rivoluzionari* (Armed Revolutionary Nuclei, NAR) developed a romanticized idea of activists as 'legionnaires', fighting for a hopeless cause.

The 'armed spontaneity' of the late 1970s (Ferraresi 1995: 189) paved the way for the formation of small autonomous groups operating independently and understanding street violence as a first step in a revolutionary progression that would comprise terrorism and culminate in guerrilla warfare. The failure of this strategy to integrate the extreme right into a collective movement, and the countless victims it produced culminating in the massacre at Bologna's train station (85 deaths on 2 August 1980), ultimately led to the demise of Italy's armed neo-Fascism in the 1980s. The dismantlement of most extra-parliamentary right-wing organizations, the fall of the Berlin wall and the changing global context progressively made confrontation with communism and street violence lose momentum. By the early 1990s, the MSI had gradually turned into a focus for protest by legal means, unambiguously denouncing violence and clearly distancing itself from extreme-right fringes.

As MSI candidates achieved resounding success in local elections, the party greatly improved its coalition potential (Ignazi 1998). Taking advantage of these opportunities, the 1995 congress in Fiuggi marked the transition of the MSI into a modern European radical right party, *Alleanza Nazionale* (National Alliance, AN) that could now present itself as a legitimate ally for the emerging mainstream right coalitions that would rule Italy in the following decades (Lazaridis et al. 2016). AN's last leader, Gianfranco Fini, officially detached the party from the legacy of historical Fascism in October 2003, when, during a visit to Israel, he declared that 'Fascism was the absolute evil' (*La Repubblica* 2003). A few years later in 2009, AN disappeared as the party merged into Silvio Berlusconi's coalition The People of Freedom (*Popolo della libertà,* PDL).

2.2 The contemporary scenario

In the early 1990s, the transition of the MSI into mainstream conservative politics inevitably triggered reactions among the right-wing milieu. Indeed, numerous activists and several party officials who did not support the rejection of the revolutionary features of Fascism founded the *Movimento Sociale-Fiamma Tricolore* (Social Movement – Tricolour Flame, MS-FT). While AN progressively took a clear stand against biological racism and anti-Semitism, MS-FT did not renounce references to Fascism, nor to its social foundations and revolutionary principles (Castelli Gattinara et al. 2013). The group benefited from considerable popularity in the early years among marginalized groups in metropolitan areas, thanks to its radical positions against globalization, immigration and the liberal economy, which define the party as a clear example of extreme-right politics (Ignazi 2003). MS-FT in fact successfully elected one Member of Parliament at the 1996 general election, and one Euro-MP at the 1999 European Parliament election. Over the years, however, the party lost momentum, as other actors in the same area increasingly challenged its distinctive profile.

In the same years, former members of post-war fascist militant organizations founded the party *Forza Nuova* (New Force, FzNv). At its origins, the group formed the grassroots faction of the MS-FT. Subsequently, it splintered from the party to develop an agenda of its own, focusing primarily on street activism and protest politics, and promoting a series of campaigns against abortion, euthanasia and same-sex marriage. FzNv's politics hence combined historical Fascism ideals with ultra-catholic values, which set it apart from the secularist tradition of Italy's post-war fascist sector. During the 1990s and early 2000s, FzNv infiltrated organized soccer clubs to recruit militants among hooligans and the skinhead music subculture to attract young activists (Caldiron 2013). At the same time, the group also tried to gain legitimacy in the electoral arena, by collaborating with small splinter groups originating from the AN. After 2008, FzNv fielded candidates using their own independent lists in national and local elections, generally with little success. Throughout the 1990s and 2000s, FzNv displayed characteristics that are similar to some factions of post-war Italian Fascism, in that it was contradictory in nature, seeking respectability as a political party in the electoral arena, but also claiming a 'revolutionary' spirit, open to violence (Campani 2016).

In the early 2000s, therefore, both FzNv and MS-FT transitioned to the electoral arena, where they repeatedly established national and local alliances with the mainstream right coalition of Silvio Berlusconi. As will be discussed in the next section, the origins of CasaPound are tightly embedded in this political climate and are related to the tensions generated by the decision of most actors of the Italian far right to enter elections. The right-wing coalition between Silvio Berlusconi's personal party, the Northern League, and various other conservative and Christian-democratic groups, in fact, produced a progressive blurring of the distinction between mainstream and far-right politics in Italy (Albertazzi and McDonnell 2010; Fella and Ruzza 2013). While this led to the marginalization of at least some extreme-right movements at the fringe of the political spectrum, it also contributed to mainstreaming a number of far-right narratives. Notably, the promotion of openly xenophobic vocabularies by mainstream right actors provided radical movements with public credibility in national and local debates over migration and diversity (Castelli Gattinara 2016).

Over the following years, Italy was at the core of two major critical events, the Eurozone crisis and the EU migration policy crisis (Castelli Gattinara 2018; Kriesi and Pappas 2016; Mudde 2016). As well as contributing to a further weakening of the mainstream parties, these issues also reshaped the opportunities for far-right mobilization. While the linkage between 'crises' and the breakthrough of the far right remains contested (Mudde 2013), critical events of this sort offer new opportunities to political actors to diversify their engagement across political arenas, as well as across socio-economic and socio-cultural issues. With respect to the far right, previous research suggested that political crises might induce far-right parties to use street organizations as a route into society, thus facilitating coexistence, if not cooperation, across arenas of engagement (Pedahzur and Weinberg 2001). Indeed, today the Italian far right benefits from the growing public resonance of issues like immigration, security and opposition to the establishment. This boosted the electoral support of the most influential party actor of this area, the increasingly right-wing populist *Lega Nord* (rebranded *Lega* in 2018), while also granting political leeway to the smaller *Fratelli d'Italia* (Brothers of Italy, FdI). This came to the detriment of mainstream right and conservative actors, which are more and more marginal in Italy's increasingly polarized political system. The intensive media coverage of these parties further expanded the opportunities for other far-right groups to take action, including extremist and violent events (The Washington Post 2018). In this context, taking advantage of the inefficient implementation of anti-racist and anti-fascist sanctions, a multiplicity of anti-democratic, autocratic and ultra-nationalist organizations have managed to obtain access to the public domain (ECRI 2015; Human Rights Watch 2011).

Overall, contemporary right-wing mobilization in Italy is faced with a rather favourable pattern of political opportunities, which facilitates the participation of small grassroots groups in national politics, and their access to the public sphere (Caiani et al. 2012). While radical right populist parties (RRPPs) enjoy considerable electoral support, in fact, they also sustain a privileged channel of communication with the social movement arena. In return, social movement organizations can count on the presence of far-right parties in institutions to gather the necessary resources to increase their visibility in the public sphere (Rao 2014; Wetzel 2009: 337). As we shall illustrate in the next section, the emergence of CasaPound in the early 2000s is strongly linked to the process of institutionalization of pre-existing extreme-right actors. Yet, the rapid growth of CPI and the visibility of its social movement campaigns is also related to the availability of favourable opportunities for mobilization and access to the media.

2.3 The origins of CasaPound Italia

CasaPound Italia was officially established in 2008 as a charitable organization. The origins of the group, however, must be found in the socio-political context of the late 1990s, when CPI's current president Gianluca Iannone founded the music band *ZetaZeroAlfa* (ZZA), which would come to represent an important cultural phenomenon within the Roman right-wing landscape. Over the following years, the ZZA became a core identity feature of a small group of young extreme-right militants (see Chapter 5), meeting at the *Cutty Sark* pub (now managed by CPI), to discuss the history of Fascism, football, love, violence and

FIGURE 2.1 The logo of *ZetaZeroAlfa*.

globalization. As reported in the website of CasaPound, the texts of ZZA's songs gave voice to the demands of those young activists who did not feel represented by the far-right parties of the time, and who identified more with the extra-parliamentary right than with the electoral tradition of the MSI as a political party (CPI 2012a).

In the early 2000s, the group engaged in a number of showcase political actions, which marked their diversity from the style of action of most existing far-right actors. Faced with the need to find a place to meet and gather, they started occupying abandoned buildings. Social-centre squatting in Italy has its roots in the mid-1970s, as a radical left mobilization to 'claim the city' (Della Porta and Diani 1999). By the 1990s, the movement had reached its apogee, with the widespread occupation of public spaces and empty buildings throughout the country (Piazza 2011), but until then right-wing squats had been fairly exceptional, and generally short-lived (Rao 2014). The group led by Iannone set out to change this tradition. First, in 2002, they targeted a building in the suburbs of Rome, which they named *CasaMontag* (The House of Montag, CM) and used it to organize music gigs and cultural events.[2] This was the first of a series of *Occupazioni non Conformi* (Non-Compliant Occupations) that took place in the early 2000s, and which would come to represent a fundamental pillar for CPI's activism and propaganda. Yet CM did not have, at least initially, a political aim; rather, it served as a meeting space, in which activists could gather to debate politics, play music, draw and read

FIGURE 2.2 The logo of *CasaPound Italia*.

comics. The set-up of *CasaMontag*, which lasted for about a year, was the result of an immediate, direct action, presented as a concrete answer to an urgent need: that of finding a place to meet and gather with other like-minded activists and sympathizers. Only later would CPI develop the understanding of occupations as a political response to the housing crisis, and of squatting as a form of political activism (see Di Stefano 2013).

The origins of *CasaPound* are therefore connected with the progressive politicization of squatting practices. On 26 December 2003, a group of activists led by Iannone decided to occupy an apartment block in the *Esquilino Hill* neighbourhood, close to the main train station in Rome. This time, the motivation for the squat – which would be named *CasaPound* ('The House of Pound') – was political and, most notably, linked to housing issues. It was the first of CPI's *Occupazioni a Scopo Abitativo* (Occupations for Housing Purposes), and housed the national headquarters of CasaPound Italia, together with 23 families – including those of prominent members of the organization (*Il Riformista* 2010). The political nature of this CasaPound squat was radically different from that of CasaMontag. Now, the occupation was motivated by the need to deal with the housing crisis in Rome, as shown in the banner that was hung outside the occupied building: 'Rent is usury. Stop the increase in the cost of living!' (Di Nunzio and Toscano 2011: 25).

Despite several judiciary and political attempts to evacuate the building until 2018 (*La Repubblica 2018*), at the time of writing the CasaPound squat is still at the core of CPI politics. The building physically hosts the headquarters of the organization, and most of the national events organized by CPI. Symbolically, the occupation reinforces the social movement image of CPI even though in more recent years the group has been progressively engaging in the election arena. Indeed, while CPI leadership proudly claims that they are and will always be *different* from traditional parties (Rao 2014), CPI's relationship with electoral politics has not been so linear. A few years after the squat of CasaPound, Gianluca Iannone and his group officially joined the MS-FT and rapidly became the dominant minority faction of the party, especially within the youth wing. In 2006 Iannone himself ran as an independent candidate for MS-FT, but this relationship was short-lived. Already in 2008, CPI splintered from the party due to disagreements concerning its organization and decision-making. According to CPI leaders, MS-FT did not allow young people to express themselves and engage in politics in an autonomous and non-conventional way.[3] Specifically, Iannone was expelled from MS-FT after he led the occupation of the party's national headquarters demanding the organization of a new congress. The statement released by Iannone on that occasion is emblematic:

> Today, 23 May 2008, the 'men of action' [...] have occupied the national headquarters of the *Fiamma Tricolore* (Tricolour Flame, FT) party – which two years ago was smashed and to which we had given a new dynamism, ideas, and political credibility. This action responds to the work we have

> been doing for years, with the spirit of self-sacrifice and sense of belonging that characterises us. A spirit constantly betrayed by an 'apparatus' that does not even abide to the obligations imposed by the party statute – the highest normative source for a party. An apparatus that is insensitive to the demands for meritocracy that its movement-wing has been advancing for a long time. An apparatus […] that is only interested in selling to the highest bidder a political leeway that we have built with our militancy and that, today, we take back.
>
> *(CPI 2008)*

Acknowledging that MS-FT had become old hat, in terms of symbols, ideas and modes of action,[4] the splinter group would thus quit the party to found CasaPound Italia. As can be noted in the quote above, CPI's leaders emphasize the tension between their propulsion towards social movement activism, on the one hand, and the slow, old-fashioned, exclusive nature of party politics, on the other. This ambiguous relationship with both protest and party politics will become a crucial feature of CPI in the following years, as we shall illustrate in the next section.

2.4 From local to national, from single-issue movement to political party

In its early years, CPI was active almost exclusively in one city: Rome. It configured as a typical case of a single-issue actor, mobilizing almost exclusively on one issue: housing rights for Italians. Over time, however, the group expanded its political platform and reached out to other cities.

The territorial expansion depended on available resources and the opportunity to set up a local chapter.[5] Although irregular, this expansion has been sizable: as shown in Map 2.1, in 2013 CPI could count on 60 local sections in Italy, whereas in 2018 it had 154 local sections.

Looking at the development over time, it can be seen that CPI has extended its territorial reach, progressively becoming a national movement. If in 2013 the group existed mostly in the region of Rome and in a few northern cities, in 2018 CPI chapters are found in most regions in the centre of Italy, but also in the south and now more extensively in the north. This also led the group to extend its name, from simply 'CasaPound' to 'CasaPound Italia'. At the same time, the two maps show that CPI remains an urban phenomenon, since its chapters are mostly located in regional capitals and major cities, and less so in smaller towns and rural areas.

Through its local branches, CasaPound recruits militants and sponsors activities linked to its main national campaigns (see Chapters 4 and 5). In this respect, the territorial organization of CPI does not differ much from that of political parties. Yet the local branches also invest in two types of initiatives that are less political in nature. On the one hand, they promote socialization among militants and sympathizers through leisure activities, pubs, music events and sport clubs, in line with

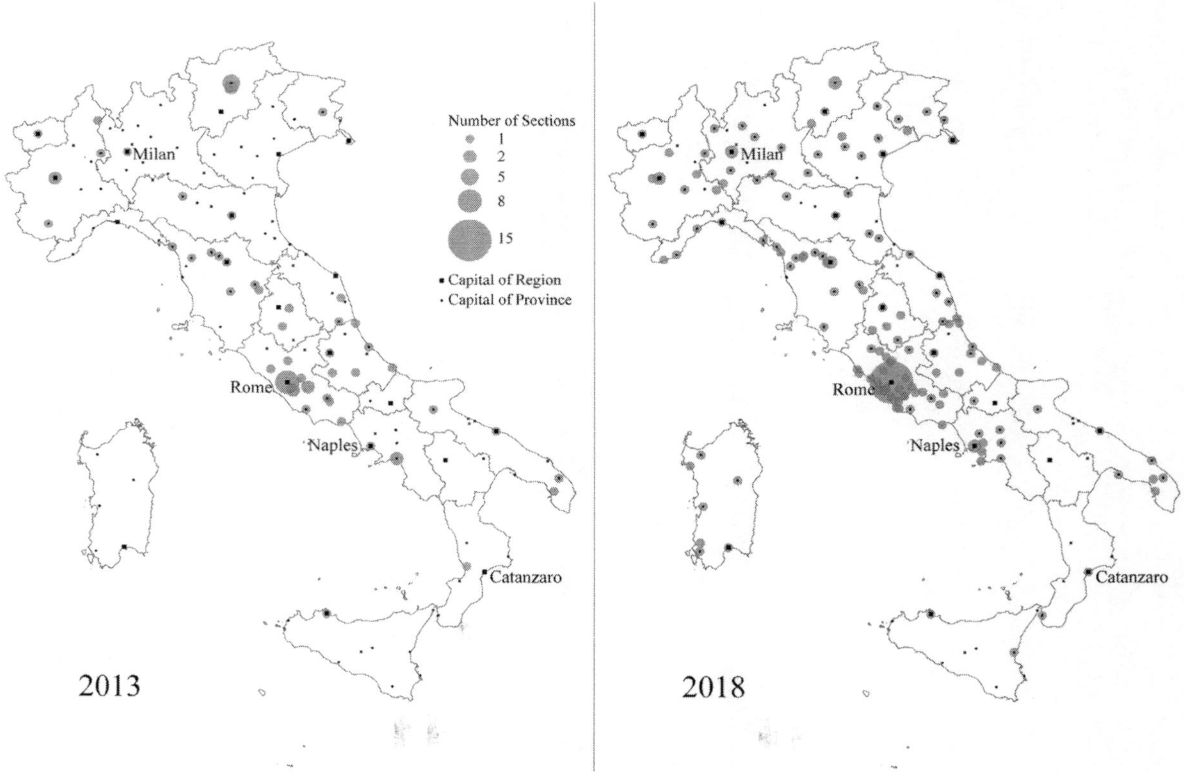

MAP 2.1 Local sections of CasaPound Italia: geographical distribution in 2013 and 2018.

the general idea of CPI as a community. On the other, they promote direct forms of engagement on local problems perceived as urgent, a repertoire which previous literature named Direct Social Actions (DSA) (Bosi and Zamponi 2015). Notably, local CasaPound activists intervene to offer a material contribution to public problems of security, emergency and environmental deterioration, among others (Froio and Castelli Gattinara 2017). While DSA are not the bulk of CPI's mobilization (see Chapter 6), they serve to permeate contexts that are unfavourable to the group, or where the opportunities to open a local branch are minimal due to the presence of political opponents. This was the case of Naples, where CPI faced much opposition and thus opted to mobilize on social issues, by distributing food to (Italian) families, by offering counselling to (Italian) workers and unemployed people, and by trying to open a clinic for (Italian) people who struggled to access public health services.

> We have set up a centre that, from the beginning and still today, has offered services, from tax advice to employment assistance to counselling. It might seem silly, since today is all about numbers and profit (…) but we just want to give people the possibility to come and talk to us, to unburden themselves of their problems. There are people that no one wants to hear. Often they just come to us and talk about their personal problems: their son who takes drugs or who cannot find a job.[6]

In this respect, the progressive national expansion of CPI also had consequences on the group's political offer, and on its preferred modes of action. As noted earlier, in its early years CPI preferred the protest arena to the institutional one, and stood out for its predisposition towards non-conventional repertoires, showcase protests, occupations and other political and cultural activities. The imagery and symbols of its protests contributed to building a radical image of CPI and its network of political and cultural movements, granting recognizability within and without the extreme-right milieu (Rao 2014). Over time, however, CPI increasingly combined grassroots engagement with activities in the electoral arena. While the results have been generally very poor (see Chapter 6), the electoral shift forced the group to expand its programmatic agenda to issues that had remained until then on the margins of its political agenda. In 2011 and 2012, a number of candidates from CPI ran as independents within centre-right coalitions, as Gianluca Iannone had done with MS-FT in 2006. From 2013 onwards, however, CPI presented its own electoral list and refused to ally or build coalitions with other candidates at the local and national levels. A few local councillors were elected throughout Italy. The increased attention on the election arena, however, was accompanied by sustained mobilization in the protest arena, including a number of episodes of violence (see Chapter 6).

A trace of this hybrid institutionalization can be noted in the way in which the group officially presents itself to the outside world. The 'FAQ' section of CPI's website, in fact, includes questions that 'define' the group, its organization and main goals. Comparing the text that appeared in 2012 (when we started this research) with the one currently displayed (January 2019 at the time of writing), a number of substantial changes are evident. The first change concerns the question 'What does CPI do?'. Both in 2012 and in 2018, the answer emphasizes the extra-political, social and cultural nature of CPI politics. Yet, in 2012, the answer concluded in a way that made CPI almost incompatible with electoral politics. Tellingly, the last sentence of the 2012 quote is omitted in the 2018 version, signalling a change in strategy and the progressive transition towards electoral politics (CPI 2012b).

> *What does CPI do?* Politics. That is, the good of the polis. That is, to give hope, dignity, strength and will to an exhausted and bloodless people. CPI acts in society with a single will expressed by a thousand voices: exhibitions, conferences, study groups, artistic experiments, concerts, pubs, youth communities, gyms, volunteering, trade unionism, media provocations. And also elections. If and when necessary. If and when there is room for manoeuvre beyond the usual mob of businessmen. This means: very rarely.

A second change concerns CPI as an organization. In the early years, the group presented itself as *alternative* to the model of extra-parliamentary movements but also to that of traditional political parties. Two subsequent questions asked if CPI was 'an extra-parliamentary movement' and whether it was 'a political party'. In both cases, the answer was 'Absolutely not'. Again, this changed over time and the paragraph here, from 2012, no longer appears on the website in 2018:

> *Is CPI a party?* Absolutely not. CPI is transversal, free, and creative. CPI has militants and programmes; it offers ideas, not career opportunities. Therefore, it cannot be a party. This does not mean that it does not engage in politics. To think that only a party can do so is to have an idealised view of contemporary political dynamics, stuck in the nineteenth century, and unaware of contemporary dynamics.
>
> *(CPI 2012b)*

Finally, a third change concerns the way in which CPI relates to extra-parliamentary politics. As can be noted in the following excerpts, in 2018, as in 2012, CPI refuses to be considered as an extra-parliamentary movement, but it does so based on quite different reasons.

> *Is CPI an extra-parliamentary movement?* Absolutely not. CPI has militants, supporters, and friends who are active in institutional politics, mainstream culture, and in associations defining the social life of the nation. It is not a group of subversive outcasts, crazy terrorists, hotheads looking to pull a stunt.
>
> *(CPI 2012b)*

FIGURE 2.3 Posters of CasaPound's territorial festivals.

On the left, the poster of the 2016 festival in Tuscany entitled *Direction: Revolution*. On the right, a 2018 event in Isernia (Molise) entitled *Direction: Parliament*.

> *Is CPI an extra-parliamentary movement?* Absolutely not. CPI is a political community that regularly presents itself in elections and aspires to enter Parliament to undermine the power systems that paralyze this nation. It is not a group of subversive outcasts, crazy terrorists, hotheads looking to pull a stunt.
>
> *(CPI 2018)*

A final, exemplary, sign of CPI's progressive transition to the election arena is provided by the choice of the slogans for its campaigns. Traditionally, CPI employs a sensationalizing strategy, using a shocking visual and linguistic repertoire to get the attention of the media (see Chapter 7). In 2013, the slogan accompanying CPI's national festival was *Direzione Rivoluzione* (Direction: Revolution), underlying the group's ambition to radically transform Italy and Italian politics. Tellingly, by 2018 the slogan was amended to *Direzione Parlamento* (Direction: Parliament).

Conclusive remarks

The rise of CPI represented a novelty in the Italian extreme right, especially considering the ideological stagnation of far-right parties in Italy since the early 1980s. This contributed to capturing the attention of the media, other extreme-right organizations and the broader public. In this respect, CPI's trajectory illustrates how the group managed to build an image *of its own* within the crowded field of far-right politics in Italy. As we have shown, CPI acquired a unique position thanks to its simultaneous engagement in the social movement and electoral arena, and thanks to its unconventional narrative inspired by different political and cultural traditions.

Today, CPI occupies a peculiar position with respect to various other extreme-right parties that did not accept the transformation of the post-fascist MSI throughout the 1990s and 2000s. The recent history of these groups has been characterized by a continuous ideological and strategic fragmentation, by personal and political disputes among party leaders, and by the failed attempts to find a strong figure to bring together its different factions. While the transformation of the Italian political system should have pushed the Italian extreme right towards a profound organizational renovation, instead, most parties failed to rethink themselves and their way of doing politics, thus crucially dampening their public appeal, mobilization potential and capacity for recruitment. At the time of its foundation, therefore, CPI was able to benefit from a lack of competition from the other organizations of the Italian extreme right. But its breakthrough has also to do with strategic choices. Despite emerging from the same neo-fascist milieu as other extreme-right parties, CasaPound set out on a completely different route, and invested most of its resources into the redefinition of its ideological and organizational profile. This granted the group unparalleled visibility in the media, facilitated its expansion on Italian territory, and triggered the engagement in electoral politics.

CPI's high profile in the Italian public sphere is confirmed by the increasing emulation of its strategy by other organizations and groups. Most notably, with the emergence of the so-called refugee crisis in Italy, *Forza Nuova* militants returned to social movement activism, and employed mobilization techniques that reproduced the imagery of CasaPound, such as the use of masks and smoke bombs. Similarly, they developed media-oriented strategies aimed at producing controversy and getting the spotlight (*L'Espresso* 2017), such as the public contestation of mainstream media whom they accused of carrying out independent investigations into the international connections and financing channels of the Italian extreme right (more on this in Chapter 7).

Whether or not these developments will ultimately reconfigure the composition of the Italian far right, rebalancing the relative weight of its electoral and social movement components, is a question that goes beyond the scope of our analysis. However, the trajectory of CPI since its foundation represents a major change for far-right politics in Italy. In this chapter, we have shown that the political and cultural context in which CPI emerged can help make sense, at least to a certain extent, of its politics. The question of precisely how embedded these hybrid politics are in the group's ideology will be the focus of the next chapter.

Notes

1 The 'Third Position' perspective reflected the opposition to both capitalism and socialism, and therefore to the political left and right (Ferraresi 1995; Griffin 2003).
2 The name refers to Guy Montag, the protagonist of Ray Bradbury's novel *Fahrenheit 451* (1953).

3 Interviews no. 1b, 1c, 1d, 19/04/2012.
4 Interview no. 1b, 19/04/2012.
5 This was the idea expressed by an official who, when narrating the beginnings of CasaPound in his own city, told us that the local office was established due to his own personal efforts: 'I borrowed a sum of money to open the office – which has existed for three years, this is our fourth year. That was because I wanted to live like a warrior, to assault the trench. The problem was that I owed large debts that I could not repay. I then asked Gianluca for help. I called him and he brought the ZetaZeroAlfa here. The comrades and I worked hard, rented the largest club in the area – 600 people attended! – earned money and paid back the outstanding debts!' (Interview no. 3a of 01/06/2012).
6 Interview no. 5b of 28/06/2012.

References

Albertazzi, D., and D. McDonnell. 2010. 'The Lega Nord Back in Government', *West European Politics* 33(6): 1318–40.

Bar-On, T. 2012. 'The French New Right's Quest for Alternative Modernity', *Fascism* 1(1): 18–52.

Bosi, L., and L. Zamponi. 2015. 'Direct Social Actions and Economic Crises: The Relationship between Forms of Action and Socio-Economic Context in Italy', *Partecipazione e Conflitto* 8(2): 367–91.

Caiani, M. et al. 2012. *Mobilizing on the Extreme Right: Germany, Italy, and the United States.* Oxford: Oxford University Press.

Caldiron, G. 2009. *La destra sociale: da Salò a Tremonti.* Rome: Manifestolibri.

———. 2013. *Estrema destra.* Rome: Newton Compton Editori.

Campani, G. 2016. 'Neo-Fascism from the Twentieth Century to the Third Millennium: The Case of Italy', in G. Lazaridis, et al. (eds), *The Rise of the Far Right in Europe. Populist Shifts and 'Othering'.* London: Palgrave Macmillan, pp. 25–54.

Castelli Gattinara, P. 2016. *The Politics of Migration in Italy: Perspectives on Local Debates and Party Competition.* London: Routledge.

———. 2018. 'Europeans, Shut the Borders! Anti-Refugee Mobilisation in Italy and France', in D. Della Porta (ed.), *Solidarity Mobilizations in the 'Refugee Crisis'.* London: Palgrave, pp. 271–97.

Castelli Gattinara, P. et al. 2013. 'The Appeal of Neo-Fascism in Times of Crisis: The Experience of CasaPound Italia', *Fascism*, 2(2): 234–58.

Cento Bull, A. 2007. *The Strategy of Tension and the Politics of Nonreconciliation.* Oxford: Berghahn Books.

Chiarini, R. 1995. *Destra italiana: dall'Unità d'Italia a Alleanza Nazionale.* Venice: Marsilio.

CPI, 2008. 'CasaPound Occupa La Sede Di Fiamma Tricolore [CasaPound Occupies the Headquarters of Fiamma Tricolore]'. URL: www.vivamafarka.com/forum/index. php?topic=29274.0 (consulted July 2013).

———. 2012a. 'Una Terribile Bellezza è Nata [A Terrible Beauty Was Born]'. URL: www.casapounditalia.org (consulted August 2012).

———. 2012b. 'Le FAQ Di CasaPound [CPI's FAQ]'. URL: www.casapounditalia.org/p/le-faq-di-cpi.html (consulted October 2012).

———. 2018. 'Le FAQ Di CasaPound [CPI's FAQ]'. URL: www.casapounditalia.org/p/le-faq-di-cpi.html (consulted April 2018).

De Felice, R. 1969. *Le interpretazioni del fascismo.* Bari: Laterza.

Della Porta, D., and M. Diani. 1999. 'Forms, Repertoires and Cycles of Protest', in D. della Porta and M. Diani (eds), *Social Movements: An Introduction*. Oxford: Blackwell, pp. 165–92.

Di Nunzio, D., and E. Toscano. 2011. *Dentro e Fuori CasaPound: Capire Il Fascismo Del Terzo Millennio*. Rome: Armando Editore.

Di Stefano, S. 2013. 'I Colori Del Nero' [The Colours of Black], URL: www.youtube.com/watch?v=KE8VV46_0f0 (consulted May 2017).

ECRI. 2015. *Report on Italy*. Strasbourg: European Commission Against Racism and Intolerance.

Fella, S., and C. Ruzza. 2013. 'Populism and the Fall of the Centre-Right in Italy: The End of the Berlusconi Model or a New Beginning?', *Journal of Contemporary European Studies* 21(1): 38–52.

Ferraresi, F. 1995. *Threats to Democracy: The Radical Right in Italy after the War*. Princeton, NJ: Princeton University Press.

Froio, C., and P. Castelli Gattinara. 2017. 'Direct Social Actions in Extreme Right Mobilisations: Ideological, Strategic and Organisational Incentives in the Italian Neo-Fascist Right', *Partecipazione e Conflitto* 9(3): 1040–66.

Gentile, E. 2013. *Fascismo: Storia e interpretazione*. Bari: Laterza.

Giugni, M. 2009. 'Political Opportunities: From Tilly to Tilly', *Swiss Political Science Review* 15(2): 361–7.

Griffin, R. 2003. 'From Slime Mould to Rhizome: An Introduction to the Groupuscular Right', *Patterns of Prejudice* 37(1): 27–50.

Human Rights Watch. 2011. *Racist and Xenophobic Violence in Italy*. URL: www.hrw.org/publications/reports?topic=All&region=194 (consulted August 2016).

Ignazi, P. 1998. *Il Polo escluso: profilo storico del Movimiento Sociale Italiano*. Bologna: Il Mulino.

———. 2003. *Extreme Right Parties in Western Europe*. Oxford: Oxford University Press.

Il Riformista. 2010. 'Se CasaPound Diventa Un Caso Letterario', 11 February.

Koopmans, R., and P. Statham. 1999. 'Political Claims Analysis: Integrating Protest Event and Political Discourse Approaches', *Mobilization: An International Quarterly* 4(2): 203–21.

Kriesi, H. 1989. 'The Political Opportunity Structure of the Dutch Peace Movement', *West European Politics* 12(3): 295–312.

Kriesi, H., and T.S. Pappas. 2016. *European Populism in the Shadow of the Great Recession*. Colchester: ECPR Press.

La Repubblica. 2003, 'Fini in Israele: Il Fascismo Fu Parte Del Male Assoluto', November 24.

———. 2018. 'Sgomberate La Sede Abusiva Di Casapound L'appello Del Sindaco Di Cerveteri Pascucci a Salvini e Raggi', April 8.

Lazaridis, G. et al. (eds). 2016. *The Rise of the Far Right in Europe. Populist Shifts and 'Othering'*. London: Palgrave Macmillan.

L'Espresso. 2017. 'Fumogeni e Maschere: Blitz Di Forza Nuova Sotto La Redazione de l'Espresso e Repubblica', June 12.

Mammone, A. et al. 2013. *Varieties of Right-Wing Extremism in Europe*. London: Routledge.

Marchi, V. 1997. *Nazi-Rock. Pop Music e Destra Radicale*. Rome: Castelvecchi.

McAdam, D. et al. (eds). 1996. *Comparative Perspectives on Social Movements: Political Opportunities, Mobilizing Structures, and Cultural Framings*. New York: Cambridge University Press.

Mudde, C. 2013. 'Three Decades of Populist Radical Right Parties in Western Europe: So What?', *European Journal of Political Research* 52(1): 1–19.

———. 2016. *The Populist Radical Right: A Reader*. London: Routledge.

Payne, S.G. 1996. *A History of Fascism, 1914–1945*. Madison: University of Wisconsin Press.

Pedahzur, A., and L. Weinberg. 2001. 'Modern European Democracy and Its Enemies: The Threat of the Extreme Right', *Totalitarian Movements and Political Religions* 2(1): 52–72.

Piazza, G. 2011. 'Which Models of Democracy? Internal and External Decisionmaking Processes of Italian Social Centres in a Comparative Study', *Center of Studies on Politics and Society –WP Series* 1(1): 3–54.

Picco, P. 2018. *Liaisons Dangereuses. Les Extrêmes Droites En France et En Italie (1960–1984)*. Rennes: Presses Universitaires de Rennes.

Rao, N. 2014. *Trilogia della celtica*. Milan: Sperling & Kupfer.

Tarchi, M. 1995. *Esuli in patria: i fascisti nell'Italia repubblicana*. Milan: Guanda.

———. 1997. *Dal MSI ad An: organizzazione e strategie*. Bologna: Il Mulino.

———. 2010. *La Rivoluzione Impossibile. Dai Campi Hobbit Alla Nuova Destra*. Firenze: Vallecchi.

Tarrow, S. 1996. 'States and Opportunities: The Political Structuring of Social Movements', in D. McAdam, et al. (eds), *Comparative Perspectives on Social Movements*. New York: Cambridge University Press, pp. 41–61.

The Washington Post. 2018. 'An Italian Neo-Fascist Shot 6 Immigrants So Why Won't Italy's Political Parties Condemn Xenophobia?', February 9.

Weinberg, L. 1995. 'Italian Neo-Fascist Terrorism: A Comparative Perspective', *Terrorism and Political Violence* 7(1): 221–38.

Wetzel, J. 2009. 'Country Report Italy', in Bertlesmann Stiftung (ed.), *Strategies for Combating Right-Wing Extremism in Europe*. Gütersloh: Bertlesmann Stiftung, pp. 327–74.

3
IDEOLOGY

In this chapter, we focus on hybridization in the ideology of CasaPound Italia (CPI). Following extant literature on the far right (Mudde 2007), we adopt a minimal definition of ideology as a worldview encompassing a set of normative beliefs about the role of man in society and about how contemporary societies shall be organized. Our main goal is to present CPI's specific ideological traits and illustrate how the group uses references to historical Fascism to address themes that become prominent in contemporary public debates. To do so, we build on a set of interviews with the leadership of CPI and on the group's internal literature, which we examine with reference to the scholarship on the far right and its ideology. The chapter opens with a discussion of how CPI articulates the two core ideological features of the far right: nativism and authoritarianism (sections 3.1 and 3.2). Section 3.3 examines CPI's stances on economic and social issues, before moving to the other themes (3.4), such as European Union (EU) integration, the environment, gender and international relations, which CPI interprets in terms of its Fascist worldview. The concluding section highlights that CPI combines references to historical and post-war Fascism with other themes that resonate with topical events in public debates. Accordingly, CPI's platform displays a patchwork of ad hoc issues that the group addresses strategically, and that it interprets ideologically based on normative beliefs mediated from the tradition of historical Fascism.

3.1 Nativism and the people: 'Italians first!'

The literature on the ideology of the far right recognizes the primacy of nativism, as 'an ideology positing that states shall be inhabited exclusively by members of the native group (the nation) and that non-natives (personas or ideas) are a threat for the homogeneous nation-states' (Mudde 2007: 19). Nativism is a core feature of CPI's ideology. The group's idea of national belonging, however, goes beyond biological racism, and is informed by the *Nouvelle Droite*'s racial doctrine of 'ethnopluralism' (Bar-On 2018; Froio 2018; Rydgren 2008; Taguieff 1985, 1987).

Ethnopluralist understanding of group differences are mainly inspired by the writings of traditionalist thinkers, notably Julius Evola[1] (1898–1974) and after 1968 Alain de Benoist.[2] Their works posit that human beings can only develop fully within a community defined by shared *traditions*, understood as a set of perennial ethnic, cultural and religious characteristics that are specific to each community. This interpretation of nativism is endorsed by CPI, which – therefore – justifies differences between communities based on a mix of ethnic and cultural factors. As explained by CPI's culture officer:

> Identity is the result of three factors: nature, culture and will. Nature refers to the most strictly physical, biological and racial characteristics of the people, their most concrete essence, or 'human matter'. Culture represents the unique and original way in which each community perceives the world. It enables to reach self-consciousness through a confrontation with the Other. [The will] indicates awareness about the other two elements: it is the act of giving meaning to the physical and cultural factors.
>
> *(Scianca 2008)*

In this interpretation, ethnic and cultural characteristics define who is part of the nation (us) and who is not (them). Put differently, in CPI's worldview, individuals are linked to *their* nation by a 'civilizational nexus' (*Nesso di Civiltà*) (Scianca 2016), according to which every person is considered to 'belong' to a specific place and culture. This is at odds with international migration as mobility threatens the culture and security of receiving societies, while also spoiling migrants of their own national and cultural identity.[3] Thus, CPI's position is reminiscent of de Benoist's idea that peoples belonging to different communities and traditions shall not be mixed within the same territory. This interpretation does not posit (at least explicitly) the superiority of one race over the others unlike, for instance, the ideals of white supremacists or pre-war racists. Rather, the argument is that traditions belonging to different communities are incompatible with one another and therefore shall not be mixed.

For CPI, identity differentiates the nation (and its people) from a territory (and its population). The recognition, and defence, of national identities is at the core of the group's ideology, which refers to it as *Fronte dell'essere* (Front of being). Yet, at the time of our first fieldwork in 2012, CPI's agenda appeared somewhat disconnected from the policy issue that is generally associated with nativist politics: immigration. Migration and related identity concerns did not, in fact, emerge as a cornerstone of CPI's politics. Even though the national headquarters of the organization are located at the heart of Rome's multicultural district, in an area characterized by a high density of migrant shops and residents, the group expressed little interest in issues of cultural diversity. This was even more surprising considering that virtually all other far-right organizations in Italy and Europe accord much importance to these themes.

CPI leaders framed immigration as an economic issue, seeing it in terms of job-market competition between native and foreign workers. Specifically, CPI used an ethnopluralist utilitarian narrative criticizing the exploitation of migrants by capitalist entrepreneurs (albeit without expressing any empathy towards them). In this interpretation, migrants represent an economic threat to Italians' housing and workers' rights, because the economic elites are interested in repopulating Italy with foreign workers with low living and working standards (Froio 2016). In this understanding, migrants are not only responsible for worsening the labour conditions of native workers, but are also privileged beneficiaries of social services and public housing. In CPI's words, migrants are a 'reserve army' of unprivileged workers for national industry (CPI 2013a), which also drains the welfare resources that native Italians can no longer access.[4]

> Immigrants are simply slaves of the third millennium. […] Beyond the humanitarian narrative used by lefty people, the only reason that justifies the multiracial society is the need to import low-cost, non-unionized labour into western Europe.
>
> *(Radio Bandiera Nera 2015)*

> Immigrants are indeed a resource not only for progressive parties and Catholic organizations such as *Caritas* [Confederation of Catholic relief organizations], but also for *Confindustria* [General Confederation of Italian Industry] and the patronage system. They are the ones benefitting the most from this new slave economy and the reserve army of labour made from a mass of underprivileged people looking for work. These oligarchs fuel the war of the poor against the poor that feeds mutual resentment and creates a 'multiracist' society.
>
> *(CPI 2013a)*

This interpretation of migration, however, did not cope well with the increasingly security-oriented and cultural reading of migration that emerged in the context of the European asylum policy crisis, and even more so after the Islamist attacks that struck Europe from 2015 (Castelli Gattinara 2017a). Accordingly, CPI started to emphasize various other implications of migration as well. To begin with, following a practice that is standard for right-wing parties (Castelli Gattinara 2016), CPI associated immigration with criminality and urban insecurity. Being 'foreign to our [Italy's] land and history' (CPI 2013b), migrants are deemed responsible for drug dealing, prostitution and urban decay. While targeted groups may vary (asylum seekers, second generation migrants, irregular migrants or migrants *tout court*), special emphasis is on ethnic minorities and in particular the migrant Roma, addressed as 'Gypsies' and portrayed as criminal social parasites taking advantage of state anti-discrimination benefits.

In addition, CPI emphasizes the cultural differences between foreigners and autochthones, notably in terms of religious and dietary habits, as well as dressing styles. This was done within the framework of widespread conspiracy theories about the 'Kalergi plan' and the 'Great Replacement', according to which there is an international plot to substitute European peoples and their 'civilization' with peoples from non-European countries (i.e. Arab and African migrants) and/or holding allegedly non-European beliefs (i.e. Islam, but also multiculturalism and feminism). In this understanding, migration represents a threat to the homogeneity and distinctiveness of Italy's national culture. This national diversity must be defended against the cultural and ethnic homogenization generated by immigration and multiracial societies, both fuelled by globalization. Put differently, for CPI globalization may lead to the extinction of national specificities and cultural diversity between ethnic communities (Scianca 2011a). While globalization turns *all* migrants into 'individuals without roots',[5] the most threatening are migrants coming from outside Europe, as they are incompatible with the shared history and traditions at the origins of Europe's cultural distinctiveness (Bar-On 2008).

CPI blames global migration on governing parties and the main targets of its campaigns are international lobbies and humanitarian non-governmental organizations (NGOs). In CPI's interpretation, foreign lobbies and neoliberal elites would promote migration to undermine national sovereignty and increase profits on low-skilled workers. Left-wing political elites, instead, would defend mass migration based on a normative conviction that multicultural societies are morally superior to culturally homogeneous ones, since they are imbued with naive 'do-goodism' (*buonismo*). Together, they are accused of sponsoring international NGOs who would allegedly collude with smugglers to bring migrants into Europe. The diagnosis of the migration problem by CasaPound is thus almost entirely in line with most far-right parties in Italy and beyond.

On the one hand, the group calls for a stop to all migratory flows to prevent the creation of a 'Third World' of 'slaves and criminals' within Europe (CPI 2013a). Accordingly, CPI integrated its agenda with a critique of the Italian migration law, which is accused of being too permissive towards foreigners wishing to acquire Italian citizenship. According to CPI, it should simply not be possible for foreigners to become part of a national community which is different from that of their birth. This is why the group rejects both assimilationist and multiculturalist citizenship models and opposes any proposal to base the Italian citizenship law on the model of *Ius Soli*, providing birthright nationality to anyone born on Italian territory (Scianca 2016: 231–4). As explained by Gianluca Iannone, the leader of the group: 'For CPI only those whose parents are Italian is and can be considered an Italian citizen. Citizenship cannot be offered as a present' (CPI 2015).

On the other hand, CPI began protesting against the Islamization of Western societies, notably by celebrating the suicide of Dominique Venner – defined as a 'Samurai of the West' (CPI 2013c).[6] On Islam, CPI defends a position that is at odds with the strategy of similar groups in Italy, Europe and the United States (Brubaker 2017; Castelli Gattinara 2017b; Froio 2017; Zúquete 2015). CPI does not endorse Huntington's theory of the 'Clash of Civilizations'. Rather, it developed a neo-racist interpretation of the 'right to difference' (see Froio 2017). Accordingly, Muslim communities have a right to preserve their identity and habits, yet they must do so outside Italy and Europe. It follows that they believe it is preferable 'to stop importing people from alien cultures rather than to open the doors and then expect that these people will conform to allegedly liberal values' (*Il Primato Nazionale* 2015). This logic also informs CPI's intense mobilization in support of Bashar al-Assad (see section 3.4.4).

As a result, CPI's ethnopluralist worldview accommodates both utilitarian and cultural concerns to oppose migration. It must be noted, however, that CPI activists often struggle to articulate these lines of reasoning, and ultimately rely on more simplistic understandings of diversity. As regards migration, one interviewee reported that, according to him, migrants 'are not poor or exploited in their countries. They just want an easy life here; they are just cowards! If you are a man, how can you leave behind your family and kids?'[7] With respect to cultural diversity, a local leader explained:

> Immigrants do not want to integrate in my culture. If I go to the house of someone who does not eat meat, I do not ask to eat meat for lunch. You see, I am not a racist in the sense that I think that you stink or that you are stupid because you are black. I am a spiritual racist because I believe that if you are black you are different from me and my culture.[8]

A topic related to nativism that did not emerge during the fieldwork was that of the Jews in general and of Israel in particular. The relationship between Italian Fascism and anti-Semitism is in fact a subject on which CPI's leadership displays a strategic ambiguity, even though some 'old rust' remains (Rosati 2018: 156–9; see also Zúquete 2018). At the official level, CPI rejects anti-Semitism and it condemns Mussolini's racial laws as a 'historical mistake'. In 2012 Gianluca Iannone declared that 'the racial laws alienated the Hebrews from the Fascist revolution, of which they had been among the protagonists since the march on Rome (1922)'.[9]

Yet CPI finds it unproblematic to build its ideology on the intellectual figure of Ezra Pound whose writings attacked the 'Jewish monetary system' and accused Judaism to be 'not a race but a disease'. Over the past years, moreover, a number of CPI's activists have been at the core of news stories and trials for incitement to racial hatred, and a group of militants was arrested in 2013 for allegedly plotting to rape a Jewish student in Naples.[10] CPI's position on Israel is not clear either. While CPI used to be officially pro-Palestinian, in 2018 the vice-president publicly defended Benjamin Netanyahu's anti-Arab policies.[11]

3.2 Authoritarianism: historical Fascism and law and order

A second core feature in the ideology of the far right is authoritarianism. As stated in Chapter 1, authoritarianism may refer to a call for establishing an authoritarian political order, or it may refer to a belief in a strictly ordered society glorifying punishment of outsiders in the name of some moral authority (Adorno et al. 1969). In CPI's 'Fascism of the Third Millennium', authoritarianism relates to both of these interpretations.

To begin with, CPI takes explicit inspiration from the authoritarian political order of Fascist Italy and its ideologues (see Chapter 2).[12] Among the readings suggested by CPI to its activists, one may find Mussolini's own writings, those of the American poet Ezra Pound and other texts by historical and contemporary extreme-right thinkers, such as Alessandro Pavolini,[13] Julius Evola, Alain de Benoist, among others. In addition to general references to historical Fascism, CasaPound's ideological platform also includes references to post-war Fascism in Italy and Europe, in particular the line of thought pursued by organizations and intellectual movements such as *Giovane Europa*,[14] the French *Nouvelle Droite*, and the Italian *Nuova Destra* (New Right, NDE).[15] More precisely, CPI reaffirms ideas which characterized the first phase of post-war Fascism,[16] as opposed to the successive attempts by extreme-right parties to gain legitimacy by denying some central features of historical Fascism. In this respect, CPI's culture officer Adriano Scianca criticizes post-war extreme-right militancy for its 'individualistic withdrawal' to subcultural milieus, but also pointed out that the idea of renouncing Fascism as an ideological cornerstone is 'pretentious, intellectualistic and shameful' (Scianca 2011b).

As regards the belief in a strictly ordered society, CPI refers to the 'law and order' dimension of the fascist regime, and to its 'movement spirit'. For the group, the strong role that historical Fascism gave to the state in terms of crime repression and social policies is what is needed to ensure security, the 'certainty of punishment'[17] and well-being in Italy. While CPI does not endorse the death penalty, its motivation is not one of mercy but because 'in prison criminals suffer more'.[18]

Ideological authoritarianism also stems from CPI's fascination for the movement phase of Italian Fascism, briefly outlined in the previous chapter. CPI refers to the revolutionary spirit that characterized historical Fascism during its early years, and its desire to break from the structured demands of representative democracy, unions and of established political parties. According to De Felice (1975), early historical Fascism was characterized by strong romanticism and intense violence against political opponents and established political parties.[19] The Fascism from which CPI takes its inspiration is that of *action squads* (*Squadre d'Azione)* and of grassroots mobilization (De Felice 1975), corresponding to an explosion of violent social anger against ongoing social transformations and the inadequacy of liberal political structures (Sabbatucci 2005). In this sense, references to the revolutionary spirit of historical Fascism inform CPI's anti-establishment rhetoric. CPI describes democracy as a political model that is ill-suited to respond to the will of the citizens[20] and sees mainstream political parties (and in particular governing ones) as the origin of the loss of national sovereignty. Opposing democracy and criticizing representative democracy from a fascist-revolutionary perspective, while regularly running for elections (see Chapter 6), is perhaps the most important element that CPI openly borrows from the authoritarian tradition of historical Fascism.

3.3 Welfare and the economy: state-led (domestic) laissez-faire

Economic and social concerns, notably housing rights, welfare and state interventionism, play a crucial role in CPI's ideological platform.

The importance of housing in the ideology of CPI is established by the very name that the group chose – CasaPound – and by its symbol, the arrowed turtle. In fact, 'Casa' is the Italian word for 'house' and Pound is a reference to the poet Ezra Pound (1885–1972). Ezra Pound was born in the United States but moved to Italy in 1924. He supported Benito Mussolini and wrote several publications (notably the *Cantos*) on housing rights and ownership, understood as basic human needs (Redman 1991; Gallesi 2005). Housing is so important for CPI that it is embedded in the very logo of the group: a turtle – an animal that always has a roof over its head.

> The turtle was chosen as the logo of CPI because it is an animal constantly carrying its home, the animal that turned a residence into a shelter. In this sense, the home refers not only to an idea of society, but also to a daily practice closely connected to the concrete, existential needs of citizens.[21]

CasaPound considers home ownership a sacred right on which to establish the family unit; it is an inviolable right central to a person's dignity. It follows – in line with the preaching of Ezra Pound – that rent is seen as usury, as it represents the exploitation of something that should not be monetized (*Cantos*). The explicit reference to the public housing projects of the 1920s and 1930s is used to support CPI's main policy campaign: the Social Mortgage (*Mutuo Sociale*). Rather than proposing public housing, however, CPI calls for a subsidized home-buying scheme to encourage individual private property (see Chapter 6).

As regards state interventionism, CPI's position is ambiguous: it calls simultaneously for a strong state to protect the national economy from external challenges, and for laissez-faire policies at the domestic level. This peculiar vision is inspired by historical Fascism but also by the tradition of the 'social right' *(Destra Sociale*), the post-war wing of the extreme right that stressed the 'social doctrine' of Italian Fascism (Caldiron 2010). The main reference is thus the social legislation of the Fascist regime, namely the Labour Charter of 1927[22] and the *Verona Manifesto* (1943).[23] Within these complex pieces of legislation, however, CPI picks only a carefully selected sample of elements considered to be politically useful, such as the introduction of mutual aid societies, state policies on land and infrastructure, and the idea that entitlement to welfare assistance should be linked to citizenship rather than to taxation.

The intervention of a strong state is called for by CasaPound as a necessary means to protect Italian workers and products against unfair and foreign competition. In the aftermath of the Great Recession in Italy, CPI's activists engaged in the creation of a workers' union (*Blocco Lavoratori Unitario* – United Workers' Bloc, BLU) and promoted measures to reduce conflict on labour issues, taking inspiration from the Verona Manifesto. The 1943 Manifesto was the act that established the Italian Social Republic (*Repubblica Sociale Italiana*, RSI) and is a crucial cultural reference for Italy's Social Right in the post-war years. CPI's internal literature emphasizes its most innovative aspects (in particular the collectivization of businesses for the good of the nation), while ignoring the fact that none of the Manifesto's proposals were actually implemented, due to the collapse of the RSI (see De Bernardi 2001).

At the same time, CPI articulates a relatively positive view of private initiative and the free market, at least *within* the nation state. This sets CPI apart from other (and more established) far-right parties which progressively moved from laissez-faire positions (favouring lower taxes, smaller governments and deregulation of the economy) to interventionist and protectionist ones (Otjes et al. 2018; Ivaldi 2015). In CPI's worldview, the economy is just a means at the service of the nation: accordingly, it calls for the nationalization of businesses that operate for the 'vital interests of the nation'[24] such as the Bank of Italy, telecommunications, postal and transportation services. In this respect, the economy would be governed by the State in order to defend the economic interests of Italian natives, whether Italian citizens in need of welfare provision or Italian businesses demanding tax-cuts to contribute to the growth of the nation.

The same double-edged logic applies to redistribution and, more generally, to CPI's view of capitalism. Concerning the first, CPI denounces social inequality, but it opposes redistribution through taxation (Scianca 2011a). More precisely, it calls for state protection of specific social groups of Italians (families, women, persons with a disability and the elderly) *and* for tax-cuts or for a non-redistributive tax system with a constant marginal rate or 'flat' tax (*Il Primato Nazionale* 2014). At a more general level, CPI does not oppose market capitalism per se: it is critical of a deregulated international trade system, but it supports the idea that national economies are run by private initiative in a free domestic market.[25]

> We are not inventing anything new. Fascism protected private property, the entrepreneurial spirit, etc. ... We are anti-capitalist only as far as capitalism means as much market as possible and as little state as possible. We are opposed to capitalism if it means that every aspect of daily life is commodified, and that everything can be transformed into a commodity. We are anticapitalistic only when labour itself is seen as a commodity.[26]

The ambiguous position of CPI concerning the role of the state in the economy makes it difficult to locate the group on the Left–Right political spectrum, at least on a purely economic basis. This corresponds with the information emerging from our interviews, since CPI militants and leaders reported that they identify with a variety of political cultures: some reluctantly accepted the 'right-wing' label,[27] others told us that they identified as 'socialist',[28] and yet one interviewee went as far as to affirm that, in the 1970s, people would have called him a 'Nazi Maoist'.[29] In fact, 'right-wing' is a qualification that CPI's leaders and activists generally reject. Their self-understanding is as 'fascists', and thus beyond the 'right and left categories',[30] an interpretation heavily inspired by the 'meta-political' approaches to political action of the New Right. This implies that, as a political movement, CasaPound prioritizes engagement in the cultural sphere over strictly elections-oriented activism. Inspired by the Marxist philosopher Antonio Gramsci, meta-politics thus refers to an ideological investment in non-political activities addressing schools, universities, the cultural world and the press as a prerequisite to all forms of engagement in the institutional parliamentary arena. For CPI, meta-politics implies creating the cultural conditions for the return of the Fascist state model that, in turn, will allow social and class divisions to be overcome through the creation of an organic state.[31]

3.4 Other themes

Nativism, authoritarianism and socio-economic stances are at the core of CPI's ideological worldview, but the group also refers to historical Fascism to position itself on issues that acquire relevance in public debates. We focus, in particular, on four key themes: European integration, the environment, gender and international relations.

3.4.1 European integration: for Europe but against the EU

On European issues, CPI makes a clear distinction between its support for Europe as a nation or as a 'civilizational area', and strong opposition against the EU integration as a political and economic process. On the first aspect, CPI's positions configure what Bar-On summarizes as a 'dream of a pan-European empire' (Bar-On 2008). On the second, instead, CPI progressively radicalized its positions, attributing increasing importance to the EU in its political campaigns, and moving towards a hard form of Euroscepticism in the wake of the European sovereign debt crisis. In this section, we discuss CPI's positions on Europe and the EU separately and look at the interrelations between the two.

CPI imagines Europe as the cradle of Western civilization: a spiritual space built on shared and immutable traditions. In line with the above-mentioned ethnopluralist worldview, European traditions constitute the identity of the 'West' (as opposed to the 'East'), and they are increasingly threatened by the arrival of non-Europeans with their own (incompatible) traditions. This vision is indebted to the theory of the so-called 'Great Replacement', discussed earlier in this chapter. According to CPI, the progressive eradication of native peoples from their land (which CPI calls 'an ethnocide') is accelerated by supra-nationalization, and specifically by EU integration and globalization (Froio 2017).

> Today, the greatest danger for European civilization is represented by the Great Replacement of its populations, organized by right-wing economic elites colluding with the left-wing cultural caste. They promote the idea that our lands can be repopulated by foreign masses of people coming from who knows where.
>
> *(Scianca 2016)*

To contrast the Great Replacement project, European peoples only have one option, according to CPI: building a strong, homogeneous 'pan-European empire' that can defend European civilization from the threats posed by destructive cosmopolitan ideologies such as liberalism, conservativism, communism and social democracy (Bar-On 2008: 327).

It follows that CasaPound challenges all supra-national processes that could endanger the nativist equation of Europe as a civilizational space based on ethnicity and territory, and thus on tradition.

At the same time CPI does not endorse Huntington's theory of the clash of civilizations, which acquired prominence in the Italian public debate through the writings of Oriana Fallaci and Magdi Allam (Cousin and Vitale 2014) and influenced the campaigns of other far-right organizations (notably *Forza Nuova*, *Fratelli d'Italia* and the *Lega*).

> There is no Islamic invasion at the door and there is no crusade setting out against Islam. The ultimate enemy of our people and traditions is not another people or another tradition, but something that is hostile to all peoples and all traditions. This enemy is the project of homologation called 'globalization'. A two-headed monster made of two complementary forces: liberalism, which is the capitalist idea of a market without rules ('right-wing globalism'); and cosmopolitan culture, which is internationalist and multiracial ('left mondialism').
>
> *(Radio Bandiera Nera 2015)*

In sum, for CPI the ultimate enemy of all peoples and nations is mobility (in CPI's words 'the eradication of peoples' roots'), which is fostered by globalization, and fuelled by the mixing of different communities and traditions. This extreme view inevitably shaped CPI's vision of the EU integration project. On this ground, CPI's activists joined the #DefendEurope campaigns that started in August 2017, organized by the Identitarian movement to oppose migration from Northern Africa and the Middle East (Zúquete 2018).

Similar to other far-right parties (Pirro and Kessel 2017; Vasilopoulou 2017) however, the positions of CPI on the EU have oscillated between soft and hard forms of Euroscepticism. While Euroscepticism broadly refers to all negative attitudes towards EU integration, scholars usually distinguish varying degrees of opposition (Taggart and Szczerbiak 2008). So-called *hard Euroscepticism* designates a principled opposition to the EU (e.g. parties that believe that their countries should withdraw from EU membership), whereas *soft Euroscepticism* represents a qualified opposition to the EU, often concerning specific policy areas or aspects (e.g. the idea that 'national interests' are at odds with EU policies). CPI's Euroscepticism radicalized over time passing from soft to hard forms. This is also visible in the mobilizations and policy proposals of the group (see Chapter 6). Today, the EU is a major concern for CPI, which envisages it as the 'Trojan horse' of globalism, fostering people's movement and thus the eradication of national traditions. As we discuss in more detail in Chapter 6, this was not previously the case; EU politics were basically irrelevant in the agenda and internal material of the group.

The turning point seems to have been the appointment of the technocratic government of Mario Monti (2011–2013), and the grand-coalition governments that ruled Italy over the following years. Until then, CPI had been much softer on EU issues. Three examples are helpful to better illustrate this. First, until 2013, CPI never sought Italy's exit from the EU, despite denouncing a democratic deficit in EU institutions and decision-making. Second, the early platforms of CPI did not advocate for the replacement of the Euro currency, but rather for the introduction of a local complementary currency (the *Equo*). And third, until 2013 CPI did not call for the abolition of the Schengen Treaty, but rather for a revision that would however preserve a closed trade area within Europe.[32] CPI's position on EU integration was thus rather original if compared to similar extreme right-wing groups:

> The Europe stemming from the Maastricht treaty is the right thing done in the wrong way. [...] The old microstate sovereignty often invoked by 'nationalists' against the EU seems to us utterly obsolete. Nation-states have all the flaws of the current EU but none of its potential [...]. Those who oppose [the EU] are engaged in a reactionary struggle that does not belong to us and does not interest us. This does not mean that CPI will stop claiming that the EU is a tool of globalist demands. Yet, for us a bad Europe is still better than no Europe at all.
>
> *(Ideodromo CasaPound 2013)*

Thus, before 2013 CPI already described the EU as a threat to Italy's sovereignty and to the tradition of European peoples. Yet, it voiced an internal opposition to EU policies rather than a principled rejection of the EU as a polity (Mair 2007). This changed with the intensification of the social and political consequences of the Great Recession in Italy, ultimately leading CPI to a fully-fledged Euroscepticism consisting of symbolic actions (e.g. the tearing down of an EU flag from the Commission's office in Rome; see *Il Messaggero* 2013a), forming international

FIGURE 3.1 Poster for CasaPound's 2014 EU election campaign, with the slogan: 'Enough of the EU: we are Europeans, not slaves'.

It states six main demands that CPI aims to 'say out and loud to the EU: under these circumstances, we want to exit the euro; we do not wish to work at the slave wages of Eastern Europe; we want to print our own currency with a sovereign central bank just like Hungary and the UK; we want to eat first our own agricultural products, and only later produce from other countries; we want to protect our industry and our workers from foreigners and unfair competition; we do not wish to destroy the future of our children by paying 50 billion per year for the Fiscal Compact'.

partnerships (e.g. with Nigel Farage during the Brexit campaign; see *Il Primato Nazionale* 2016) and policy proposals calling for the 'unilateral exit of Italy from the EU' (CPI 2018: 3).

3.4.2 The environment: for a nativist ecology

While ecology is not a prominent theme for CPI, the group occasionally engages in environmental politics. This happens mostly when the issue acquires importance in public debates at the local or national level, and notably in response to the environmental campaigns of the Five Star Movement (*Movimento 5 Stelle*, M5S), debates on animal rights, and more recently the Fridaysforfuture campaign. Through its internal associations, CPI supports what it calls 'a non-compliant ecology' (*ecologia non conforme*) – a nativist interpretation of environmental politics.

In the Italian far right, attention to environmental issues is not new. Early references can be found already in the late 1970s, in the activities of the intellectual Environmental Research Groups organized by Pino Rauti's youth movement[33] and later by the *Nuova Destra* (Tarchi 2010). These experiences paved the way to much theoretical and intellectual reflection on the link between right-wing politics and the environment, but left only minor traces in CasaPound's worldview. CPI in fact defends a vision of the environment that is not naturalistic, in the sense that it does not put men and the environment on the same level, unlike the Nazi vision of 'deep ecology' (see Voss 2014). Rather, it conceives the environment as subordinate to the needs of men and

FIGURE 3.2 Poster from CasaPound's NGO *La Foresta che Avanza* celebrating Arbor Day (2011).

The quote by journalist Arnaldo Mussolini (younger brother of the Duce) says 'A new belief must arise in Italy, which I would call the cult of the tree.'

interprets it along the lines of its understanding of national communities. Since the environment mirrors the characteristics and traditions of specific lands and human communities, its inhabitants shall not be mixed with species and traditions originating in different settings. In this sense, CPI does not support the elimination of meat from the diet, but it is against large-scale industrial meat production because it reduces animals to objects, 'eradicating them from their natural habitat, and forcing them to live a miserable life' (*La Foresta che Avanza* 2013). Rather, CPI calls for a nativist 'Mediterranean diet' based on the abandonment of 'imported trans-Atlantic diets, which after World War II caused a surge in the percentage of meat consumption' (*La Foresta che Avanza* 2013). The same argument justifies CPI's opposition to vivisection, the use of animals in pharmaceutical experimentation and their exploitation in festivals and circuses.

3.4.3 Gender: tradition against individualism

As is the case for the environment, gender relations are not at the core of CPI's ideology, but the group took a position on both issues as they acquired increasing relevance in the Italian debate. Ultimately, CPI interprets gender equality as a deviation from tradition.

Before 2016, CPI's internal material rarely dealt with issues related to social constructs and power relations between the sexes, to women's rights and homosexuality. Here too, CPI was set apart from most other extreme-right groups in Italy (e.g. FzNv), for it did not express a principled opposition to either abortion or euthanasia, nor any reference to religious values in politics.[34] Gender issues acquired importance for CPI from 2016 onwards. This coincided with the discussion, and then approval, of the first law on same-sex unions (Law 20 May 2016, no. 76); subsequently, it related to the controversies concerning the teaching of so-called 'gender theory' in public schools (Garbagnoli and Prearo 2018); and, more recently, following the *#metoo* campaign on Twitter. The emergence of these issues forced CPI to take a clear stance on gender-related matters, reflecting its opposition to gender equality.

CPI's view on gender relations can be extrapolated from a book published by one of the national leaders of the group, which is entirely dedicated to this issue. Once more, gender is interpreted through the same ideological scheme that drives CPI's worldview. The demands for gender equality are the result of a 'dominant individualistic ideology' that wishes to alienate individuals from the 'culture' and 'traditions' provided by nature, that is, their biological sex.

Accordingly, CPI's view on the role of women in society is traditionalist, claiming 'the right to difference between the sexes' (Scianca 2011a: 120). Unlike conservative and ultra-catholic positions, however, CPI does not consider women exclusively as mothers: it recognizes that women can work and have a career, and therefore does not suggest that they should be discouraged from work or treated as 'mothers to be'. Despite this, for CPI, women bear the main responsibility for family care, the education of children and domestic work. In this respect, a prominent campaign of CPI focuses on family policy and labour rights for women. The policy proposal called *Tempo di essere madri* (Time to be mothers) targets (Italian) working mothers, offering reduced working hours and economic compensation so that women can keep their jobs while also performing their domestic duty as mothers (*Tempo di Essere Madri* 2013).[35] At the same time, CPI is against all forms of gender quotas, in the labour market and in education.

Furthermore, CPI explicitly supports the idea of 'traditional' families consisting of a man and a woman, but it does not consider civil and religious marriages important and it does not oppose divorce (Scianca 2017). While homosexuality is depicted as an expression of neoliberal individualism which poses a threat to the nation and menaces reproduction, CPI does not promote explicitly homophobic views:

> That same-sex couples exist is a fact. Of course, not all of them live their condition with moderation and good taste, but the same can be said of too many heterosexual couples – and in any case, good taste is a question of style, and certainly cannot be enforced by law. We do not consider it a problem that such unions may receive civil and administrative recognition, with the attribution to the couple of specific rights and obligations. However, we are fully opposed to any hypothesis of adoption of children by gay couples.
>
> *(CPI 2013d)*

While these interpretations are CPI's official position on these issues, activists often struggle to integrate them. In fact, CPI has been at the centre of several episodes of intolerance and discrimination – including homophobic insults (SkyNews Italia 2013) and threats against the former governor of the Apulia Region, Nichi Vendola, one of the first openly homosexual Italian politicians (*Il Messaggero* 2013b).

3.4.4 International relations: nostalgia for empires (with Putin and Assad)

For CPI, international relations are primarily about the promotion of the nation's interests and sovereignty. Specifically, CPI's worldview is informed by 'third-position' understandings developed in the 1970s, according to which Italy should represent an alternative to both the US and Soviet models. Applied to the contemporary scenario, this results in a set of loosely connected proposals calling for the withdrawal of Italy from NATO, the reintroduction of compulsory military service, higher spending for the army and for the development of war technologies.[36] Additionally, the dream of reinstating the Fascist colonial empire has inspired some recent claims that Italy must 'go back to northern Africa' (CPI 2018) to establish colonies that would also help to halt immigration from Eritrea, Somalia and Libya.

FIGURE 3.3 Poster publicizing a debate on civil rights promoted by CasaPound Salerno, featuring guests from the mainstream right Italian party *Il Popolo della Libertà* (2011).

In terms of world politics, CPI did not celebrate the election of Donald Trump as president of the United States, nor did it welcome the grand tour of Europe by the American Steven Bannon. In line with third-position views, CPI considers the United States as an imperialistic power threatening Italy's sovereignty and civilization. Notably, the NATO bases on Italian territory are considered to represent a breach of national sovereignty and a threat to security by an occupying power.[37] While CPI does not support Russia either, it appreciates the figure of its current president Vladimir Putin, for his strategic position on the recent conflicts in Donbass, Crimea and Syria (CPI 2018), and for his idea of reinstating the imperial Russia that was overthrown by the 1917 Bolshevik revolution. On the one hand, the idea of a Russian empire resonates with CPI's 'civilizational' nationalism; on the other, Putin's international politics promote the idea of 'a new multipolar world that is alternative to the unipolar one dominated by the US and the dollar'.[38] In this sense, for CPI, Putin is mainly the icon of a nationalist 'cultural project alternative to US globalism' (CPI 2018).

Similar arguments explain why CPI supports the Syrian dictator Bashar al-Assad. As an authoritarian leader fighting both US imperialism and ISIL's religious fundamentalism, Assad promotes a secularist nationalist understanding of society that resonates highly with CPI's worldviews. Indeed, CPI promoted numerous solidarity actions in support of the Syrian regime through its association, *Solidarité Identités* (Sol.Id.) (see Chapter 4), and within the framework of the European Solidarity Front for Syria – a network of political associations from several countries supporting the government of Bashar al-Assad.[39] 'For Syria, for Assad!' is also the title of one of the songs on the 2017 album by CPI's band *ZetaZeroAlfa*.

Support for authoritarian regimes around the world also has a pragmatic dimension, in that CPI advocates for the stability of emigration countries as a way to halt the inflow of asylum seekers to Europe. This resonates with CPI's ethnopluralist understanding of society, and the idea that 'the problem is not Islam per se, but Islam here in Italy'. Accordingly, there is some evidence that supporters and activists of CPI have occasionally participated, as volunteers or observers, in recent conflicts in Syria, Donbass and Crimea (*L'Espresso* 2018).

FIGURE 3.4 Poster publicizing a debate on 'Assad's Syria: a bulwark of freedom', promoted by CasaPound and the Fronte Europeo per la Siria (2013).

Conclusive remarks

Studying the ideology of a political group is never an easy task. Not only because the role of ideologies in contemporary politics is changing drastically, but also because ideologies encompass complex, and often contradictory, belief systems. In this respect, this chapter offers a plea to move beyond simplistic interpretations of CPI's ideology as simply a copycat of historical and post-war Fascism. At the same time, we remain somewhat sceptical as regards the 'innovative' nature of CPI's ideology, and refrain from describing it as completely disconnected from the past.

CPI does not dismiss references to inter-war ideologies. Rather, it explicitly endorses historical Fascism, and its normative beliefs about democracy, the nation and the organization of society. These references are crucial to define CPI's ideological nativism and authoritarianism, and confirm the definition of the group as 'extreme right' (as opposed to 'radical', see Chapter 1). From Fascism, CPI borrows not only nativism, the authoritarian stance and a principled opposition to democracy, but also some elements concerning welfare and state interventionism in the economy.

In addition, CPI takes explicit inspiration from multiple strands of post-war right-wing extremism, including the European intellectual movement of the New Right, the Third Position's approach to international relations and the Social Right understanding of socio-economic affairs. Above all, CPI is heavily indebted to the post-war *Nouvelle Droite*, which has inspired its understanding of Europe as a 'civilizational' project, and the ethnopluralist understanding of ethnic and cultural communities. Furthermore, CPI's economic platform is very ambiguous, calling simultaneously for welfare expansion (for natives only) and tax reduction within a system of domestic laissez-faire.

We also found that CPI's platform includes a patchwork of ad hoc issues that the group addresses strategically when these are salient in the public debate. Ethnopluralism is thus used by CPI as a frame to articulate a 'Fascist' understanding of issues as diverse as welfare, the environment and gender. Ethnopluralism grants ideological consistency across different themes, upholding a reference to historical Fascism while avoiding appearing anachronistic, explicitly racist or openly homophobic. In this respect, the impact of CPI's hybridization strategy on the ideological domain has been limited. The group's worldview is generally consistent and rooted in the tradition of the extreme right. Yet, it strategically mixes insights and positions from different strands of historical Fascism and post-war extremism (Fascism as a movement, the Social Right, the Third Position, etc.), and articulates them to address issues that become prominent in public debates.

This chapter argued that while CPI maintains some ideological references to historical and post-war Fascism, it has embedded other elements too. The hybridization strategy of CPI juxtaposes aspects of historical and post-war Fascism, as well as issues at the top current of public debates. The question therefore is how CPI manages to transmit this hybrid, heterogeneous worldview to its activists. The next chapter addresses this question in detail, focusing on how CPI organizes internally.

Notes

1 Giulio Cesare Andrea Evola, better known as the Baron Julius Evola (1898–1974) was an Italian philosopher, writer and esotericist. His writings have often been referred to by far-right groups.
2 Alain de Benoist (b. 1943) is a writer and one of the founders of the *Nouvelle Droite* in France.
3 Interview no. 2b of 27/04/2012.
4 Interview no. 2b of 27/04/2012.
5 Interview no. 2a of 27/04/2012.
6 Dominique Venner (1935–2013) was a historian and writer close to the French *Nouvelle Droite*, and the editor of two renowned Europe-wide historical magazines. In 2013, he took his life by shooting himself in Notre Dame Cathedral in Paris, in a gesture of protest against the decline of Western society and its founding values (which Venner, despite being openly pagan, traced back to the pre-Christian societies of Northern Europe).
7 Interview no. 1a of 30/03/2012.
8 Interview no. 3a of 01/06/2012.
9 See http://espresso.repubblica.it/palazzo/2012/02/08/news/roma-casapound-spiazza-tutti-1.40175http://espresso.repubblica.it/palazzo/2012/02/08/news/roma-casapound-spiazza-tutti-1.40175 (accessed 10/09/2019).
10 See https://napoli.repubblica.it/cronaca/2013/01/24/news/arrestati_estremisti_di_destra_c_anche_la_figlia_di_un_ex_senatore-51175878/ (accessed 10/09/2019).
11 See the interview with Simone di Stefano at: https://www.lospecialegiornale.it/2018/04/03/migranti-israele-casapound/ (accessed 10/09/2019).
12 Benito Mussolini seized power officially on the 29 October 1922 and stayed in office until the end of the regime that took place formally on 25 July 1943. From the time of the German occupation in 1943 until 1945, Mussolini led the Italian Social Republic (*Repubblica Sociale Italiana*, RSI) also known as the Republic of Salò.
13 Alessandro Pavolini (1903–1945) was an Italian journalist and writer who served as minister for Popular Culture and secretary of the Republican Fascist Party.
14 *Giovane Europa* (Young Europe) was a movement founded in Belgium in 1962 by Jean Thiriart. Its tendencies were neo-fascist, despite eclectic variations in its thought. The organization's central idea was the construction of a united, non-federal Europe, outside the two blocs of the Cold War. Such an idea attracted a few young people in Italy, who criticized the MSI's line as conservative.
15 The *Nuova Destra* (New Right) was an intellectual far right movement formed in Italy during the 1970s, inspired by the French *Nouvelle Droite* and developed through the journal *Diorama Letterario*, edited by Marco Tarchi. The *Nuova Destra* came into being during the first Hobbit Camp (1977), an event organized by the minority component of the MSI headed by Pino Rauti. Between 1977 and 1981, the *Nuova Destra* organized a series of youth summer camps named Hobbit Camps, from Tolkien's *Lord of the Rings* characters (Revelli 1985). For an overview of the origins of the *Nuova Destra* and of the Hobbit Camps phenomenon, see Tarchi 2010; Capra Casadio 2014.
16 The imagery of historical Fascism's supporters as inhabitants of the 'sewers' derives from the notorious anti-fascist slogan ('fascist scum, go back to the sewers') which inspired the name of the satiric journal founded by Marco Tarchi in 1974, *La Voce della Fogna* (The Voice of the Sewer).
17 Interview no. 2b of 27/04/2012.
18 Interview no. 2b of 27/04/2012.
19 While the 'movement' phase of historical Fascism lasted from 1920 to 1925, from 1926 onwards it developed into a regime. The transition was symbolically marked by the approval of the *Leggi Fascistissime* (the 'most fascist' laws), introducing strict government control over the press and abolishing the right to strike. In 1928, Mussolini's

government passed a new electoral law which guaranteed de facto the victory of a single party, the *Partito Nazionale Fascista* (National Fascist Party, PNF). In 1939, the government created the Grand Council of Fascism which formally suppressed democratic electoral competition.

20 Interview no. 5b of 28/06/2012.
21 Interview no. 2b of 27/04/2012.
22 The Charter of Labour (1927) was a piece of legislation introduced by Benito Mussolini to regulate the labour market. It recognized private initiative as the most efficient to strengthen the economy.
23 The Verona Manifesto (1943) was an 18-point document that outlined the policy agenda of the Italian Social Republic, the RSI. It recognized private property.
24 Interview no. 2b of 27/04/2012.
25 Interview no. 2b of 27/04/2012.
26 Interview no. 2b of 27/04/2012.
27 'We don't like the "right-wing" label very much, but it's a word you need to use … How else to explain where I am more or less positioned to someone that doesn't understand?'. Interview no. 2 of 27/04/2012.
28 Interview no. 2c of 27/04/2012.
29 Interview no. 1a of 30/03/2012. Nazi-Maoism was a minor post-war intellectual movement on the neo-fascist right of the 1960s and 1970s. The first organization to adopt these positions in Italy was *Giovane Europa*, which abandoned rather hastily the right-wing label, even though it included within its ranks many dissidents and political exiles from the MSI and its youth organizations. In the documents of the time, the claim of equal distance from the Left and the Right was presented as the natural evolution of the socialist roots of historical Fascism. Towards the end of the 1960s, *Giovane Europa* sought a convergence with fringes on the far left, especially those inspired by Maoism, and called for a common opposition to both American and Soviet imperialism (Carioti 2011).
30 Interview no. 2b of 27/04/2012. References to 'neither left nor right' recur systematically in all the interviews conducted by the authors.
31 Historical Fascism claimed to represent the overcoming of the class contradiction and of the democratic resolution of conflicts – in other words, it proposed an *organic* vision of the state (see Gentile 1929). In this respect, historical Fascism envisaged the social and political organization of the state in emulation of the functioning of a biological body: just as a human body needs a brain to work, a brain without body is, to all intents and purposes, useless. In the Fascist state, the leader represented the *brain*, whose guiding function would be useless without the support of the *body*, i.e. the nation.
32 Interview no. 2b of 27/04/2012.
33 Notably through the magazine *Dimensione Ambiente*.
34 Interview no. 2c of 27/04/2012.
35 Interview no. 2c of 27/04/2012.
36 Interview no. 2c of 27/04/2012.
37 Interview no. 2c of 27/04/2012.
38 Interview no. 2b of 27/04/2012.
39 See the website of the organization, at: www.esfsyria.org/ (accessed 18/04/2019).

References

Adorno, T.W. et al. 1969. *The Authoritarian Personality*. New York: John Wiley.

Bar-On, T. 2008. 'Fascism to the Nouvelle Droite: The Dream of Pan-European Empire', *Journal of Contemporary European Studies* 16(3): 327–45.

———. 2018. 'The Radical Right and Nationalism', in J. Rydgren (ed.), *The Oxford Handbook of the Radical Right*. Oxford: Oxford University Press, pp. 17–41.

Brubaker, R. 2017. 'Between Nationalism and Civilizationism: The European Populist Moment in Comparative Perspective', *Ethnic and Racial Studies* 40(2): 1191–226.

Caldiron, G. 2010. *La destra sociale da Salò a Tremonti*. Rome: Manifestolibri.

Capra Casadio, M. 2014. 'The New Right and Metapolitics in France and Italy', *Journal for the Study of Radicalism* 8(1): 45–86.

Carioti, A. 2011. *Gli Orfani Di Salò. Il Sessantotto Nero Dei Giovani Neofascisti Nel Dopoguerra 1945–1951*. Milan: Mursia.

Castelli Gattinara, P. 2016. *The Politics of Migration in Italy: Perspectives on Local Debates and Party Competition*. London: Routledge.

———. 2017a. 'The Refugee Crisis as a Crisis of Legitimacy', *Contemporary Italian Politics* 9 (3): 318–31.

———. 2017b. 'Framing Exclusion in the Public Sphere: Far-Right Mobilisation and the Debate on Charlie Hebdo in Italy', *South European Society and Politics* 22(3): 345–64.

Cousin, B., and T. Vitale. 2014. 'Le magistère intellectuel islamophobe d'Oriana Fallaci', *Sociologie* (no. 1, vol. 5).

CPI. 2013a. 'Una Nazione: Il Programma Politico Di CasaPound Italia'. URL: https://www.docdroid.net/Bg8qGdw/programma-casapound-2013.pdf#page=2 (consulted August 2017).

———. 2013b. 'Sul Fronte Dell'Essere: Le Proposte Di CasaPound Italia Sull'Immigrazione'. URL: www.casapoundlombardia.org/images/IMMIGRAZIONE/immigrazionepdf.pdf (consulted August 2018).

———. 2013c.'Francia: "Dominique Venner, Samurai d'Occidente", l'omaggio Di CasaPound Con Striscioni in Tutta Italia'. URL: www.casapounditalia.org/2013/05/francia-dominique-venner-samurai.html (consulted August 2017).

———. 2013d. 'Intervista Con Gianluca Iannone'. URL: www.vivamafarka.com/forum/index.php?topic=104372.0 (consulted July 2013).

———. 2015. 'Ius Soli, CasaPound Tappezza Le Città Di Manifesti per Promuovere Il Referendum Abrogativo'. URL: https://www.facebook.com/notes/casapound-bolzano/ius-soli-casapound-tappezza-le-citt%C3%A0-di-manifesti-per-promuovere-il-referendum-a/898705973509996/ (consulted November 2018).

———. 2018. 'Presentazione Del Libro "Putin Contro Putin" Di A. Dugin, Con A. Scianca'. URL: https://www.youtube.com/watch?v=u4DL4fqFftA (consulted December 2018).

De Bernardi, A. 2001. *Una Dittatura Moderna. Il Fascismo Come Problema Storico*. Milan: Mondadori.

De Felice, R. 1975. *Intervista Sul Fascismo*. Rome-Bari: Laterza.

Froio, C. 2016. 'Who Are "They"? Continuities and Changes in the Discourse of CasaPound Italia on Migration and Otherness', in M. Fielitz and L.L. Laloire (eds), *Trouble of the Far Right*. Bielefeld: Transcript, pp. 87–97.

———. 2017. 'Nous et les autres', *Réseaux* (202–203): 39–78.

———. 2018. 'Race, Religion or Culture? Framing Islam between Racism and Neo-Racism in the Online Network of the French Far Right', *Perspectives on Politics* 16(3): 696–709.

Gallesi, L. 2005. *Le origini del fascismo di Ezra Pound*. Milan: Ares.

Garbagnoli, S., and M. Prearo. 2018. *La Crociata «anti-Gender». Dal Vaticano Alle Manif Pour Tous*. Turin: Kaplan.

Gentile, G. 1929. *Orgini e Dottrina Del Fascismo*. Rome: Libreria del Littorio.

Ideodromo CasaPound. 2013. 'L'Europa: Domande e Risposte'. URL: https://www.ideodromo.it/Europa-domande-c/678/ (consulted December 2014).

Il Messaggero. 2013a. 'Casapound, Di Stefano Condannato a Tre Mesi per Il Furto Della Bandiera Ue'. URL: https://www.ilmessaggero.it/roma/cronaca/casapound_di_stefano_condannato_tre_mesi_furto_bandiera_ue-235484.html (consulted November 2014).

———. 2013b. 'Casapound su Facebook insulti Omofobi a Vendola'. URL: https://www.lastampa.it/2013/02/03/italia/casapound-su-facebook-insulti-omofobi-a-vendola-Q56YWpdTKooKyCQnD0pZnJ/pagina.html (consulted November 2014).

Il Primato Nazionale. 2014. 'Flat Tax? Sì, Ma Solo Se c'è Sovranità Monetaria'. URL: https://www.ilprimatonazionale.it/economia/flat-tax-si-se-ce-sovranita-monetaria-11652/ (consulted November 2014).

———. 2015. 'La Storia Dell'islam "Moderato" è Una Cagata Pazzesca'. URL: https://www.ilprimatonazionale.it/politica/islam-moderato-34763/.

———. 2016. 'Trappolone Inglese: Così Stanno Sabotando La Brexit'. URL: https://www.ilprimatonazionale.it/esteri/trappolone-inglese-cosi-stanno-sabotando-la-brexit-52425/ (consulted December 2016).

Ivaldi, G. 2015. 'Towards the Median Economic Crisis Voter? The New Leftist Economic Agenda of the Front National in France', *French Politics* 13(4): 346–69.

La Foresta che Avanza. 2013. 'Il Programma'. URL: www.laforestacheavanza.org/2013/04/il-programma.html (consulted November 2015).

L'Espresso. 2018. 'Fascisti a Damasco Casapound e Forza Nuova in Siria per Assad'. URL: http://espresso.repubblica.it/attualita/2018/11/09/news/fascisti-a-damasco-casapound-e-forza-nuova-in-siria-per-assad-1.328510 (consulted November 2018).

Mair, P. 2007. 'Political Opposition and the European Union', *Government and Opposition* 42(1): 1–17.

Mudde, C. 2007. *Populist Radical Right Parties in Europe*. Cambridge: Cambridge University Press.

Otjes, S., G. Ivaldi, A.R. Jupskås, and O. Mazzoleni. 2018. 'It's not Economic Interventionism, Stupid! Reassessing the Political Economy of Radical Right-wing Populist Parties', *Swiss Political Science Review* 24(3): 270–90.

Pirro, A.L.P., and S. van Kessel. 2017. 'United in Opposition? The Populist Radical Right's EU-Pessimism in Times of Crisis', *Journal of European Integration* 39(4): 405–20.

Radio Bandiera Nera. 2015. 'Sul Fronte Dell'Essere: Immigrazione, Identità, Cittadinanza'. URL: www.radiobandieranera.org/immigrazionepdf.pdf (consulted April 2018).

Redman, T. 1991. *Ezra Pound and Italian Fascism*. Cambridge: Cambridge University Press.

Revelli, M. 1985. *La cultura della destra radicale*. Milan: Franco Angeli.

Rosati, E. 2018. *CasaPound Italia. Fascisti del Terzo Millennio*. Sesto S. Giovanni: Mimesis.

Rydgren, J. 2008. 'Immigration Sceptics, Xenophobes or Racists? Radical Right-Wing Voting in Six West European Countries', *European Journal of Political Research* 47(6): 737–65.

Sabbatucci, G. 2005. 'La Democrazia Liberale e i Suoi Nemici', *Mondo Contemporaneo* (3).

Scianca, A. 2008. 'La Battaglia Identitaria'. URL: https://www.centrostudilaruna.it/battagliaidentitaria.html (consulted October 2018).

———. 2011a. *Riprendersi tutto: le parole di CasaPound: 40 concetti per una rivoluzione in atto*. Società editrice Barbarossa.

———. 2011b. 'Braccia Sottratte Ai Campi. Hobbit'. November. URL: http://robertoalfattiappetiti.blogspot.fr/2011/11/braccia-sottratteai-campi-hobbit-di.html (consulted February 2012).

———. 2016. *L'identità sacra. Dèi, popoli e luoghi al tempo della Grande Sostituzione*. Cusano Milanino: AGA.

———. 2017. *Contro l'eroticamente Corretto*. Milan: Bietti.

SkyNews Italia. 2013, July 23. 'Vendola Minacciato Dai Militanti Di CasaPound Perché Gay'. URL: https://video.sky.it/news/cronaca/vendola_minacciato_dai_militanti_di_casapound_perche_gay/v149529.vid (consulted October 2014).

Taggart, P., and A. Szczerbiak. 2008. 'Introduction: Opposing Europe? The Politics of Euroscepticism in Europe', in P. Taggart and A. Szczerbiak (eds), *Opposing Europe? The Comparative Party Politics of Euroscepticism, Volume 1: Case Studies and Country Surveys*. Oxford: Oxford University Press, pp. 1–15.

Taguieff, P.-A. 1985. 'Les Nouvelles Idéologies de Droite en France (1976–1984)', in J.-Y. Potel (ed.), *L'Etat de la France et de ses habitants*. Paris: La Découverte, pp. 446–50.

———. 1987. *La Force Du Préjugé : Essai Sur Le Racisme et Ses Doubles*. Paris: La Découverte.

Tarchi, M. 2010. *La Rivoluzione Impossibile. Dai Campi Hobbit Alla Nuova Destra*. Firenze: Vallecchi.

Tempo di Essere Madri. 2013. 'Il Programma'. URL: www.tempodiesseremadri.org/ilprogetto.html (consulted March 2017).

Vasilopoulou, S. 2017. *Far Right Parties and Euroscepticism*. Colchester: ECPR Press.

Voss, K. 2014. *Nature and Nation in Harmony: The Ecological Component of Far Right Ideology*. PhD dissertation defended at the European University Institute, Florence.

Zúquete, J.P. 2015. 'The New Frontlines of Right-Wing Nationalism', *Journal of Political Ideologies* 20(1): 69–85.

———. 2018. *The Identitarians*. Notre Dame, IN: Notre Dame Press.

4

INTERNAL STRUCTURE

How is CasaPound Italia (CPI) organized internally? Building on the literature on political parties and social movements, this chapter presents CPI's internal configuration based on evidence from online data, open participant observation and face-to-face interviews with activists and high-ranking officials. Specifically, it discusses how strategic hybridization in the group organization have allowed CPI to gather the financial, human and symbolic resources that have granted its survival expansion, and recognition. We begin by presenting the formal hierarchical structure of CPI, focusing on its territorial and thematic organization (4.1). We then move on to analyse how CPI copes with the problem of collective choice (Kitschelt 2006) and present the rules governing leadership, personnel selection and internal decision-making (4.2). Two specific sections are devoted to recruitment: comparing group strategies and individual motivations to join the group (4.3); and the modes of engagement with CPI – paying special attention to youth, women and football fans (4.4). In the concluding section, we argue that the high profile currently enjoyed by CPI is due, at least to a certain extent, to its hybrid organizational configuration. Combining the features of political parties and social movements, the internal structure of CPI facilitates the recruitment and engagement of activists, as well as ensuring financial resources from different venues.

4.1 Formal organization: territorial and thematic units

Since CPI does not provide public information about its internal organization, neither on the Web nor in its internal literature, we had to reconstruct its organizational features starting with the information gathered during our participant observation and interviews.

Formally, CPI is registered as an *Associazione di Promozione Sociale* (Association for Social Promotion), which is the legal status of non-profit associations in Italy. The advantage of this status is that it allows CPI to gather financial resources through donations and the so-called 'five-per-thousand' law, under which Italian taxpayers devolve a compulsory share of their annual income tax to an association considered of public interest. Since CPI leadership was reluctant to provide information about the composition of its finances, we could not assess the extent to which this form of funding contributes to CPI's budget. Tellingly, the ID code for devolving funds to CPI does not mention the name of CPI, but a more neutral *L'Isola delle Tartarughe* (The Island of Turtles: the arrowed turtle being the logo of CPI).[1]

As an organization, CPI is strongly hierarchical and centred on the figure of its founding leader, Gianluca Iannone, and on an advisory body made up of a few individuals in charge of the core activities and ideas of the group. Internal debates originally took place through a blog managed by the leadership, but now mostly appear in CPI's newspaper *Il Primato Nazionale*, which is available both online and in print format (see Chapter 7).[2] Overall, CPI is organized much like a mass political party, with a central headquarters (in Rome) and series of hierarchically subordinate local chapters (see Chapter 2). The internal organization follows two logics: a territorial division of responsibilities, and a thematic distribution of responsibilities. Geographically, CPI organizes like a party, with a number of local branches responding directly to the central organization. Thematically, CPI is more unusual, featuring a youth wing similar to that of most political parties, and a series of parallel project-based organizations or issue-specific associations.

The geographic organization of CPI is rather simple. All local chapters have a similar structure including a local leader and an advisory body in direct touch with the central authority in Rome. The Roman chapter oversees the planning of CPI's major activities at the national and local levels, and notably the training of activists, and the management of recreational events, demonstrations and other campaigns. The hierarchical organization of local chapters thus ensures that all decision-making is centralized on the national headquarters, especially concerning the training of activists and the organization of events.

As explained by two local leaders, in fact, most decisions concerning the recruitment and training of local activists and the funding of local events have to be approved in Rome:

> Intellectual education is a mainstay for CPI. From the national headquarters they send us lists of books, themes, and films for activists. Moreover, since we also manage a pub, we organize other types of events too, such as the 'Irish month', for which we ask [the national headquarters] for funding.[3]

Hence, similar to the model of the post-war mass parties, all local officials are trained in Rome by means of ad hoc sessions organized by the national leadership. The sessions include training on event management (concerts, movie projections, celebrations), but also working groups on the readings to suggest to activists and newcomers.[4] These courses are then reproduced locally for local activists.

> We organize training courses for militants at the local level, but local leaders go to Rome every now and then for a few days for their own training and an update. Here we have organized about thirty training meetings [*the interviewee shows a folder with all the leaflets, catalogued by date, from the various meetings*].[5]

> We organize training courses about history and culture … but also practical things, such as sewing for instance. And then we discuss important issues, like welfare state or immigration, and we discuss with the activists how to address them.[6]

On these occasions, national leaders set the strategy for local political meetings focusing on broad political issues considered relevant for CPI in general. At the time of our fieldwork, the main issues were the Italian sovereign debt crisis, housing rights and the need to restore economic protectionism; local leaders can articulate the discussions around local issues (e.g. local social housing projects, local industrial plans, etc.). Overall, besides the themes sponsored by the national leadership, local leaders can also promote others, as long as these are considered to be coherent with CPI's general agenda.

> To tell you the truth, we can propose any reading we want about Fascism and the core ideas of CPI. For instance, here in [*city of the local branch*], we meet once a month and comment on a book we have read. It may be one of the titles included in the list suggested from Rome, but we can also choose another topic related to CPI's political goals … for example I can suggest to activists: next time we discuss the history of the Social Republic. Or something on Ezra Pound or the like.[7]

As for the thematic organization of CPI, the group features a youth organization (*Blocco Studentesco*, Student Bloc, BS) and a series of associations promoting political participation on specific issues. Table 4.1 lists their names, the activities proposed, their legal status and the numbers of chapters they can count on.

Besides the youth wing (which counts 53 chapters: see section 4.3), CasaPound promotes seven other associations. The most prominent ones – which recurred frequently in our interviews – are CPI's humanitarian charity *Solidarités-Identités* (Solidarity – Identity) and *La Salamandra* (The Salamander), a unit of volunteers aiming to support Italy's Civil Protection (*Protezione Civile*) in the prevention and management of exceptional events and natural disasters. The other associations were initially formed under the initiative of single individuals or smaller groups of activists. This includes various types of groups which enable CPI to mobilize on different issues, using a different (and less stigmatized) name,

TABLE 4.1 CasaPound Italia's associations

Name	*Field*	*Legal status*	*Nr of chapters*
Blocco studentesco	Students' association	None	53
Solidaritès Identitès Onlus	International Humanitarian volunteering	Legally registered association	5 abroad (Syria, Birmania, Kosovo, Palestine, South Africa)
La Muvra	Mountain Hiking, sport	Legally registered association	15
La Foresta che avanza	Environmental association	Legally registered association	20
GR.IM.ES	Health assistance	None	Not available
Il Circuito	Combat sport	None	Not available
Impavidi Destini	Disability	None	Not available
La Salamandra	Domestic Humanitarian volunteering (civil protection)	None	Not available
Scuderie7Punto1	Bikers	None	Not available

and creating links with civil society. For instance, *Impavidi Destini* (Fearless Fates) is an NGO assisting persons with disabilities and campaigning for their rights; *GR.I.ME.S.* (Special Team on Social Medicine) is a group of medics and paramedics who, through CPI, organized free services for health counselling; whereas *La Foresta che Avanza* (The Advancing Forest) is a volunteer association focusing on the environment and animal rights. In addition, CPI promotes sport activities notably through *Il Circuito* (The Circuit – the network of CPI gyms) and excursions through *La Muvra* (The Mouflon – for mountain hiking). While some of these associations are now established, involving several activists and counting on official websites and a relatively professional staff, others can only count on Facebook pages and are relatively inactive unless individual militants invest in organizing events (see Chapter 7).

The rationale for the thematic organization of CPI's internal units is threefold. First, as noted, these associations help CPI to recruit sympathizers, by offering engagement opportunities on specific themes, and services available to the public. Second, these associations help to craft the identity of militants, offering specific trajectories of militancy within the political framework offered by CPI (see Chapter 5). And third, and perhaps most importantly, these associations are important for the funding of CPI. Since CPI cannot count on the state funding associated with electoral participation, it gathers financial resources from non-electoral activities. Three of these associations, in fact, are registered and are able to receive donations through the tax return system outlined above. Furthermore, they can participate in public calls for tenders (*gare d'appalto*), and their charitable

FIGURE 4.1 Posters from CasaPound Italia's associations.

On the left a *Sol.Id.* initiative advertising a food drive for Syria (2015); in the middle, the membership campaign of *La Salamandra* (2017); on the right, a poster from *La Foresta che Avanza* calling for the end of animal suffering in circuses (2011).

activities can be funded. The advantage for CPI is that these associations do not display the logo of CPI and thus escape the stigmatization of the right-wing extremist worldviews of the group. With reference to these linkages, the mayor of a small town in central Italy explained to us that he funded CPI's association *La Foresta che Avanza* for a project of environmental requalification, without knowing that it was related to CPI.

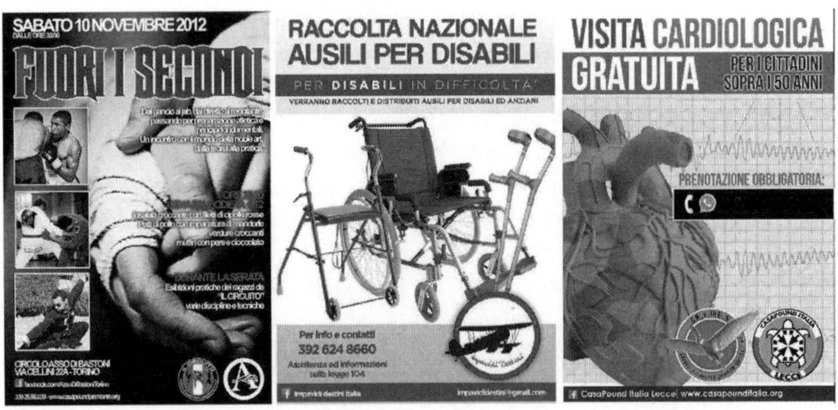

FIGURE 4.2 Posters from CasaPound Italia's associations.

On the left, the poster of a boxing initiative by *Il Circuito* in Turin (2012); in the middle, a campaign to collect equipment for the disabled organized by the NGO *Impavidi Destini* (2016); on the right, a poster from *GR.I.ME.S.* promoting free cardiology check-ups for people over 50 years of age (2018).

4.2 Leadership, decision-making and personnel selection

CPI presents a hierarchical structure with neither formal decision-making procedures, nor discernible internal democracy. In this section, we shall discuss three crucial factors in the internal structure of CPI: the leadership and its relationship with the base; the organization of the internal decision-making process; and the definition of organizational roles.

Leadership in CPI is embodied by the president, Gianluca Iannone, who is also the founder of CPI and a widely recognized figure in the subcultural milieu of the Italian extreme right. His involvement in the everyday politics of CPI has however decreased over time; most of the ordinary business is now delegated to the vice-president, Simone Di Stefano, who acts as spokesperson, and runs as candidate in national and major local elections. But Iannone remains the most widely recognized figure of CasaPound, and he takes the stage whenever there is any controversy about the group, such as in the aftermath of the 2011 shootings in Florence.[8]

All the activists we met and interviewed during fieldwork agreed that the leadership held a complete, unchallenged steering role over the organization and its activities. The interviewees described Iannone as a 'natural' charismatic leader, and accepted his leadership because of his direct connection with the base and the militants. While acting as the leader, Iannone is also perceived as part of the CPI community, thanks to his direct, personal engagement in CPI's major political activities, social voluntary work and leisure activities – notably through the ZetaZeroAlfa concerts and music. The leader is thus described emphatically as 'Soldier, brother and friend' at the same time.[9] Our open participant observation, however, provided a somewhat different image of the relationship, and proximity, between the leader and its base. Notably, during our visit at one of the prominent squats of the group – *Area 19*, a disused metro station which hosted CasaPound's three-day festival in September 2012 – we were able to note that the leadership was very cautious about mingling with the rest of the militants. Rather, Iannone and the other high-ranking officials were reserved a specific place, physically separated from the crowd. The same was confirmed at CPI's national demonstration, where Iannone and Di Stefano led the parade but did not join the ranks of the activists and sympathizers.

In addition to playing a symbolic role as a model and a point of reference for activists (Eatwell 2002), the coterie charisma of CasaPound's leader is crucial for internal decision-making and for the selection of personnel. As noted earlier, all strategies and policy proposals are decided by the inner leadership in Rome, and are simply communicated to members, militants and local branches. The central body then sets up a number of cabinets in charge of coordinating activities across main policy areas, notably housing. While decentralized grassroots initiatives are possible, they have to be ratified by the offices in Rome. For instance, CPI's decision to run for national elections was communicated during the 2012 national festival at a public debate and national officials did not attempt to justify the choice. When we asked one of the local leaders who was present at the debate whether he agreed with the decision, his answer was simple:

> We do not take part in these decisions. I cannot take decisions like that! Gianluca [Iannone] decided and then he told us. He says that this is good for CPI, and I trust him. He knows what is good for CPI.[10]

The definition of organizational roles and duties in CPI follows similarly strict and informal procedures. Again, all procedures take place under the explicit initiative and unique responsibility of the leader. National and local officials are thus co-opted within the leadership based on Iannone's own judgement. Militants are promoted to officials or assigned specific roles based on ad hoc decisions and then justified according to their educational or professional competencies. As a result, officials often perform tasks that correspond to their professional or educational skills: the communication manager is a professional journalist, whereas the cultural manager graduated in philosophy.

Appointments and promotions do not depend much on the experience and seniority of militants, nor on collective decision-making procedures, but simply on the relationship between militants and the national leadership. Still, CPI activists consider that personnel selection in the group conforms to meritocratic standards, rather than to co-optation: unlike the processes in political parties, it is claimed, in CPI the length of militancy does not necessarily lead to a leadership role.

> There's clearly a substantial difference compared to parties, in the sense that there is not some big shot that can recruit members and use them to impose his will on a local congress.[11]

> Consider that, once elected, our councilmen give everything or almost everything to CasaPound. They do not keep anything for themselves. There are no professional politicians like in the other parties.[12]

Our interviewees justified this choice based on ideology, referring to Julius Evola's concept of 'personal equations', according to which each individual (and, thus, each militant) is defined by a pre-established set of intellectual and spiritual inclinations (Furlong 2011).

> Everyone chooses his or her own way (…) according to his or her personal equation, as Evola used to say. Everyone has his or her own way of being an activist, his or her own competencies and skills.[13]

Still, while certain skills can be learned through militancy, others are characteristics that are innate to only a few. The most important quality of a militant is leadership, which cannot be learned.

> CasaPound's structure is both hierarchical and meritocratic. Essentially, we have no high ranks and no congresses. We do not even have colonels. Instead, those of us who commit the most, and better than the others, will be recognised as leaders, and followed by everyone.[14]

This 'objective' understanding of meritocracy is closely intertwined with CasaPound's leadership principle according to which the national leader possesses all the qualities necessary to select the cadres, identify the needs of the organization and judge the abilities of each individual militant. As a result, CPI does not envisage the possibility of internal factions, either formally or informally. All national officials have had and still have personal exchanges with the national leader, and most of them were directly recruited by him. The leader is thus in charge of not only the strategic and practical running of CPI but is also responsible for the effectiveness of its decision-making and internal cohesion.

4.3 Recruitment strategies

A third crucial aspect of CPI's internal structure has to do with the group's recruitment practices. So far, the literature on the far right has paid little attention to the question of how and why people join these groups (Klandermans and Mayer 2006). In this section we address these questions on the basis of militants' experiences as described in the interviews.

As regards recruitment, there are two main ways to join CPI. First, as in the case of normal political parties, individuals can visit a local chapter or one of the associations of CPI, and ask to be registered. Through this formal procedure, newcomers receive an official membership card. The cost of the card can vary, but normally it ranges between 10 and 15 euros. Similarly, sympathizers can ask to become 'web supporters', paying a reduced fee and getting a different type of membership card.[15] Unlike actual members, who are expected to participate in most activities and be active militants, web supporters are only in charge of promoting CPI's messages and images online. Second, similar to social movements, individuals can join CPI by getting involved in the social activities of the group. Depending on one's interests, individuals can join any of the various associations mentioned above.

Hence, people can join CPI through voluntary social work, environmental protection activities, as well as through cultural and sports events. In this way, CPI offers multiple non-political access routes to individuals who wish to approach the group. The underlying idea is that outsiders would gradually transition into sympathizers, and sympathizers into activists, by means of participation in initiatives of an increasingly political nature. Accordingly, CPI's chapters are thought of as places to socialize. They are expected to facilitate the arrival of new recruits, initially through their interest in the recreational activities offered by CPI, or by the prospect of being part of a community. This is why the chapters of CPI do not use the often-impersonal looking rooms of party chapters, mainly utilized for hosting political meetings and other conventional party events. Instead, their meeting places are often bars, gyms, theatres, music halls or tattoo shops.

> I was not very interested in politics, because I always thought that it was a waste of time or just too complicated for me. I was always interested in boxing and *Il Circuito* offers good venues to train for decent prices. Here I met some *camerati* (comrades) who helped me with the training and often we also discussed politics. I understood that I can actually do something to change things. I learned that I should not be passive, and I got the card of CPI.[16]

In addition to these physical spaces, the Web constitutes a crucial venue for recruitment. Among the people we met during fieldwork, however, many used online platforms to get information and news about CPI, but only a few had been actually recruited online.

> I grew up in a small village where no one cares about politics. There were no places to engage in politics, apart from short chats at the bar and ridiculous local campaigns. I discovered the CPI website and its political platform and its events and I was fascinated. When I moved to Rome for my studies, I decided to visit CPI's headquarters and … here I am.[17]

CPI's recruitment strategies, therefore, are based on a hybrid system of venues of access, which facilitate individual, non-political trajectories of adhesion to the group. The intention is that of constructing a close community, which is as compact on the inside as it is insulated towards the outside world. This emerges quite clearly from the ways in which individual activists describe how they joined the group. For our interviewees, in fact, joining CPI is mainly about identity, and less about ideological or instrumental motivations. Movement participation in CPI can therefore be distinguished in line with the seminal work of Klandermans and Mayer (2006: 8). First, there are *identity motivations*, which explain movement participation as an expression of personal identification with the group; second, *ideological motivations* describe participation as a search for meaning for one's own views; and finally, *instrumental motivations* see participation as an explicit attempt to change the political and social environment.

Most militants we were able to meet during our fieldwork emphasized identity motivations, and notably the need to be part of a family-like community with whom they can share ideas that are stigmatized by others (Orfali 1990, 2012). A community of like-minded people enables the building of solidarity through political and non-political activities but also prevents factionalism. Thus activism is primarily an existential choice: it is 'primarily a way of life'[18] and activists are aware that 'CPI is a monolith … if you are in you are in, if you are out you are out'.[19]

Identification with the community is so important that even when speaking about their individual experiences in CPI, activists rarely used the pronoun 'I' while many used 'we' even when speaking about their individual experiences.

> There is a very tight relationship among us, the activists. It's not by chance that we feel like we are brothers. And that's with every one of us, irrespective of whether we fancy each other or not.[20]

> Here [*in CasaPound*] the career is not like in the other parties. Our only reward is to make ourselves available to the whole group.[21]

Ideological motives for movement participation emerge as well, notably when militants emphasize their need to share their views with like-minded people. This has special importance for a group, like CPI, that promotes highly stigmatized ideas, builds upon controversial figures and symbols, which many militants do not feel comfortable sharing with people outside CPI.

> Finally, I had the opportunity to express my true self within the community (...). What I have found within the community of CasaPound, and which I consider truly exceptional, is that every cultural and social barrier is overcome – which for me is fundamental.[22]

In addition to identity and ideological motivations, some activists also had instrumental reasons. They referred to the need to change Italian politics and its establishment, defined by political representatives, cultural elites and the media. Many describe being an activist as a mission, which does not imply any personal reward. Many describe their involvement as a pure act of commitment:

> You don't join CasaPound to make a career for yourself, here there are no congresses, no factions. You're in or you're out (...), either you live with the community and for the community, or you don't become a leader.[23]

4.4 Modes of engagement

The hybrid range of CPI recruitment strategies is mirrored by the multiple modes of engagement offered to its militants and sympathizers. A variety of daily activities are in fact envisaged, with the goal of creating solidarity bonds within the group, and strengthening collective identity (Castelli Gattinara and Froio 2014; Di Nunzio and Toscano 2011).

CPI defines itself as a community that takes care of the material as well as spiritual needs of its members: there is no aspect of the everyday life of activists that CPI does not attempt to imbue with political content (see Chapter 5).

Accordingly, CasaPound organizes a multiplicity of collective activities open to all members. Activists are expected to spend most of their free time within the group. The idea is that militants perform most of their everyday activities within *the community* rather than elsewhere. Many of the activists we met during our fieldwork participated regularly in these activities and frequented CPI's social spaces – shops, gyms, concert halls – on an everyday basis.

Once an individual has become a member of CPI, activism becomes extremely demanding. Militants engage in conventional activities, such as electoral campaigning, political meetings, organization of public events, as well as in various forms of protest politics, and cultural activities such as art exhibitions, book presentations, concerts and movie projections:

> Becoming a political activist means devoting most of your free time to CPI. Of course, those who want can simply be sympathizers or just vote for us. That is fine, but being an activist is a different thing. It is an existential commitment: you have to share with the community your daily routine, your passions and fears, everything. With us, you do politics not only by voting or by taking part in a demonstration. You must take part in all of our activities, our debates, our concerts, our exhibitions and so forth.[24]

According to one national leader, by engaging in the different activities proposed by CPI and its associations, activists expand their political knowledge and skills. Joining CPI is thus the first step of a process of personal growth inside the community, made up of 'thought and action'.[25] Being an activist implies enrolment in traditional activities, but also requires a substantial commitment to the process of learning and sharing the group's values, ideas and practices: 'To be with us, there should be sacrifice and the effort to improve oneself to become part of a community.'[26]

Despite CPI's official emphasis on the communitarian dimension of engagement, at least three specific patterns of participation can be distinguished, deserving specific attention. The first concerns the way in which the youth and student activism are integrated within CPI. The second concerns female activists and their roles in the group. And the third is the link between football fans and activism in CPI.

4.4.1 The youth wing

Just like the vast majority of traditional political parties, CPI has its own youth wing: the Student Bloc (Blocco Studentesco, BS). Founded in the summer of 2006, BS is active in the field of education policies, addressing youth in middle and high schools, and in universities. The logo of the BS is an encircled lightning flash that, according to one of its national leaders, should indicate the 'collective action of students'[27] and its 'dynamic spirit'.[28] The choice of the logo is ambivalent: while it does not recall the iconography of the Italian extreme right, it is rather similar to the emblem of the British Union of Fascists.

FIGURE 4.3 The logo of CasaPound Italia's youth branch: the Blocco Studentesco.

Overall, the Bloc aims to improve the quality of education for (Italian) students, increasing the number of student representatives in schools and universities and reducing the cost of studying. The Bloc's programme focuses on public education (for Italian students only), against private education and the private funding of research. While defending public and free education, the Bloc supports a 'meritocratic university model' (Blocco Studentesco 2008a) based on excellence scholarships (for Italians only). It also calls for the introduction to the educational system of trips and ad hoc programmes to 'rediscover the holy places of the nation' (Blocco Studentesco 2015) and an increase in the hours of physical training in high schools. The main political goals of CPI's youth wing are listed on the group's website:

> The BS is a revolutionary movement that wants to change the existing schooling system: the corporate schools which censor ideas, where students are powerless, and where 1968 teachers and principal-managers rule. (Blocco Studentesco 2008b)

While the leaders of the Bloc are not the same as those of CPI, they still refer to them to coordinate their actions and programmes. During an interview with a national leader of the BS, he explained that the Bloc was born to bring CasaPound into schools and universities, which are usually associated with progressive-left movements and collectives. The official slogan of the BS – 'Power to Youth' – is also an ironic distortion of the May 1968 slogan 'Power to imagination'. In this respect, the BS was born to challenge:

> the pretended hegemony over education and intellectual activities of the left who believe that schools and universities belong to them. We also have things to say but to do so we must remove the cultural hegemony of the generation of May' 68 who monopolizes schools and universities.[29]

As is the case with CPI in general, the majority of the BS activists do not have the appearance of the 'male skinhead, heavily tattooed, heads freshly shaven' (Mudde 2014: 1). Mainly belonging to younger generations, the BS activists that we met during fieldwork use the same dress codes as CPI activists, exhibiting coded symbols and slogans easily recognizable only by other activists or sympathizers (see Chapter 5).

The first action that gave visibility to BS took place in 2006, when some activists occupied a high school in Rome for six days (*La Repubblica* 2009). In October 2008, the BS obtained national coverage after the highly mediatized clashes between right-wing and left-wing students in Rome, which resulted in 37 people being put under investigation, 21 of whom belonged to BS (*La Repubblica* 2009). A few days later, the Bloc stormed the studios of the public television (Rai) programme *Chi l'ha visto?* to denounce the show's interpretation of the events. Shortly afterwards, CPI aired amateur footage reconstructing the events with images and testimonies.[30] In 2009, the BS obtained the presidency of several local student councils (*La Repubblica* 2009), and in 2010 it elected its first members on the councils of universities in Rome, Verona and Palermo (Di Nunzio and Toscano 2011). As regards the National Council of University Students (CNSU), however, BS never gained more than 2 per cent of the votes, which is far below most other student lists. In March 2010 however, the leaders of BS participated in an official meeting with the then minister of education Mariastella Gelmini and presented a series of proposals to improve education in the Veneto region (*Il Giornale* 2010).

Over time, however, it appears that BS lost the momentum it had acquired through their participation in violent and confrontational events. In this respect, Map 4.1 illustrates the territorial distribution of BS chapters in Italy, measured at two points in time. BS chapters that existed in 2013 are marked in white, whereas those present in 2018 are grey (the chapters existing both in 2013 and 2018 display a grey ringed circle). As can be noted, BS is mainly concentrated in central Italy, and in large urban areas. In over five years, between 2013 and 2018, the BS founded only six new chapters – which is remarkably little if compared with the much faster growth of CPI, discussed in the previous chapters.

4.4.2 Women in CasaPound

The 'gendered-dimension'[31] of far-right politics is considered to be increasingly important by academic scholarship and the media (Köttig et al. 2017; Spierings et al. 2015). While extant studies have focused on female leaders within established right-wing parties, little is known about the participation of women in the usually male-dominated grassroots extreme right (Avanza 2008; Blee 2002, 2017; Scrinzi 2017).

As regards the gender composition of CPI's electoral lists, women are fairly well represented. This is no surprise, considering that Italy has a legal mechanism

MAP 4.1 The local sections of the Student Bloc in Italy in 2013 and 2018.

designed to ensure gender equality in electoral lists, whereby each sex cannot be represented in excess of 60 per cent.[32] Accordingly, 47 per cent of the 716 candidates who stood for CPI during the 2018 general elections were women, which is slightly higher but more or less in line with most other parties. Considering that CPI did not elect any MPs, and that national electoral lists are often made up of sympathizers who are participating symbolically, we should not make too much of these results.

Still, in light of the presence of this gender quota, CPI's choice of transitioning to the electoral arena certainly had consequences for the engagement and participation of women. Indeed, a number of women ran as main candidates for CPI in local elections, notably at the 2018 regional elections in Lombardy. Others acted as spokespersons for male candidates, sometimes managing to obtain national visibility despite the suburban scope of the elections, such as in the case of recent elections in the Roman suburb of Ostia (Torrisi 2018). Like other far-right groups and parties, CPI tries to give visibility to female militants and candidates, as well as sympathizers, in the belief that they appear to have greater legitimization than their male counterparts, who are more directly associated with violence and extremism.

In terms of movement participation, however, female activists display specific activist trajectories, both in terms of their motivations to join, and their modes of engagement within CPI. Unlike men, who stressed primarily the identity dimension of being members of CPI, the women we interviewed focused on personal factors and ideological motivations.

> CPI is the real alternative for Italy. It brings fresh air compared to the MSI. I know the history of the MSI well – my father was a Senator for that party. It is thanks to him that I am here. He transmitted important patriotic values to me, and a love for the Italian nation. However, I also know that, to survive, these values can not be presented like 40 years ago. I am in CPI because I want to protect the Italian nation and not because I am a woman![33]

> I am an activist because I want to be a mother and a worker, but it is difficult to be able to do both things at once. To be a mother, first you need a house, a job and a salary. These are the proposals of CPI.[34]

At the same time, female activists are integrated into the movement following the same personalized trajectory we have observed in the previous sections; their personal interests are progressively integrated into the political activities of the group:

> I joined CPI thanks to M. [name of partner, a local leader]. When we met, he was already a local official for the movement. Thanks to him, I discovered a group of fighters, who take the side of the Italian people. Here, they also gave space to my interests, to my studies on regional poetry. I join demonstrations and I also promote cultural activities such as reading sessions to discuss regional poetry.[35]

Female interviewees thus describe their membership in CPI ideologically, as a form of legitimization of beliefs that they possessed even before becoming members. On the one hand, unlike men, they do not describe their approach to

CPI as an individual trajectory culminating in a collective identity, but rather as an intermediated process, channelled by the presence of men: their partner, their husband or their father. On the other hand, they confirm the idea of CPI as a hybrid container, where activism can take multiple forms to accommodate the needs and preferences of individual militants.

This, however, corresponds only in part to the evidence we collected through participant observation. While most of the female activists that we interviewed claimed that men and women should have an equal say, both within and outside CPI, they also stressed that 'unlike feminists' CPI activists 'do not hate men'.[36] The rationale is that women have prescribed roles, which distinguish them from men in the context of the family – as mothers; and in society – as the biological reproducers of the nation.

> During demonstrations we stand side by side with our male *camerati* because we are all the same, we are all activists, we fight for the same objectives – to protect our nation, have a house, a job and a family. But women are also the guardians of life. This is why it is silly to claim that men and women are just the same. I believe that women are different and that they are complementary to men.[37]

In general, activism in CPI is interpreted within a masculine framework, mobilizing the strength of the militant, his fearless nature and his image as the 'hero of the nation'. In this respect, women often describe themselves using similar attributes: 'Activism for me is a fight. It is a struggle and I am strong.'[38] At the same time, they do not participate in the games and social activities that reproduce models of masculinity based on physical strength and aggressiveness. During pogo dancing and violent rites of identity building (Chapter 5), women do not mingle with men, but simply look at them from a distance, because 'it is their game and we watch them having fun'. While women are occasionally involved in most of CPI's activities, in fact, their presence is consistent in only two specific areas. First, they promote and manage the initiatives of CPI's project for women's right '*Tempo di essere madri*' (discussed in Chapter 2 and Chapter 6). Second, they take care of domestic tasks during social events (see Blee 2002), including cleaning, cooking, and serving food and beer.

4.4.3 Football fans

The link – actual or alleged – between right-wing extremism and football fans is often at the core of academic and political debate.[39] Notably, the neo-fascist tenets manifested by ideologically extreme-right groups of *ultras* are often interpreted as a fascist-inspired resistance against dominant socio-cultural models and political values in contemporary Italy (Testa and Armstrong 2008). Since the composition of *ultras* groups in Italy tends to reflect the character of the communities from which they are drawn, football hooliganism in Rome often unites a dual passion for the local teams and the political ideas of neo-fascism. However, the relationship between CPI and the stadium is ambiguous. During the 1990s and early 2000s, CPI's competitors from *Forza Nuova* successfully infiltrated organized soccer clubs and the stadiums in Rome to recruit militants among hooligans (Caldiron 2013). But in more recent times actors seeking to recruit in these milieus often faced open hostility (Testa and Armstrong 2010).

Hence, the milieu of the *curva*[40] is not central for political engagement in CPI, because the group offers its activists and supporters dedicated spaces and activities aimed at linking political views and group identity. While important, the stadium does not represent the main arena to articulate and express CPI's political identity.

> Of course, I go to the stadium, but, for me, doing politics is different from simply going to the stadium wearing a t-shirt with the logo of CPI and of my football team.[41]

However, the stadium plays an important role for recognition by outsiders of CPI and its members. In this respect, in the late 2000s some groups of *ultras* sought association with CPI, as they recognized it as a group mainly engaged in social activism, rather than being interested in purely ideological projects, or oriented towards the elections. Over the years, the movement style of CPI, and its propensity towards bottom-up action, turned it into one of the most respected political groups within the *ultras* environment (Testa et al. 2013). CPI therefore developed an ad hoc strategy towards political participation in Italian stadiums. When the circumstances were favourable, it built links with pre-existing football groups (e.g. in Rome), or alliances with groups that had connections with the *curva*, such as in the case of the youth centre *Cuore Nero* (Black Heart) in Milan. In other cases, and notably in some cities in Tuscany, it created sub-groups of supporters that directly connected with the central organization.

> We only go to the *curva* where it is permitted to enter as a political group. I mean without … starting a war! We did it in Rome, with *Padroni di Casa* [The Landlords]. In Arezzo we have a group called *Io e i miei amici* [My Friends and I],[42] whose members have certain political ideas and certainly belong to CasaPound.[43]

CPI has used the stadiums strategically to achieve visibility and recognition within a milieu in which the extreme right had been long present, but was often ostracized by open hostility towards political parties and 'the system'. Getting into the *curva* was thus functional to CPI's project for hegemony over the far-right milieu, precisely to mark its difference from the existing parties of the Italian extreme right. In this way, CPI sought to bring the world of the *ultras* closer to its own social activism outside the stadiums, promoting its distinctive profile and youth-oriented approach to politics. Indeed, the *ultras'* world features prominently in the novel written by a leading figure of the movement, which describes, in a romanticized way, the stages that could lead a young person to become a CPI militant. The main character of the novel, which is titled *Nessun Dolore: Una Storia di CasaPound* (No Pain: A Story of CasaPound), describes coming into contact with CPI at the stadium:

> They had created their own group of supporters: the Landlords. Being one of them meant having a different style, within and outside the stadium. [...] It was a style of supporting, but also a way of life, based on a few strict rules. [...] Those roughly one hundred young men were not merely organized supporters: they represented the arrowed turtle of CasaPound and the encircled lightning flash of the Student Bloc. (Di Tullio 2010: 93)

Conclusive remarks

This chapter has described the main organizational features of CasaPound, focusing on its formal organization, leadership, recruitment strategies and modes of engagement. For each of these dimensions, it illustrated that CPI organizes internally by strategically hybridizing the configurational models of both political parties and of social movements. By looking at the internal structure of CPI, our analysis argued that these two models can coexist. This, in turn, provides recognition to the group.

Like political parties, CPI organizes territorially around one central headquarters and several local branches, hierarchically subordinated to Rome but whose functions are linked to the recruitment of supporters and collecting membership fees. Furthermore, it promotes a formally organized youth wing, which responds directly to the national offices. Other features distinguish CPI from the usual internal structure of far-right political parties. It does not foresee any formal representation of local units at the national level, nor does it envisage any formal mechanism dealing with questions of collective choice, internal democracy and personnel selection. As the group does not count on a professionalized staff, the leader distributes tasks depending on activists' skills and competences. Similarly, recruitment strategies combine conventional activities typical of party campaigning, and the dense informal networks of social movements. This is sustained by a set of thematic associations that take responsibility for specific projects and try to draw individuals into activism through informal and non-political activities in various fields (environment, community service, etc.). Additionally, CPI promotes spaces devoted to the socialization of activists, including subcultural activities, gyms and organized football groups.

Overall, the chapter argued that CPI's ability in recruiting sympathizers and sustaining activists' engagement rests precisely on its hybrid organizational configuration. By facilitating the involvement of activists and attracting financial resources from different sources, hybridization has contributed to sustain CPI's organization and public profile. Moving to a discussion of CPI's collective action, Chapter 5 examines how individuals relate to CasaPound as an organization, discussing hybridization in the symbols and practices that define CPI's collective identity.

Notes

1 In 2017, a journalistic investigation by the magazine *L'Espresso* reported that CPI uses its funds for purposes that go beyond its everyday political goals (*L'Espresso* 2017).
2 In the past, this was done on a website related to CPI called the *Ideodromo* and through a blog called *Vivamafarka* which, however, are no longer active.
3 Interview no. 3a of 01/06/2012.
4 Interview no. 3a of 01/06/2012.
5 Interview no. 3a of 01/06/2012.
6 Interview no. 2b of 27/04/2012.
7 Interview no. 1b of 19/04/2012.
8 In the city of Florence on 13 December 2011, Gianluca Casseri, a CPI sympathizer, shot dead two market traders from Senegal, Samb Modou and Mor Diop, before committing suicide. The video of Gianluca Iannone's interview on TV is available at www.youtube.com/watch?v=WPlYIFqR2CE (accessed 24/07/2013).
9 The expression 'Soldier, Brother, Friend' was used by an activist during interview no. 3a of 1/06/2012.
10 Interview no. 1b of 19/04/2012.
11 Interview no. 2c of 27/04/2012.
12 Interview no. 1b of 19/04/2012
13 Interview no. 2b of 27/04/2012
14 Interview no. 1b of 19/04/2012.
15 It was not possible to find reliable figures for the number of CasaPound members (beyond those provided by CPI itself). During fieldwork, we were told that CPI had 10,000 registered members but this figure could not be verified.
16 Interview no. 6a of 20/09/2012.
17 Interview no. 2b of 27/04/2012.
18 Interview no. 5c of 26/06/2012.
19 Interview no. 2c of 27/04/2012.
20 Interview no. 5a of 26/06/2012.
21 Interview no. 1c of 19/04/2012.
22 Interview no. 5b of 26/06/2012.
23 Interview no. 2c of 27/04/2012.
24 Interview no. 5c of 26/06/2012.
25 Interview no. 1b of 19/04/2012.
26 Interview no. 2c of 27/04/2012.
27 Interview no. 2c of 27/04/2012.
28 Interview no. 2c of 27/04/2012.
29 Interview no. 2c of 27/04/2012.
30 Interview no. 2d of 27/04/2012.
31 While the reality may be more complex than the simplification we have adopted, we use the term 'sex' for men, women and transsexuals to refer to biological distinctions and 'gender' to refer to social constructs not biologically linked to sexes but shaped by social structures, norms and institutions. The gendered dimension of CPI's ideology is examined in Chapter 3.
32 The law mentions a number of mechanisms making sure that each party or coalition does not have more than 60 per cent of candidates of the same sex.
33 Interview no. 5b of 28/06/2012.
34 Interview no. 5b of 28/06/2012.

35 Interview no. 6b of 20/09/2012.
36 Interview no. 5b of 28/06/2012.
37 Interview no. 5b of 28/06/2012.
38 Interview no. 5b of 28/06/2012.
39 As confirmed by the information and security policy report issued by the Italian Presidency of the Council of Ministers in 2008 (Presidenza del Consiglio dei Ministri 2008).
40 Literally the curved ends of a stadium, where the most fanatical supporters (*ultras*) stand.
41 Interview no. 3a of 1/06/2012.
42 This is also the title of a song by ZZA.
43 Interview no. 1b of 19/04/2012.

References

Avanza, M. 2008. 'Un Parti Qui 'l'a Dure' Les 'Femmes Padanes' Dans La Ligue Du Nord', in O. Fillieule and P. Roux (eds), *Le Sexe Du Militantisme*. Paris: Presses de Sciences Po.

Blee, K. 2002. *Organized Racism: Women and Men in the Hate Movement*. Berkeley: University of California Press.

———. 2017. 'Similarities/Differences in Gender and Far-Right Politics in Europe and the USA', in M. Köttig, et al.(eds), *Gender and Far Right Politics in Europe*. Cham, Switzerland: Springer International Publishing, pp. 191–204.

Blocco Studentesco. 2008a. 'Università'. URL: www.bloccostudentesco.org/universita.html (consulted April 2018).

———. 2008b. 'Chi Siamo'. URL: www.bloccostudentesco.org/universita.html (consulted April 2018).

———. 2015. 'Programma Scuola'. URL: www.bloccostudentesco.org/scuola/programma.html (consulted April 2018).

Caldiron, G. 2013. *Estrema destra*. Rome: Newton Compton Editori.

Castelli Gattinara, P., and C. Froio. 2014. 'Discourse and Practice of Violence in the Italian Extreme Right: Frames, Symbols, and Identity-Building in CasaPound Italia', *International Journal of Conflict and Violence* 8(1).

Di Nunzio, D., and E. Toscano. 2011. *Dentro e Fuori CasaPound: Capire Il Fascismo Del Terzo Millennio*. Rome: Armando Editore.

Di Tullio, D. 2010. *Nessun Dolore. Una Storia Di CasaPound*. Milano: Rizzoli.

Eatwell, R. 2002. 'The Rebirth of Right-Wing Charisma? The Cases of Jean-Marie Le Pen and Vladimir Zhirinovsky', *Totalitarian Movements and Political Religions* 3(3): 1–23.

Furlong, P. 2011. *Social and Political Thought of Julius Evola*. London: Routledge.

Il Giornale. 2010. 'A Verona Il Ministro Gelmini Incontra Il Blocco Studentesco', March 14.

Kitschelt, H. 2006. 'Movement Parties', in R.S. Katz and W. Crotty (eds), *Handbook of Party Politics*. Thousand Oaks, CA: Sage, pp. 278–90.

Klandermans, B., and N. Mayer. 2006. *Extreme Right Activists in Europe: Through the Magnifying Glass*. New York: Psychology Press.

Köttig, M. et al.2017. *Gender and Far Right Politics in Europe*. London: Palgrave Macmillan.

La Repubblica. 2009. 'Elezioni Della Consulta Provinciale Blocco Studentesco: Nostro', *La Repubblica*, November 25.

L'Espresso. 2017. 'Così Casapound Prende Soldi Con Il 5 per Mille', August 11.

Mudde, C. (ed.). 2014. *Youth and the Extreme Right*. London: Routledge.

Orfali, B. 1990. 'Le FN Ou Le Parti-Famille', *Esprit* 164(9): 15–24.

———. 2012. *L'adhésion à l'extrême Droite: Etude Comparative en France, Hongrie, Italie et Roumanie*. Paris: L'Harmattan.

Presidenza del Consiglio dei Ministri. 2008. 'Relazione Sulla Politica Dell'informazione per La Sicurezza'. URL: https://www.sicurezzanazionale.gov.it/sisr.nsf/wp-content/uploads/2009/02/relazione-2008.pdf (consulted April 2019).

Scrinzi, F. 2017. 'Gender and Women in the Front National Discourse and Policy: From "Mothers of the Nation" to "Working Mothers"', *New Formations* 91: 1–25.

Spierings, N. et al.2015. 'Gender and Populist Radical-Right Politics: An Introduction', *Patterns of Prejudice* 49(1–2): 3–15.

Testa, A., and G. Armstrong. 2008. 'Words and Actions: Italian Ultras and Neo-Fascism', *Social Identities* 14(4): 473–90.

Testa, A. and G. Armstrong. 2010. 'Purity and Danger: Policing the Italian Neo-fascist Football UltraS', *Criminal Justice Studies* 23(3): 219–37.

Testa, A. et al.2013. 'The Ultras: The Extreme Right in Contemporary Italian Football', in A. Mammone (ed.), *Varieties of Right-Wing Extremism in Europe*. London: Routledge.

Torrisi, C. 2018. 'How Italian Media Glamourise Fascism', *Open Democracy*, January 29, URL: https://www.opendemocracy.net/5050/claudia-torrisi/italian-media-casapound-glamourise-fascism (consulted April 2019).

5
COLLECTIVE IDENTITY

Previous chapters discussed how historical Fascism inspires CasaPound's worldview and its hybrid organizational configuration, which is somewhere between the forms of political parties and of social movements. To continue the investigation, this chapter examines hybridization in the formation of a collective identity within CPI. We define collective identities as the sense of common purpose and shared commitment to a cause (Melucci 1995; Olson 1965; Pizzorno 1996). According to Melucci (1995) collective identities are formed through shared definitions of the goals, means and tactics to which activists apply a common language, rituals, practices and cultural references. Collective identities generate and sustain individuals' commitment to a given group or cause over time, by providing resources that make it easier for activists to face the risks involved in joint action (Olson 1971).

Building on the literature on collective identities in social movements, we examine shared meanings, symbols and practices in CPI's activism (Polletta and Jasper 2001; Snow 2001) that crucially contribute to the public visibility of the group. We use evidence gathered through participant observation and face-to-face interviews as well as qualitative content analysis of written material, namely the lyrics of the songs of ZetaZeroAlfa and CPI's internal literature. This allows us to disentangle the symbols, rituals and narratives through which activists attribute meaning to collective action, and thus understand, negotiate and inform themselves as part of the community. Specifically, the chapter looks at four vectors of identity formation: imagery, in the form of references to shared items and visual symbols (5.1); style, understood as a common identifier establishing shared aesthetic and clothing codes (5.2); music, as an expression and result of shared subcultural belonging (5.3); and violence, understood as a way for activists to behave (5.4). The chapter argues that commitment to CPI results from shared hybrid images and practices, which trigger a network of relationships of trust among activists. Collective identity in CPI is thus not only explained by the adherence to a set of classic extreme-right symbols and rituals, but by a more complex combination of extreme and coded references, mediated by different political cultures. This mix of extreme right, pop-culture and left-progressive references supports the engagement of individuals in CPI, by consolidating the group's internal identity and by ensuring public recognizability.

5.1 Imagery

Symbolic resources act as signifiers of collective identity and shared symbols are crucial to sustain individuals' commitment to a group (Hirsch 1990; Hunt and Benford 1994; Klandermans 1997). In this respect, CPI exhibits hybrid features, combining symbols belonging to different (if not opposite) political cultures: while CPI's imagery and aesthetic codes are crucially inspired by the tradition of historical Fascism, the choice of specific symbols and ways to promote engagement in the community recalls the political culture of left-wing movements. This unusual symbolism came to represent a trademark of the group.

The bulk of CPI's imagery, used for both external and internal communication, includes classic symbols of historical Fascism (see Figure 5.1). By exhibiting Mussolini's icon, or the monumental heritage of ancient Rome, CasaPound differs from the majority of contemporary far-right parties, which avoid using the symbols of the inter-war regimes. These symbolic choices locate CPI in the nostalgic milieu of the Italian extreme right. References to classic Fascist symbols include easily recognizable images of the *squadristi* (blackshirts, on the bottom left in Figure 5.1),[1] glorification of fascist architecture (in particular the *Palazzo della Civiltà Italiana* in Rome, the top-right flyer in Figure 5.1) and the use of slogans such as 'Spring of Beauty' (*Primavera di Bellezza*). Also derived from historical Fascism and neo-Fascism are the gestures used as a greeting in CPI public and closed events. CPI activists are seldom seen making the 'Roman salute' at public occasions (the arm is held out straight forward, with palm down and is more common during private events). Instead, they often make use of the so-called 'legionary handshake' (performed by clasping the forearm instead of shaking hands). In a similar fashion, CPI graphic style is directly inspired by the aesthetic codes of the Italian futurist school of the early twentieth century, which emphasized notions such as youth, speed, violence and technological progress (Ferrarotti 2016). While the connection between Italian Futurism and historical Fascism is known, CPI leaders justify this choice ideologically: Futurism represents CPI's 'constant search for dynamism'.[2] Futurist images, paintings and sculptures encourage the observer to join the action rather than remain a passive observer. Similarly, for CPI, 'beauty is in the action not in contemplation'.[3]

Next to an imagery clearly inspired by the Fascist and neo-Fascist traditions, however, CPI utilizes symbols that are generally associated with the political left, including communist icons and ideologues, figures belonging to the anarchist

FIGURE 5.1 References to historical Fascism in CasaPound's posters and events.

Top left: public debate on 'Benito Mussolini: father of the nation' (2010), Lamezia Terme (Calabria); top right: CasaPound's campaign against the eviction of Italian citizens in Rome (2016), showing the *Palazzo della Civiltà Italiana*/Squared Coliseum; bottom left: poster advertising a 2010 debate on the book *Diary of a Tuscan Blackshirt* in Siena (Tuscany); bottom right: inauguration of the local chapter in Cisterna di Latina (Latium), in 2018.

sphere, and modes of action associated with progressive movements. To forge the group's public profile, CPI appropriated several images commonly associated with the left, including political figures like Che Guevara and Karl Marx, music stars such as Rino Gaetano, and pop-culture icons like the comic books hero Corto Maltese (see Figure 5.2). Our impression is that this choice of hybrid imagery complements CPI's predisposition to use tactics that are generally associated with left-wing social movements (see Chapter 6). In fact, associating a given imaginary with a specific repertoire of contention offers a basis on which to build collective identities, as in the case of direct activism among the the Black Bloc (Jasper 1997). Indeed, CPI's imagery during street actions and meetings does not aim to disseminate extreme-right aesthetics and symbols, but

FIGURE 5.2 References to left-wing symbols in CPI's posters and events.

Posters of CasaPound advertising public events related to Rino Gaetano, Che Guevara, Karl Marx and Corto Maltese.

rather to make the protest sensational, and thus catch the attention of large segments of the Italian public and quality media (see Chapter 7).

On the one hand, unlike other extreme-right groups in Italy, which invest considerably in commemorations and other symbolic gatherings, CPI manages to organize events featuring public figures who are not associated with the extreme-right, such as well-known gay rights activists, mainstream journalists and the president of the Chinese community in Rome.[4] On the other hand, CPI promotes spectacular tactics that can maximize the media impact of collective actions: it hung mannequins from buildings (CPI 2008a) and left messages in hundreds of bottles in fountains as a protest during the housing crisis (*Il Cannocchiale* 2008), and has occasionally stormed the political meetings of opponents (*Il Messaggero* 2013), TV shows (*L'Occidentale* 2008) and public schools, thereby gaining visibility in the quality media (Rai News 24 2012). The peculiarity of CPI's hybrid imagery stems precisely from its ability to borrow the icons and tactics of the political left and to combine them with the extreme-right references mentioned above. The result is a clearly defined, highly recognizable profile, which facilitates the identification of CPI by insiders, as well as outsiders such as the media, political opponents and the public.

5.2 Style

Activists' style – their appearance and clothing – are also important common identifiers, sustaining and reproducing collective identities (Polletta 1997). Notably, clothing styles may signal subcultural identities and play a crucial role in contemporary extreme-right activism (Miller-Idriss 2018). As we shall describe, CPI's hybrid style stands out from that of most of the Italian extreme right and the group commercializes clothing and tattoos to strengthen group and to be recognizable.

Current literature on German far-right youth supporters (Miller-Idriss 2018) observed that activists are increasingly taking a distance from the traditional extreme-right skinhead style that dominated this political subculture in the 1980s and 1990s. CPI appears to be in line with this trend. Only a minority of people we met during our fieldwork were clothed in the bomber jacket, braces and shaved-hair style. Instead, most activists presented a rather conventional look and wore simple clothes, such as a pair of jeans and a t-shirt. While more varied, the clothing of women is even further removed from the common extreme-right standards. Only seldom do CPI activists wear polo shirts, braces, stockings and three-quarter-length jackets. Rather, they do not seem to follow any specific clothing code, including in the choice of colours (generally dark, but also grey and dark red).

All activists display symbols that, despite being highly meaningful for insiders, are generally more obscure for outsiders, and for non-experts probably do not appear to be associated with an extreme-right culture (e.g. the logo of ZetaZeroAalfa (ZZA), the lyrics of their songs, pirate flags, etc.). CPI itself promotes and commercializes items displaying these coded symbols, such as t-shirts, backpacks, hats and hoodies. This merchandizing plays an identity-building function, allowing activists to wear branded clothes, and to distinguish insiders from outsiders. The branded clothes are also ideologically meaningful, in that CPI activists are asked to prioritize Italian products over those of multinational corporations. In addition, these commercial products also help CPI to increase financial resources, notably through e-commerce. CPI is informally associated with the music band ZZA, which promotes its own line of accessories, whose frontman is CPI's president, Gianluca Iannone (see Chapter 2), with a publishing house (*Altaforte Edizioni*) publishing books, magazines and comics, and with *Pivert,* a clothing line for men whose registered office is the same as that of CPI's newspaper, *Il Primato Nazionale*. *Pivert* aims at reaching a broader audience than CPI activists alone: its clothes do not in fact display the logo of CPI, nor other extreme-right symbols or slogans. While mostly prevalent among the extreme-right youth subculture, a Pivert jacket was worn in public in May 2018 by the former Italian Minister of Internal Affairs, Matteo Salvini (*La Repubblica* 2018).

In addition to clothing, tattoos play an identity function, defining activists who belong to the community and making CPI adherents recognizable externally. CPI owns a tattoo shop in Rome (*Tango Core*), where activists have themselves tattooed with the group's symbol of the turtle. Other tattoos that are common among CPI members confirm the groups' hybrid imagery and include the pirate ship the *Jolly Roger* (evoking rebellion against the rules and the system), but also Celtic and ancient Roman symbols (such as the runes or the acronym SPQR), as well as historical Fascist icons (e.g. Mussolini). Activists are very proud of their tattoos and exhibited them with pride – including the most controversial ones – during the interviews. At the same time, they claim that their 'non-compliant' tattoos have nothing to do with the fashion for tattoos of so-called 'hipsters' disliked by CPI's activists.

> For us, having a tattoo is like wearing an amulet during a battle. It is something more than a medal. It has nothing to do with self-complacency or fashion. We had tattoos twenty years ago, when people considered them ugly, and having them was associated with criminality. And we will have them in twenty years from now, when the others will have had theirs removed.
>
> The tattoos are your story and you must be proud of it, because every self-respecting man or woman is made of blunders, wrong choices, incredible challenges, impossible loves, and broken dreams. Tattoos remind us that we have lived and that we are still alive. When we will not be here anymore, our tattoos will remain.
>
> *(CPI 2013b)*

5.3 Music

In addition to imagery and styles, music can offer movements a sense of group belonging, unity and strength in confronting political opponents (Eyerman 2002). It has the potential to forge collective identities in social movements in general (Born and Hesmondhalgh 2000; Eyerman and Jamison 1998) and also in the extreme right (Kahn-Harris 2007; Teitelbaum 2017). Notably, rock music has been an important channel of communication and identity-building among extreme-right groups in Italy (O'Connell and Castelo-Branco 2010).

CPI takes this form of expression into special consideration as a way to build solidarity between members. Musical entertainment is in fact fundamental not only for recruitment and funding purposes (see Chapter 4), but also to sustain commitment to the group's cause and solidarity between activists. Accordingly, the territorial chapters of CPI are often transformed into venues for music, or they become pubs serving beer in front of a small stage, tattoo shops featuring live music or places to socialize, where sympathizers, activists and leaders meet to listen to music, relax or plan a political event. It is not surprising, therefore, to learn that CPI's official pub and music band existed even before CPI was born as a political organization.

> In 1998 we became managers of the *Cutty Sark*, which was just a pub … and today it is *our* pub. … It hosted all of those people who have had enough, and broke away from the existing political groups.
>
> Before CasaPound was born, we were the community of the *Cutty Sark*: the community of the pub. We met to listen the music of *ZetaZeroAlfa* and simply hang out.[5]

Today, CPI actively engages in producing and diffusing music through its radio channel *Radio Bandiera Nera* (Black Flag Radio, see Chapter 7). In line with CPI's hybrid imagery and style, the radio broadcasts both songs by singers and songwriters associated with the progressive-left tradition, and so-called 'identity rock', a form of punk rock music accompanied by lyrics referring to core features of extreme-right ideologies. The specificity of 'identity rock' is that it carries to the extreme the often aggressive and politically incorrect dimension of the alternative music movement. Since it is linked to right-wing political and meta-political entities, identity rock 'conveys messages which are associated with a history and type of activism which many consider unacceptable by itself' (Antolini 2010: 317). The group's music codes thus constitute a cultural repertoire consisting of references to historical Fascism, left-wing groups and frustration with contemporary society.

In this respect, the ZZA are crucial to CPI's political and identity project. They allow CPI to promote its alternative cultural models and ideals, and to define the collective identity of the group around shared values such as virility, courage or voluntarism. In fact, ZZA acts as an ambassador of CPI in an extensive extreme-right subcultural scene in Italy and abroad. The music band is at the core of a relatively broad cultural network, which includes the squat for music events, *Area 19* (evicted at the time of writing), the blog *Zentropa* reporting on identity rock concerts and events in Europe, the record label *Rupe Tarpea* (Tarpeian Rock) and the cultural association *Lorien*. Furthermore, the lyrics of their songs have a pedagogical function, making clear CasaPound's position on complex issues, such as the Syrian civil war in the song *Per la Siria, per Assad!* (For Syria, for Assad!).

More broadly, ZZA represent a synthesis of the mind-set of CasaPound activists, translating into song not only their ideas, but also their passions, fears, choices and beliefs. ZZA concerts are a powerfully defining experience for activists, who express their belonging to the community via tattoos (often done during concerts), t-shirts and gadgets with song lyrics, and more generally by reproducing the band's graphic style (which in turn reflects that of all CPI material, as if it were a trademark of the group as a whole). As a result, attending a concert of ZZA represents a crucial step for people approaching CPI, as it allows them to establish a cognitive and emotional connection with the broader community.

> Imagine a few thousand people moving in unison, following the lyrics and the music of the band. Imagine a strong and mobile mass that sings together with the Captain [Gianluca Iannone] [...]. There are no individual spectators, nor groups of friends: it is a single mass embodied by a multitude of arms, heads, torsos and legs.
>
> *(Di Tullio 2010: 93)*

Through the gadgets and the band's brand of clothing, activists can participate in a creative and emotional way in the life of CPI and its political ideals while, in addition, by identifying with the subcultural music and style of ZZA, CPI's activists feel part of an alternative network of resistance against the dominant social and cultural orientations. The concerts thus combine expressivity with the sense of brotherhood typical of alternative cultures and clandestine underground phenomena (Antolini 2010: 321).

Hybrid styles of expression and music tastes are thus at the core of CPI's collective identity. It is primarily by reproducing these forms of socialization that the group has emerged and continues to build solidarity among its members. For activists, coming together through music, events and countercultural practices initiated by CPI demonstrates the will to assert the group's unique character compared to the surrounding political reality. These spaces of sociability are perceived as alternative to the 'outside world' and represent a parallel circuit that can be accessed only by 'insiders'. As explained by an activist:

> My life changed when I joined CPI. Now I can go to a pub and drink a beer, attend concerts, walk around in the city in the places where there are other *camerati*. You know, I am not like you who can go wherever you want, I have to choose my places.[6]

In this sense, music is a crucial identity resource for CPI, and allows the group to forge solidarity among its members, while simultaneously asserting their incompatibility with the dominant cultural models of the external world.

5.4 Violence

A final element contributing to the formation of CPI's collective identity is violence. The use of violence is part of CPI's conflictual understanding of doing politics, in which the opponent is an 'enemy' identified with all people and beliefs that might threaten the survival of CPI and its ideas. Although CPI claims to reject violence as a political instrument, its ideology and rhetoric inherently imply violent elements, such as the cult of the *Fasci Italiani di Combattimento* (Fasci of Combat) and the *Squadre d'azione* (Action squads). Since the group cannot afford to simply reject violence, it takes on different meanings. We focus on three dimensions here: violence as part of CPI's self-proclaimed repertoire of action; narratives of violence among militants; and practices of violence for identity-building purposes.

First, violence represents an integral part of collective action for CasaPound, and is an instrument of self-determination and self-defence for the group. On the website, the FAQ section contains a specific question asking whether CPI is a violent group and the answer:

> CPI is engaged in politics, not hooliganism. It is not interested in flexing its muscles. It calls for a tranquil strength. At the same time, it cannot allow anyone to question its right to act and exist. We want debate, but we don't shy from confrontation if this is forced upon us and if our political and physical survival is at stake.
>
> *(CPI 2016)*

A similar understanding of violence emerges from violent narratives, and notably from some of the lyrics of ZZA's songs. In these, violence represents a revolutionary instrument necessary to overthrow consumerism and cultural homologation, and, more generally, to oppose the dominant economic system. At the same time, violence is described as an instrument to pursue self-determination and fight oppression and marginalization. Self-defence and the need to protect one's safety and ideas from the external world thus become practices through which one demonstrates loyalty to the community.

> We are the ones that beat you up on Saturday night because you have forgotten good manners. We are kinder than you all in some respects, but not in others.
>
> *('Kryptonite', ZetaZeroAlfa)*

The use of violent language, however, is not limited to music. In fact, most of the activists we interviewed made use of a 'battlefield' type of language, which includes a wide array of expressions, words and concepts linked to the idea of war, conflict and struggle. CasaPound's activists define their political engagement in terms of values and concepts such as the desire to 'live like a warrior who has to storm the enemy trenches'.[7] Within this rhetorical framework, CPI's headquarters in Rome are defined as 'a trench which is under surveillance 24 hours a day',[8] while national leaders are – as we have seen – 'soldiers'.[9] In a similar way, the motto 'not one step backwards' refers to a 'street' culture – which all activists would allegedly share. Accordingly, violence and struggles would be regulated by experience, honour and courage.

Thus, activism comes to represent a collective experience of virility. On the one hand, this narrative reaffirms the idea that violence is a necessary instrument for defending the group, its ideas and its legitimacy (Di Nunzio and Toscano 2011). On the other, violence becomes a form of comradeship and a code of conduct, or a celebration of bold gestures, struggles, strength and courage.

As emerges from CPI's official novel *Nessun Dolore* (Di Tullio 2010; see Chapter 4), activists must seek to imitate the behaviour of the epic warrior fighting his enemies, because 'fascists [are] tired of hiding' (p. 71) and because 'an act of courage is an act of pure beauty' (pp. 35–6). These narratives of clashes and battles have socializing and educational functions for activists. They advocate 'lessons in kicks, punches, and life' (p. 137) where the activist-hero is irrationally brave, bold and laughing in the face of danger.

> It is the first rule they teach you: some things must be done, always. [...] Even if they [the opponents] were a thousand it would not matter, because the first rule you learn is this one, and it carves a path deep inside you, it builds a structure made of steel in your bones, and silences pain and fear. [...] What chances are left for the adversaries of those who charge them invoking the name of ancient gods, arousing the very essence of the earth, and let themselves explode with laughter?
>
> *(Di Tullio 2010: 13)*

The fight against an opponent and the experience of combat are also necessary for the group to define its nature and limits. One of the themes used by CPI in addressing young activists is the cult of the struggle, of physical confrontation and of disciplining the body during combat. 'Fighting is a destiny', reads the motto of *Il Circuito*, CPI's fighting club, echoing the lyric of a song by ZZA whose words also appear on activists' t-shirts. Indeed, the statute of *Il Circuito* specifies that:

> The *Circuito* is not a sports club, nor an amateur sports association, but is simply a coordinating structure aimed at spreading CPI's ideas through combat sport. The *Circuito* is only open to those who identify themselves with CPI's programme and social project; it cannot be the sports equivalent of a catwalk nor an instrument for personal advantage. It is a place where everyone contributes with their own sports skills and passion for martial arts in order to support sport and CPI's cause.
>
> *(CPI 2013b)*

If violence contributes to the connection between individual militants and the community during (actual or imagined) confrontations with political opponents, it also builds internal bonds through inward-oriented practices, notably pogo dancing during concerts. The exercise called *cinghiamattanza* [literally translated as: 'chain-slaughter'], perhaps the best-known practice of CPI both inside and outside the extreme-right milieu, has a similar function. Our interviewees define it as a dance – although some have described it as a type of martial art – during which a group of bare-chested men whip each other using their belts without the buckle. The goal is to regain control of one's corporeity, 'against decadence'. In one activist's description, the *cinghiamattanza* is intended to help rediscover pain, which has been banished from society, and to learn how to fight injustice:

> [The *cinghiamattanza*] is the idea of going back home with a red mark left by a blow inflicted with a belt … It's the idea of joining the fray despite the physical consequences, or the bravery to take back control over one's own body. In today's society, the fear of physical pain leads to annihilation. Even if you suffer an injustice, you never put yourself in question. Therefore [the *cinghiamattanza*] also aims to educate the guys to this….[10]

Some activists describe the *cinghiamattanza* almost with a mythological language. Those who practise it feel 'more alive than ever before' and find 'their place in the world' (Di Tullio 2010: 98).

> This is a game in which every participant is truly a winner, because there are no champions nor prizes, you know very well the enemy you need to defeat because you see him every morning in the mirror. This is not a competition for cool kids: you are not playing polo nor a card game. This is not the Thursday night five-a-side football game with the colleagues from work, nor the shadowboxing workout for showgirls that fires you up in your pseudo-exclusive gym. Here you hit and you get hit, all against all, no one against no one, brothers, warrior caste, saints of leather and flesh, blessed with the bruises of tomorrow.
>
> *(Di Tullio 2010: 96–7)*

The *cinghiamattanza* is a collective practice about which leaders and activists are very reticent to speak publicly, being aware of the risks of stigmatization. In a comment posted on CPI's blog *Ideodromo*, a CPI leader complained that 'still today many commentators see in the *cinghiamattanza* a mixture of homosexual libido and death impulses' (Ideodromo 2013).

Conclusive remarks

CasaPound's collective identity builds upon a composite repertoire of imageries, styles and practices. To overcome the risks involved in collective action, a sense of belonging among members is created through the pre-existing solidarity established by hybrid and commercialized symbols, musical references, coded clothing, tattoos and violent practices, all of which develop a sense of commitment to a shared cause. These encompass, but are not limited to, classic extreme-right features. Rather, the main element uniting these different dimensions seems to be the strategic hybridization of symbols and practices stemming from distant political cultures, including pop culture, and the progressive-left movement culture. Hence, the imagery and aesthetics of the group offer an unconventional mixture of icons, exemplified by the clothing style of CPI's militants, which has little in common with the extreme-right skinhead stereotype. Ultimately, music and violence play a crucial role in integrating individuals within the community and socializing them to the ideals and lifestyles promoted by the group.

In conclusion, the high profile that CasaPound has achieved over the years partly rests on its capacity to build a solid, clearly identifiable collective identity. This is achieved by hybridizing extreme right symbols and coded references mediated from different political cultures. CPI's coded aesthetic and stylistic choices facilitate recognizability of the group among sympathizers, and help to avoid stigmatization by outsiders. As we shall show, these codes offer a solid base for CPI's collective action, by sustaining group identification and insulating members against external influences. To disentangle how CasaPound's hybrid identity and symbolism relate to its strategies of mobilization, the next chapter focuses specifically on its repertoire of action.

Notes

1 Until 1923, the *squadristi* or blackshirts were a para-military wing of the National Fascist Party (PNF). Subsequently, they became a volunteer militia of the Kingdom of Italy (De Felice 1995).
2 Interview no. 3a of 01/06/2012.
3 Interview no. 3a of 01/06/2012.
4 For instance, the round-table discussion on civil rights in which Anna Paola Concia, member of the Democratic Party and LGBT activist, took part (see Concia 2009).
5 Interview no. 2c of 27/04/2012.
6 Interview no. 2c of 27/04/2012.
7 Interview no. 3a of 01/06/2012.
8 Interview no. 2d of 27/04/2012.
9 Interview no. 3a of 01/06/2012.
10 Interview no. 2c of 27/04/2012.

References

Antolini, N. 2010. *Fuori Dal Cerchio: Viaggio Nella Destra Radicale Italiana*. Rome: Elliot.

Born, G., and D. Hesmondhalgh. 2000. *Western Music and Its Others: Difference, Representation, and Appropriation in Music*. Berkeley: University of California Press.

Concia, P. 2009, 'CasaPound Italia Mi Ha Invitata a Partecipare Ad Un Tavolo Sui Diritti Civili e Io Ho Accettato Con Piacere', www.paolaconcia.it, September 25. URLhttps://www.paolaconcia.it/b/casapound-italia-mi-ha-invitata-a-partecipare-ad-un-tavolo-sui-diritti-civili-e-io-ho-accettato-con-piacere/(consulted April 2019).

CPI. 2008a. *Mutuo Sociale – Manichini Impiccati*. URL: www.youtube.com/watch?v=xx4XdBS6aZ8 (consulted April 2019).

———. 2013b. 'Intervista Con Gianluca Iannone'. URL: www.vivamafarka.com/forum/index.php?topic=104372.0 (consulted July 2013).

———. 2016. 'Le FAQ Di CasaPound'. URL: www.casapounditalia.org/p/le-faq-di-cpi.html (consulted February 2016).

De Felice, R. 1995. *Mussolini il rivoluzionario: 1883–1920*. Turin: Einaudi.

Di Nunzio, D., and E. Toscano. 2011. *Dentro e Fuori CasaPound: Capire Il Fascismo Del Terzo Millennio*. Rome: Armando Editore.

Di Tullio, D. 2010. *Nessun Dolore. Una Storia Di CasaPound*. Milan: Rizzoli.

Eyerman, R. 2002. 'Music in Movement: Cultural Politics and Old and New Social Movements', *Qualitative Sociology* 25(3): 443–58.

Eyerman, R., and A. Jamison. 1998. *Music and Social Movements: Mobilizing Traditions in the Twentieth Century*. Cambridge: Cambridge University Press.

Ferrarotti, F. 2016. *Futurismo Come Prefascismo. Emozione Contro Ragione. Il Filo Rosso Della Storia Italiana*. Chieti: Solfanelli.

Hirsch, E.L. 1990. 'Sacrifice for the Cause: Group Processes, Recruitment, and Commitment in a Student Social Movement', *American Sociological Review* 55(2): 243–54.

Hunt, S.A., and R.D. Benford. 1994. 'Identity Talk in the Peace and Justice Movement', *Journal of Contemporary Ethnography* 22(4): 488–517.

Ideodromo. 2013. 'Ideodromo CasaPound'. URL: www.ideodromocasapound.org/?p=430 (consulted July 2013).

Il Cannocchiale. 2008. 'Intervista a Gianluca Iannone', September 17. URL: http://nerononpercaso.ilcannocchiale.it/?TAG=casapound (consulted April 2019).

Il Messaggero. 2013. 'Casapound, Irruzione Al Comizio Di Ruotolo: Volano Sedie', November 2.

Jasper, J.M. 1997. *The Art of Moral Protest*. Chicago, IL: University of Chicago Press.

Kahn-Harris, K. 2007. *Extreme Metal: Music and Culture on the Edge*. Oxford: Berg.

Klandermans, B. 1997. *The Social Psychology of Protest*. Oxford: Blackwell.

La Repubblica. 2018. 'Salvini Versione Ultrà Allo Stadio: Tra i Vip Con Il "Giubbetto Simbolo Di CasaPound"', October 5. URL: www.repubblica.it/politica/2018/05/10/news/matteo_salvini_calcio_milan_juve_colelzione_pivert-196001095/(consulted April 2019).

L'Occidentale. 2008. 'Roma Giovani Di CasaPound Tentano Blitz in Rai Contro "Chi l'ha Visto"', April 11.

Melucci, A. 1995. 'The Process of Collective Identity', *Social Movements and Culture* 4: 41–63.

Miller-Idriss, C. 2018. *The Extreme Gone Mainstream: Commercialisation and Far Right Youth Culture*. Princeton, NJ: Princeton University Press.

O'Connell, J.M., and S.E.-S. Castelo-Branco. 2010. *Music and Conflict*. Champaign: University of Illinois Press.

Olson, M. 1965. *Logic of Collective Action*. Cambridge: Harvard University Press.

———. 1971. *The Logic of Collective Action: Public Goods and the Theory of Groups*. Cambridge: Harvard University Press.

Pizzorno, A. 1996. 'Decisioni o Interazioni? La Micro-Descrizione Del Cambiamento Sociale', *Rassegna Italiana Di Sociologia* (37): 107–32.

Polletta, F. 1997. 'Culture and Its Discontents: Recent Theorizing on the Cultural Dimensions of Protest', *Sociological Inquiry* 67(4): 431–50.

Polletta, F., and J.M. Jasper. 2001. 'Collective Identity and Social Movements', *Annual Review of Sociology* 27(1): 283–305.

Rai News 24. 2012. 'CasaPound Irrompe Al Giulio Cesare: Fumogeni, Paura, Fermi Di Polizia', October 22. URL: www.rainews24.it (consulted April 2015).
Snow, D. 2001. 'Collective Identity and Expressive Forms'. *CSD Working Papers*, UC Irvine: Center for the Study of Democracy. URL: https://escholarship.org/uc/item/2zn1t7b (consulted April 2019).
Teitelbaum, B.R. 2017. *Lions of the North: Sounds of the New Nordic Radical Nationalism*. Oxford: Oxford University Press.

6

EXTERNAL MOBILIZATION

In recent years, CasaPound started running in elections while also engaging in contentious activities. Does this mean that CPI dismissed its grassroots dimension to turn into a fully-fledged political party? Or did it rather continue to engage simultaneously in contentious protest and party politics? To understand CPI's external mobilization strategy and its impact on the group's public profile, this chapter relies on the concept of a repertoire of action and addresses its conventional and unconventional tactics (Tilly 1978). Building on data from Political Claims Analysis (PCA), the chapter first provides an overview of CPI's external mobilization strategies (6.1). The quantitative content analysis of electoral manifestos and face-to-face interviews with high-ranking officials are then used to discuss this information specifically for CPI's activities in the protest (6.2) and electoral arenas (6.3). The final sections are devoted to examining the main campaigns promoted by the group on specific themes (6.4), before drawing general conclusions on the group's hybrid mobilization strategy. Overall, the chapter shows that CPI is still torn between the need for legitimization required by engagement in electoral politics, and the propensity towards social movements' 'logic of damage' (Della Porta and Diani 2006: 170). CPI's hybrid approach to mobilization implies that while protest activism is important, this does not exclude electoral participation, so that contentious actions coexist with conventional forms of political engagement. We discuss how this hybrid external mobilization strategy contributed to building the high profile that CPI enjoys in the media, despite its minimal electoral support.

6.1 From the streets to the ballots?

The external mobilization of CPI displays aspects similar to Kitschelt's (2006) definition of 'movement parties' in that it combines activism within and outside the institutional arena, including formal activities (such as electoral campaigning and lobbying), with protest activities (squatting and vigilante operations). In Chapter 2, we argued that CPI, having emerged from a splinter of the youth section of the extreme-right party *Fiamma Tricolore* (Di Nunzio and Toscano 2011), displayed an initial predilection towards social movement forms of organization and mobilization. Disillusioned by the logic of party leadership accountability and decision-making, CPI established itself as a non-profit organization and promoted a self-styled, confrontational understanding of right-wing politics, reproducing some aspects of the repertoire of left-wing movements. Specifically, it started out as a single-issue movement focusing on 'social housing' and promoting the squatting of buildings as a protest against the housing crisis in Rome (see Chapter 3). In its early years, the group became noted for its non-conventional repertoires of contention, in particular for showcase protests, occupations of state-owned buildings for housing purposes, and squatting for political and cultural activities. The imagery and symbols accompanying these actions provided recognizability to CPI within and outside the extreme-right milieu (Chapter 5), progressively configuring a network of political and cultural movements, rooted within Italy's neo-fascist youth subculture (Rao 2014).

From 2011 onwards, however, CPI gradually diversified its strategy for external mobilization. At first, its candidates ran as independents within centre-right coalitions (2011–2012); since 2013, CPI presented its own electoral list and integrated its agenda with anti-immigration proposals. At the same time, the group also expanded its programmatic agenda on socio-economic affairs, endorsing issues that remained at the margins of its political agenda in earlier years. The evolution of CPI's strategy is evident in its changing electoral slogans over the past years: from 'Direction – Revolution' (in 2013) to 'Direction – Parliament' (in 2018). Even while participating in electoral campaigns, however, CPI has maintained a tendency to combine conventional party activities (such as handing out electoral leaflets, collecting signatures and promoting fundraising events for candidates) with contentious politics, including the storming of rival candidates' offices (CPI 2013a), clashes with anti-racist and anti-fascist groups (CPI 2013b), and direct actions and interventions (CPI 2018a). The elected officials of CPI often use their position to provide further visibility to the extra-parliamentary actions of the group (CPI 2016).

6.2 The protest arena: issues and tactics in CasaPound's mobilization

We begin the empirical investigation of CPI's repertoire of action by looking at the issues over which the group mobilizes and at the different modes of action. To identify the main issues featuring in CPI's external mobilization, we first look at the issue content of CPI's claims in the public domain, differentiating across six issue categories drawn from previous literature and detailed in the methodological appendix (3) (Kriesi et al. 2008). Instances of 'claims-making' are defined as the expression of political opinion by physical or verbal action in the public sphere, thus including verbal acts, conventional forms of intervention, as well as protest (Koopmans and Statham 1999) (see Appendix 3). Figure 6.1 reports data on CPI's issue attention as it appears in the quality paper *Il Corriere della Sera*. The vertical bar in 2013 indicates the first year that CPI ran for general elections.

As discussed in Chapter 3, claims referring to historical Fascism and socio-economic concerns related to housing rights and welfare for Italians are at the core of CPI's worldview, whereas other issues (such as the European Union and immigration) acquired importance mostly in response to external events and the content of public debates. This is confirmed by Figure 6.1. The turning point in CPI's public image took place in 2014, when the group shifted its attention away from socio-economic issues and commemorations of historical Fascism, towards issues connected to migration. In so doing, it reconfigured its profile in line with most far-right organizations in Europe. This coincides with the increasing interest of quality media in CPI. While our data covers events only up to December 2015, the public debates of the following years, notably concerning the 'European asylum policy crisis', have further accelerated this process (Castelli Gattinara 2018). Over time, CPI also diversified its strategies of mobilization. Occupying a hybrid position between party and social movement arenas, CPI could choose from a vast array of options to attract the attention of the media and the public. As Della Porta and Diani (1999: 165) have observed,

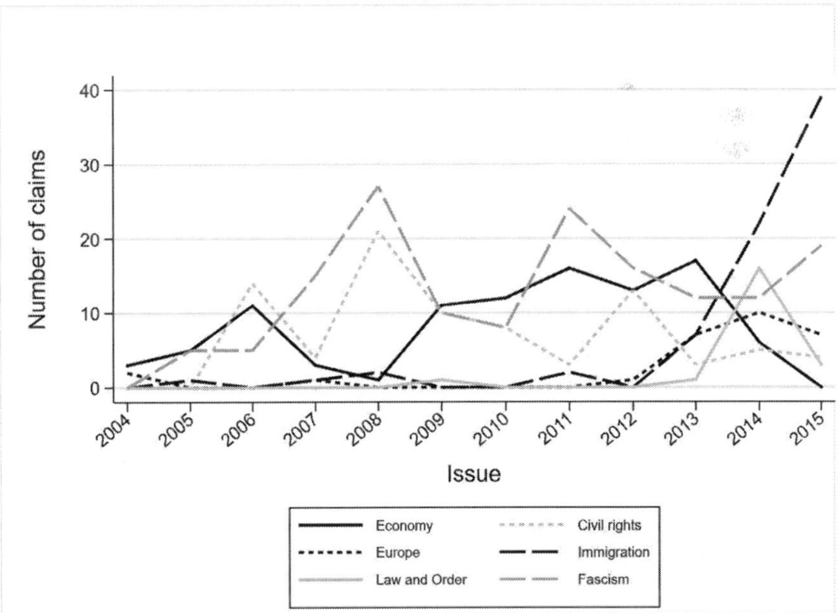

FIGURE 6.1 Issue content of CasaPound mobilization in the mass media (2004–2015). Source: Own calculation based on data from *Il Corriere della Sera*.

in choosing their repertoires of action, collective actors also make a decision as regards their degree of conventionality and the intensity of radicalism in mobilization, both of which mirror their collective identity. Figure 6.2 illustrates CPI's main forms of mobilization.

Over time, CPI increased its investment in conventional tactics (such as electoral campaigns, lobbying and petitioning). However, demonstrative actions (such as legal actions and authorized demonstrations) represent the dominant form of activism for CPI throughout the whole period. Figure 6.2 also highlights that demonstrative actions increased in importance in recent years, especially after 2013. Confrontational actions (such as illegal demonstrations and blockades) and episodes of violence (against people or things) represent a crucial part of CPI's external mobilization, constituting the second and third most important tactics for the group.

In sum, if one compares mobilization prior to and after 2013, when CPI announced its electoral switch, it appears that there has been little change in the group's repertoire of action: Political Claims Analysis shows a consistent (rather than mutually exclusive) engagement in both conventional and protest actions, and a predominance of demonstrative and confrontational activism. While CPI benefited from increased media coverage in recent years, this is mostly associated with social movement activism, such as violent events and confrontation, rather than electoral campaigning and conventional politics. In other words, CPI's

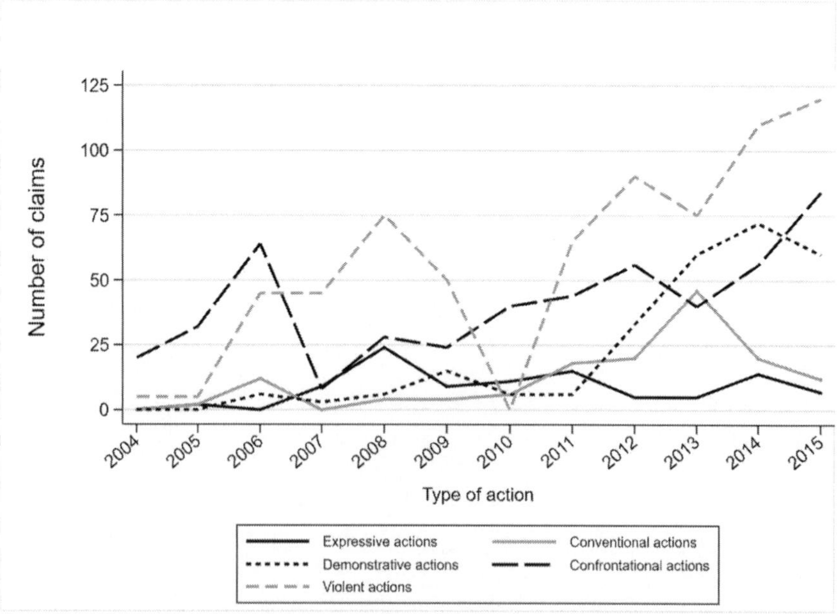

FIGURE 6.2 CasaPound's repertoire of action in the mass media (2004–2015).
Source: Own calculation based on data from *Il Corriere della Sera*.

episodic electoral participation is not accompanied by a change in the group's strategy for external mobilization. On the contrary, while the group attempts to achieve legitimation in the public sphere, it remains primarily involved in street protest and social movement activism. In this respect, two main forms of action deserve attention: direct activism and violent repertoires.

With direct activism, or 'direct social actions' (DSA), social movements' scholars refer to unconventional forms of activism that do not seek the mediation of representative authorities, but directly aim at redressing a public problem (Bosi and Zamponi 2015: 371). In the early days, DSAs were at the core of CPI's mobilization on housing rights, but then extended to other issues over time, such as security and migration, as well as environmental requalification and voluntary work to help disabled, unemployed and elderly people. The outbreak of the sovereign debt crisis in Italy after 2008 further motivated CPI towards organizing direct actions of solidary with a nativist scope: the provision of free health and fiscal services, the distribution of food to Italian families and the setting up of a unit of civil protection to work in times of emergency and distress. As the attention progressively shifted to immigration, DSAs hinged upon anti-refugee blockades, patrolling migrants' detention centres and squatting buildings originally meant for asylum seekers.

In addition, CPI's repertoire of action also includes disruptive protests such as violent confrontations with opponents and public authorities. About one-fourth of the events promoted by CPI and reported in the mass media involve at least a certain degree of violence against physical or symbolic targets. CPI's youth section engaged in violent clashes with left-wing student movements in Rome in 2008 and the group organized a number of illegal actions against the EU in 2013, which led to confrontation with the police, and the arrest of CPI's vice-president. Violence, therefore, is not confined to a simple rhetoric and to rituals used to structure a collective identity (see Chapter 5), but is also part of CPI's external mobilization.

> CasaPound's ethics code envisages that, in some cases, one can and should actually fight, in order to defend one's ability to do politics from those who want to deny it and contrast the arrogance of the intolerants. In order to save one's own life, to defend a comrade. We fight, yes. It's not beautiful, it's not polite. But it is still more vital, transparent, radiant than any moralistic farce that dehumanizes the other in the name of the 'struggle against barbarism'.
>
> *(Scianca 2011: 362)*

CPI thus holds an ambiguous stance towards violent repertoires. It tries to strike a balance between the identity needs of its community (see Chapter 5), and the structures of opportunity which it needs to confront. On the one hand, light forms of violence are deployed to radicalize the political campaigns to which CPI attaches particular importance, such as housing issues and more recently migration affairs. Furthermore, violent actions often target political opponents, especially those involved in counter-movements. On the other, the leadership of CPI condemns the most blatant episodes of violence. In December 2011, CPI argued that it bears no responsibility for Gianluca Casseri, a 50-year-old accountant and a CasaPound sympathizer, who drove to a crowded street market in the city of Florence and shot at a group of Senegalese market traders, killing two and wounding three before committing suicide. Similarly, CPI condemned 'without hesitation' the terrorist acts of February 2018, when a 28-year-old far-right activist went on a shooting rampage in Macerata, a small town in central Italy, wounding five men and one woman of African origin (*Il Secolo d'Italia* 2018). CPI thus neither endorses nor rejects symbolic and physical violence, as it considers violent confrontation part of its variegated array of strategies for doing politics. If an excess of violence is certainly condemned, light forms are an effective way for CPI to capture media attention and pressurize public opinion (Castelli Gattinara and Froio 2018).

6.3 The electoral arena: CasaPound's strategies and results

As noted earlier, CPI's engagement in the electoral arena marked an important strategic change for the group, even though it did not represent an absolute novelty. Candidates linked to CPI had in fact supported centre-right local lists since 2008, and CPI's leader Gianluca Iannone ran as an independent candidate with *Fiamma Tricolore* in 2006. By 2013, CPI could already count on at least seven representatives at the local level, elected as independents within broader right-wing coalitions (Tassinari 2011). When the decision to run at the 2013 general elections was made official (during CPI's national festival 'Direzione – Rivoluzione' of November 2012), the leadership did not discuss the actual choice to run but rather debated whether to run alone or in coalition with others. It simply informed activists that CPI will run for the general elections.

In describing what motivated this decision, Iannone referred to the participation of Italy's centre-right and centre-left parties in the parliamentary majority supporting the technocratic government led by Mario Monti (2011–2013). In a context in which mainstream parties prioritized their role as governing, rather than representative agencies (Froio and Little 2015), CasaPound intended to play the role of the outsider. Thus, in 2013, CPI decided to present their own list of candidates for the Chamber of Deputies and the Senate. Its vice-president Simone Di Stefano, moreover, ran as a candidate for governor of Lazio and mayor of Rome.

Counting on very limited resources, CPI planned its first electoral campaigns with the stated goal of driving media attention towards itself and its issues. The first campaign activity was in fact a legally authorized street demonstration (24 November 2012), with the participation of a few thousand supporters. The clamour surrounding the parade granted the group a place in a number of television programmes and debates, which CPI leaders used primarily to complain about the exclusion of their candidates from official broadcasts (CPI 2018a). At the same time, CPI organized a series of sensational events and agitprop operations aimed at increasing the group's visibility, most notably promoting smoke-bomb raids in high schools to protest against education reforms (*Huffington Post Italia* 2012). Furthermore, the group tried to get coverage by exploiting the visibility of its competitors, provoking political adversaries to trigger a reaction. CPI's vice-president Di Stefano released an official declaration urging his group's members and sympathizers to participate in the primary elections of Italy's Democratic Party: 'Our candidate is Bersani [secretary of the Democratic Party from 2009 to 2013], because we like the idea that the Democratic Party remains ancient, obtuse, and with a paradoxical view of politics' (ADN Kronos 2012). The accrued recognizability of CPI, and its centrality in the 2013 electoral campaign was further confirmed a few days before the vote, when the former leader of the *Movimento 5 Stelle* (Five Star Movement) Beppe Grillo reported that he had no problem if 'a guy from CasaPound' wanted to enter his movement (*La Stampa* 2013). Media coverage was, however, the only real success in CPI's first national election campaign. The list obtained 0.14 per cent of the vote in the lower Chamber, 0.13 per cent in the Senate and did not reach 1 per cent even in the regional and mayoral elections. While the leadership itself acknowledged that the performance was 'below expectations' (Fanpage 2013), CPI confirmed the choice of running with independent lists at the national and local level in the following years.

In the same period, at the European level, the group managed to open a channel of communication with the radical right political party *Lega Nord* (CPI 2014). During the 2014 European Parliament elections, CPI actively engaged in the campaign of Mario Borghezio. This paved the way to several joint initiatives between CPI and the *Lega Nord* throughout the year and culminated in two joint demonstrations against the Monti government (and subsequently against that of Enrico Letta) in October 2014 and February 2015. Once again, CPI was successful in gaining media visibility. But, while Mario Borghezio was elected to the European Parliament, CPI failed to consolidate the alliance with the *Lega Nord*, mainly due to the unwillingness of its leadership (Roberto Maroni first and subsequently Matteo Salvini) to abandon the centre-right coalition headed by Silvio Berlusconi.

Between 2014 and 2017, CasaPound also promoted independent lists at local elections, fielding its own candidates for the positions of mayors and regional governors. As in the national-level electoral campaigns, CPI successfully seized the attention of local media with its showcase actions, including vigilante patrols against insecurity, media stunts to criticize local administrators, and virulent campaigns against Roma people, migrants and refugees. Furthermore, the group benefited from the general dissatisfaction of Italian electorates towards mainstream parties and administrations, which produced a drastic drop in overall electoral participation, especially at the local level. In spring 2016, the CPI list obtained about 7 per cent in local elections for the municipality of Bolzano, a sizable north-eastern province towards the border with Austria, also electing one of its members to the municipal council. In June the following year, the CPI candidate was elected to the local council of the Tuscan city of Lucca, securing 8 per cent of the total preferences. Similarly, CPI candidates were elected in the central Italian town of Todi (5 per cent of the votes) and in the Calabrian province of Lamezia Terme (7 per cent). The most resounding electoral performance for CPI, however, was in November 2017, when its candidate won a seat on the municipal council of the Roman suburb of Ostia, obtaining 9 per cent of the vote.

Buoyed by rising anti-immigrant sentiment in Italy, as well as by years of economic strain and public dissatisfaction with mainstream parties, CPI hoped for a similar breakthrough in national elections in 2018. Indeed, the resounding local results further contributed to portraying CPI as a 'successful' political actor, with some national and international pundits expecting its breakthrough to the Italian parliament (Reuters 2017; *The Guardian* 2018). In this respect, CPI is certainly rooted at the local level, as confirmed by the opening of over one hundred local chapters across Italy in less than 15 years (see Chapter 4). However, CPI scores well in local elections which are usually characterized by low electoral turnout. CPI's resounding 9 per cent in Ostia (November 2017), for instance, must be contextualized in a local election where only one out of three voters participated, representing a turnout of only 36 per cent. This means that the turnout in Ostia dropped by about 20 percentage points compared to the previous local consultations in Rome – and over 40 per cent compared to the previous national elections. Importantly, it also means that the CasaPound candidate obtained in total fewer than 6,000 votes, which hardly justifies the disproportionate attention that the group received in the aftermath of the Ostia elections from national and international media.

In launching the 2018 electoral campaign, the group's candidate for prime minister, Simone Di Stefano, stated that he was certain that CPI would obtain the 3 per cent necessary to win a seat in the lower chamber. The results would soon prove him wrong. In fact, CPI had to set up a very muscular electoral campaign, to compete in a political system turning increasingly anti-immigrant and saturated by the many different components of Italy's far right, including Matteo Salvini's *Lega* and Giorgia Meloni's *Fratelli d'Italia*. Similarly, CPI's anti-establishment narrative on socio-economic issues was obfuscated by the powerful populist propaganda of the Five Star Movement. Even when it mobilized on the heritage of Fascism, CPI was generally unsuccessful in distinguishing its campaign from the nostalgic cartel established by the extreme-right *Forza Nuova* and *Fiamma Tricolore*.

CPI's electoral ambitions were thus frustrated by the results. At the 2018 national elections, the group obtained only 0.9 per cent, or 312,000 preferences, for the lower chamber, whereas the candidate for governor of Lazio won 1.9 per cent or 60,000 votes. Nonetheless, the group consolidated its preponderance over the other actors of the extreme right. At the 2013 national elections,

CPI obtained half the preferences of *Forza Nuova*, and about the same as *Fiamma Tricolore*. In 2018, it won almost three times more votes than the *Forza Nuova-Fiamma Tricolore* cartel. Moreover, compared to 2013, CPI enjoyed a six-fold increase in electoral support, from less than 50,000 votes to over 300,000. The leadership confirmed this in a Facebook post published immediately after the election, on 5 March:[1]

> Thanks to the almost 300,000 Italians who chose CasaPound. They were 48,000 in 2013, today they are six times as many; we started from 0.13 per cent, we are at almost 1 per cent now. [...] We are still weak in the South, and we must work to redress this. But the elections also confirmed a fact that we consider a victory for ourselves. Italians have demonstrated that they do not care about anti-fascism, and that they look for someone that can address their distress, as we have repeated throughout the election campaign.
>
> *(CPI 2018a)*

6.3.1 Issue attention in CasaPound's electoral campaigns

CasaPound's national electoral campaigns in 2013 and 2018 can help to make sense of the changes in the group's political offer. To illustrate this, we compare the content of the electoral platforms that the group presented for the two general elections (see appendix 4). Table 6.1 summarizes the main formal characteristics of the two documents, showing a considerable similarity between 2013 and 2018.[2]

To appreciate CPI's issue attention during national elections, Figure 6.3 compares the content of the two manifestos in terms of issue salience. It reports the aggregate percentage of quasi-sentences related to each policy area in CPI's electoral programmes for 2013 and 2018.

As can be seen, while there is no one issue that attracts most of CPI's attention, five issue categories represent about 50 per cent of the total manifesto, whereas the other 16 receive the remaining attention. The five dominant categories partially coincide with the issues over which CPI mobilizes in the protest

TABLE 6.1 Formal characteristics of CasaPound's electoral programmes

Year	2013	2018
Title	A Nation	A Nation
Prime Minister Candidate	Simone Di Stefano	Simone Di Stefano
Length (no. of pages)	17	21
Length (no. of words)	5,749	6,359
Length (no. of quasi-sentences)	252	304

Source: National electoral programmes of CasaPound Italia (2013–2018).

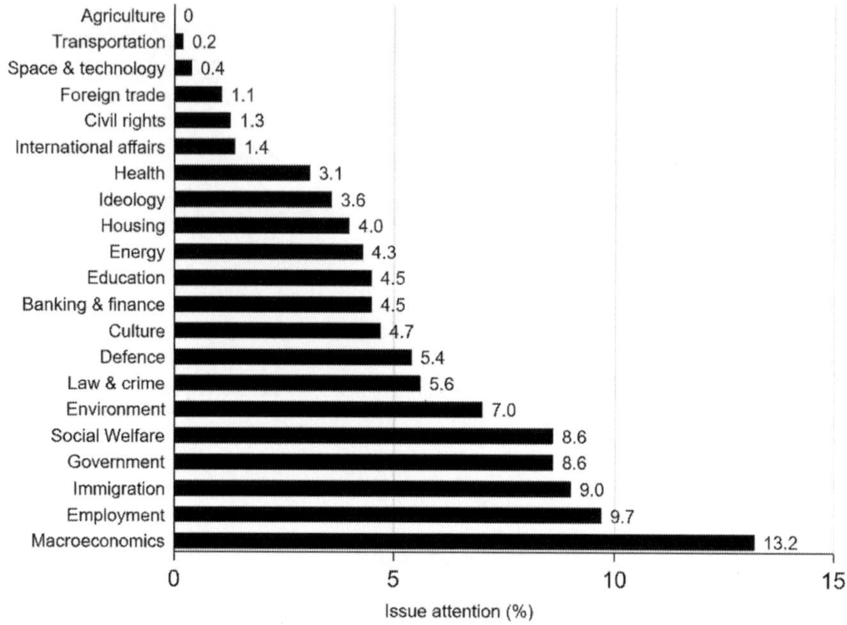

FIGURE 6.3 Issue attention in CasaPound's electoral programmes (aggregate).
Source: Own calculation based on national electoral programmes of CasaPound Italia (2013–2018).

arena: Macroeconomics (13.2 per cent of all quasi-sentences), Employment (9.7 per cent), Immigration (9 per cent), Government (8.6 per cent) and Welfare (8.6 per cent). Overall, all these issues are approached based on the group's core ideological feature of nativism (see Chapter 3). In fact, quasi-sentences on the economy attribute a strong role to the state, which is expected to serve the interests of Italian people. At the same time, CPI stands for (domestic) laissez-faire and blames Italian politicians for betraying the national interest, notably by opening borders for the international circulation of goods and people. The same approach applies to employment, welfare and immigration, where the expulsion of migrants from the country is presented as a prerequisite to labour policies aiming at the full employment of Italians, and a social welfare understood in strictly chauvinistic terms.

Other issues receive moderate attention. Notably, two issues that were at the core of CPI's mobilization in the early years – housing, and law and crime – do not feature among the main concerns in the group's electoral programmes. This may indicate a tendency of CPI towards differentiating the agenda depending on the primary arena of engagement. Indeed, CPI approaches housing issues and law and crime mainly by means of occupying abandoned buildings, street patrols and vigilante events against insecurity. CPI therefore privileges protest tactics, rather than conventional ones, to address housing and security affairs, capitalizing on direct social activism and more or less disruptive forms of confrontation with political opponents and the state.

Finally, Figure 6.4 compares issue attention in CPI's electoral programmes in 2013 and 2018 to account for change over time. The left column of the graph displays the attention provided to each issue in the 2013 platform (in percentage points), whereas the right column reports the same for 2018. The vertical axis reports the labels for each issue category, alongside the absolute change between the two elections (in brackets, ref. 2018). The figure shows that the issue content of CPI's programmes is relatively stable, albeit with a few relevant exceptions. Most notably, some issues at the core of CPI's ideology receive substantially more attention in 2018 than in 2013. These include economy-related issues – thus macroeconomics and employment – as well as housing and law and crime, which did not feature among the core issues in the 2013 platform.

Overall, the study of the electoral offer of CPI highlights two main patterns. Firstly, when running for elections CPI does not behave as a single-issue party. This is at odds with its background as a protest movement mobilizing (almost) exclusively on housing rights. Rather than focusing on only a subset of topics, CPI opted instead to develop a complex electoral programme beyond the issues classically associated with far-right groups (Mudde 1999). Secondly, the content of CPI's electoral programme and that of its protest activities tend to realign

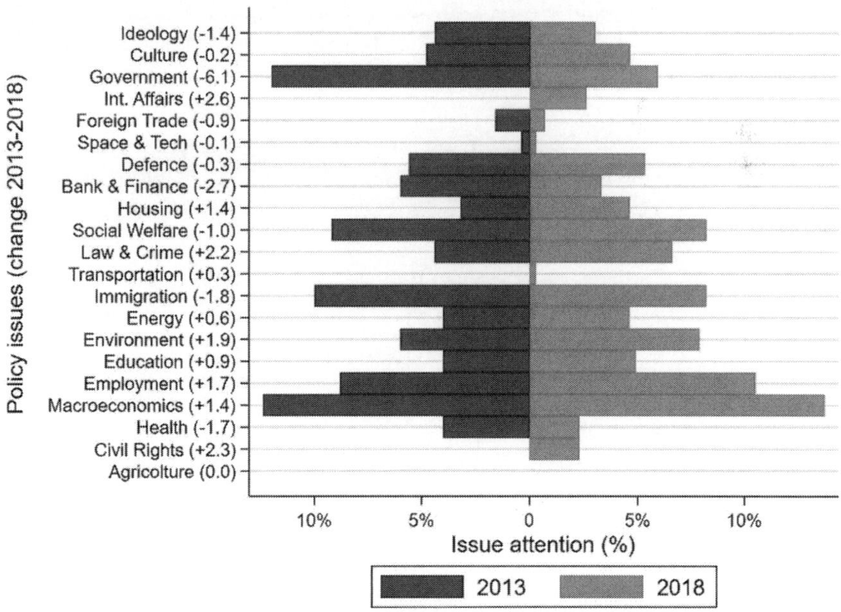

FIGURE 6.4 Issue attention in CasaPound's electoral programmes (2013–2018).

Source: Own calculation based on national electoral programmes of CasaPound Italia (2013–2018).

over time. In 2013 CPI's electoral platform deviated from the issues it promoted in the protest arena, but by 2018 its electoral pitch again emphasized housing, crime and the law – the themes that are also at the core of its street mobilization. In this respect, rather than being mutually exclusive, electoral and protest activism are complementary in CPI's external mobilization.

6.4 Protest and electoral campaigns

The hybridization of CPI's external mobilization is well illustrated by the main campaigns that the group promotes in both the protest and electoral arenas. A first set of campaigns focuses on CPI's core themes: the economy and welfare. A second set, instead, deals with issues that CPI has addressed only more recently: the European Union and migration.

6.4.1 Early campaigns: housing, welfare and austerity

As already noted, CPI's early activism responded to a need to answer traditional questions in far-right politics, while also building a distinctive recognizability within this political and cultural milieu (see Chapter 2). These incentives motivated the choice to promote the campaign 'Occupation for Housing Purposes' (*Occupazioni a Scopo Abitativo*), which addressed a traditional concern of the Italian extreme right (housing) with methods and practices (such as squatting) that had seldom been pursued by extreme-right activists. CPI's *Mutuo Sociale* project ('Social Mortgage') follows a similar rationale. Campaigning on housing rights not only enabled CPI to become easily recognizable on the Italian far right, but this specific 'brand' also provided visibility for the other themes on CPI's political agenda. Housing has in fact been a key theme in CasaPound's politics since its origins, with the concept of 'home' defining and shaping the very identity of the group, its name and its official symbol (see Chapter 3).

CPI's 'Social Mortgage' campaign calls attention to the housing crisis in Italy and claims the right to home ownership for every Italian family. It calls for a proposal for a law to create a 'Regional Institute for Social Mortgages' tasked with 'building new neighbourhoods according to traditional bio-architectural models, with a low housing density and innovative techniques in terms of renewable energy' (CPI 2018b). Housing blocks built with public funds would then be sold at cost price to Italian families that do not own a house. The social mortgage model would bypass the mediation of (private) banks, in order to allow a zero interest rate, a limit on payments to one-fifth of the total family income and the freezing of payments in case of unemployment (CPI 2018b).

While 'Social Mortgage' campaigns often imply the collection of signatures to call local referendums on public housing, CPI activists also use the idea of 'home' to justify the occupation of vacant buildings. CPI leaders in fact distinguish between 'Occupation for Housing Purposes' (OHP) – namely the spaces destined primarily to provide the occupants with a home – from the 'Non-Compliant Occupations' (NCO) – which instead have leisure purposes, and host political, cultural, sport and community activities. If the OHP reflect CPI's attention to social issues, the NCO reflect its innovative understanding of political activism. While occupations account for only a small part of CasaPound's presence on the ground (most local branches are regularly rented), they represent considerable symbolic capital for the 'Social Mortgage' campaign and the group's public image. CasaPound's notoriety owes much to its appropriation of part of the action repertoire of left-wing movements, and the establishment of what the media labelled 'right-wing social centres'. At the same time, the OHP also play an important identity function, as demonstrated by the fact that many of the group's leaders and their families live, or have lived, in occupied spaces.

With regards to social welfare, the campaign *Tempo di Essere Madri* ('Time to be Mothers') deals more closely with the sphere of labour rights for Italian women. Its aim is to 'tackle all labour issues linked to maternity and fight situations of social injustice that characterise the workplace, in particular temporary employment' (CPI 2018d). More specifically, the project calls on regional referendums to introduce part-time employment with full-time remuneration for Italian working mothers (85 per cent of the full-time salary would be paid by the employer, while the remaining 15 per cent would be covered by the State). While the same benefits would be extended to fathers, the motivations for action focus on children, who 'deserve love and attention, and need to be taken care of by the family during their growth', and on 'the role of the woman in its entirety and completeness, in its most beautiful essence, its great human and social potential' (CPI 2018d).

CPI's campaign on welfare and social housing link to another key campaign, more directly connected to the implementation of austerity measures in the aftermath of the sovereign debt crisis in Italy: *Stop Equitalia.*[3] The campaign consists of a regular law proposal, suggesting a change in the norms on tax collection by the State. The proposal calls for a limitation in *Equitalia*'s ability to mortgage first homes, forbidding the seizure of assets that are essential for businesses. The proposal also includes repealing the agency's ability to conduct financial investigations, and forces it to apply the legal interest rate when dividing credits into instalments. Its stated aim is to encourage oversight over big tax evaders rather than on small creditors. The campaign exemplifies CPI's understanding of blame and responsibility in the Italian debt crisis: it depicts tax collectors as vampires who suck blood out of employees, retirees, small businesspersons and self-employed professionals. The rationale is that the Italian State prefers to oppress 'those who maybe have little money but possess a few assets that can be seized', rather than targeting 'the real criminals and owners of business, real estate, boats, planes, luxury cars which are cleverly registered under the name of a figurehead, a relative, or Italian and foreign limited companies' (CPI 2018c).

In the early years, this logic allowed CPI to broaden its political agenda beyond the restricted area of the housing emergency, without however losing a connection with its primary issue of interest. Furthermore, it is thanks to similar campaigns that CPI extended its reach beyond Rome, setting up chapters across the country and engaging with local contexts in which the housing problem was felt less intensely than in the capital (see Chapter 2). The interviews conducted with some of CPI's leaders in the north-east confirm CPI's need to give voice to the grievances of small and medium businesses, thus intercepting the sensibilities of different contexts in Italy:

> Here, our political action does not address the housing crisis, like in Rome. Here that problem simply does not exist. Instead, we offer a response to the economic crisis, because the crisis does not only affect the banks and the world systems. For us, here, it is a crisis of small and medium-sized businesses, which produce and invest locally and are suffocated by Equitalia.[4]

6.4.2 CasaPound's recent campaigns: the European Union and immigration

As CPI engaged in the electoral arena in 2013, it also had to take a stance on themes with a high degree of prominence in national debates: the European Union and migration.

Prior to the outbreak of the sovereign debt crisis in Italy, CasaPound's position on the EU was rather original. As discussed in Chapter 3, it appeared to be a sort of 'soft Euroscepticism' (Taggart and Szczerbiak 2008; Vasilopoulou 2017). It suggested that the Maastricht treaty was 'the right thing done in the wrong way' (CPI 2013c) and advocated for 'a different idea of Europe'. Accordingly, CPI sought for unilateral cancellation of government debt and public ownership of the Bank of Italy. Furthermore, it demanded a modification of the rules of Maastricht, the establishment of a closed European trade area and the revision of the Schengen Agreements. In this framework, the people of Europe were described as 'brothers' equally oppressed by the European Central Bank (ECB) and global financial institutions.[5] In short, while opposing 'technocratic institutions', CPI did not call for the break-up of the EU.

During Mario Monti's technocratic government (2011–2013), however, CPI turned to 'hard Euroscepticism', namely a principled opposition to the EU as a polity, and consisting mainly of a critique of the unresponsiveness of technocratic government. CPI described austerity and the weakening of the welfare state as 'ultra-liberal degenerations'[6] of the EU and pointed to the responsibility of 'financial stranglers' and 'governments of bankers'.[7] In the 2013 election manifesto, CPI calls for the first time for the unilateral exit of Italy from the EU and the cancellation of all European treaties:

> The EU proved to be an enemy of our nation, and a weapon of supranational financial groups who wish to destroy our identity and economy. Outside the cage of the EU there is the rest of the world, with which we can trade and cooperate on our terms and interests.
>
> *(CPI 2013c)*

Additional evidence of the progressive radicalization of CPI's positions on the EU concerned monetary issues. Prior to the 2013 general elections, CPI campaigned for the introduction of a complementary currency, the 'equo', which would not replace the euro, but would circulate alongside it. This would allow Italy to regain its monetary sovereignty, without having to return to the lira.[8] At that time, CPI considered the idea of going back to the old currency 'ridiculous, self-defeating, and reactionary as the euro represents the first serious competitor of the dollar and the hegemony of Wall Street'.

> The euro refers to some of the best aspects of the continent's history: from Castel del Monte to Leonardo da Vinci, from Dante Alighieri to the German eagle, to futurist images. While the dollar is permeated by oligarchic and masonic symbolism, the euro is drawn from an utterly Ghilbelline, deep-rooted, proactive imagination.
>
> *(Ideodromo CasaPound 2013)*

However, on the occasion of the 2018 election campaign, CPI demanded the abandonment of the euro in favour of a new sovereign currency that would support the Italian economy and national interest.

> The Euro is a mechanism that serves the interests of private groups and hostile nations, which expropriate public goods in Italy by means of privatizations, and extort Italian citizens, extinguish their savings, multiply their debt and destroy their Welfare State.
>
> *(CPI 2018e)*

A major turning point in the relationship between CPI and the EU was represented by the 2014 European Parliament elections. It is then that the anti-EU rhetoric of CPI grew in intensity. Prior to the elections, CPI took an active part in a series of protests against the Italian government, taxation and the EU (from November 2013 to early 2014). The protests (including rallies, demonstrations and blockades of highways and rail services) were labelled 'pitchfork protests' by journalists (*Il Fatto Quotidiano* 2013) from the name of the anti-EU, autonomist and anti-tax 'pitchfork' movement. In this framework, CPI invited its sympathizers and activists to participate in the protests 'without symbols', using only a tricolour flag in support of the 'Italian truck drivers, farmers, and other professional categories [...] brought to their knees by crazy taxes that only serve to pay the interests of fraudulent debt' (CPI 2013d).

During these protests, CPI's vice-president Simone Di Stefano was arrested for replacing the EU flag with an Italian one during a sit-in in front of the head office of the European Commission in Italy (*Il Fatto Quotidiano* 2013). A first strongly critical statement against the EU accompanied the action by CPI: 'The people of 9 December rebel against the suicide of a Nation [capital in the original] which surrendered without conditions to Brussels bureaucrats' (CPI 2013e). Upon his release, Di Stefano reaffirmed CPI's opposition to the EU: 'The European flag is the flag of a technical-financial structure that is oppressing European peoples.'[9]

Despite the choice to take part in the marches devoid of the group's official symbol, the protests granted CPI considerable media attention. Activists could in fact be recognized by their tricolour painted marks, the nooses they wore around the necks, banners with slogans such as 'Some Italians do not surrender' and 'Italy, Nation, Revolution!' – as well as Mameli's hymn and other elements aimed at emphasizing Italian national identity. As a result, the 2014 European Parliament election campaign gave CasaPound the opportunity to open a channel of collaboration with Italian far-right parties (*Lega Nord*) as well as with international far-right organizations. At that time, CPI hosted international guests like Jean-Yves Le Gallou, an intellectual close to the *Nouvelle Droite*, former member of the European Parliament for the *Front National*, and theorist of national preference in the areas of welfare and labour (CPI 2013f). Similarly, CPI used EU issues to connect with Golden Dawn in Greece (CPI 2013g).

The discussion above suggests that, like other far-right parties in Europe (Pirro et al. 2018) and in line with what emerges from the analysis of the ideological themes of the group (see Chapter 3), CPI lacks a coherent position on the EU. However, the group tried to exploit the opportunities associated with EU-related themes during a time of economic hardship. By transforming its EU agenda, CPI managed to regain the visibility it had lost after its first – unsuccessful – electoral attempt. At the same time, it took advantage of common anti-EU stances to set up relationships with other political actors and movements in Italy and abroad. In so doing, CPI progressively moved beyond its original utilitarian critique of the EU, towards more ideological forms of Euroscepticism (which would be confirmed during the 2019 European Parliament election campaign).

Similar to EU affairs, also the issue of migration did not represent a cornerstone of CPI's early mobilization, even though nativism is at the core of the group's worldview (see Chapter 3). The analyses of CPI's mobilization in the protest arena (illustrated earlier in Figure 6.1), have, in fact, shown that immigration originally played a marginal role in the group's actions. From 2012 onwards, however, it suddenly turned into the second most important issue for the group. In line with what we observed for EU issues, the turning point for CPI's migration agenda coincides with the group's choice to engage in the electoral arena, which took place in a context of heated debates on immigration in Italy.

A straightforward interpretation of CPI's sudden interest in migration affairs rests in contextual factors and opportunities. The group in fact tried to capitalize on growing popular concerns linked to the European migration policy crisis. Of the one million refugees who crossed the Mediterranean in 2015, in fact, 154,000 landed in Italy, resulting in a 31 percentage-point increase in annual asylum application rates (Castelli Gattinara 2017). While the trend would slow down over the following months, Eurobarometer data shows that over 40 per cent of Italians considered immigration to be the most important problem facing Italy in 2017 (Figure 6.5). Interestingly, while the Italian average has been consistently below the European one throughout the 2000s, since the beginning of the so-called 'refugee crisis' Italy has been steadily above the EU average. As we shall discuss, CPI saw these trends as a potential window of opportunity to mobilize on migration.

In fact, the figure displays remarkable similarities with the trends in CPI's mobilization illustrated in Figure 6.1, where we showed that the group shifted its attention towards issues connected to migration. This suggests that, in entering the electoral arena, CasaPound tried to intercept the growing popular discontent with migration in Italy. On the one hand, CPI certainly adapted its political agenda to the constraints of the party system agenda (Green-Pedersen and Mortensen 2010). On the other, it did so by politicizing the issue mostly through grassroots protests.

In the electoral arena, immigration stands out as one of the most salient issues in CPI's electoral programmes in both 2013 and 2018 (although it loses salience

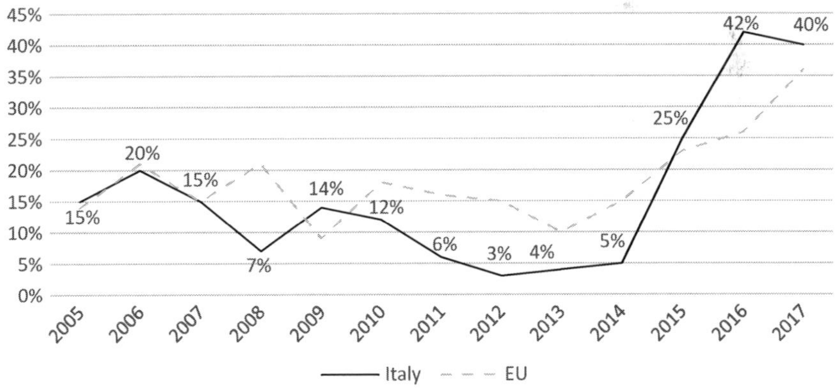

FIGURE 6.5 Share of people who consider immigration the most important problem in Italy (2005–2017).

Source: Standard Eurobarometer 2005–2017.

over time). Both manifestos enumerate several restrictive policy measures against migrants. Specifically, CPI approaches immigration as an economic issue (i.e. immigrants steal natives' jobs), as a security problem (i.e. immigrants are a physical menace) and as a cultural threat (i.e. immigrants challenge the habits of hosting societies). CPI proposes a halt to all forms of regular and irregular migration, as well as the expulsion of all irregular migrants (CPI 2013c: 4–5; CPI 2018e: 5). Furthermore, they propose stripping of their citizenship second-generation migrants who committed crimes, and introducing a reference to the *ius sanguinis* law in the Italian Constitution (CPI 2018e). As mentioned in Chapter 3 and discussed in greater detail later, CPI's manifestos also target NGOs, calling for a halt to state and private funding for those accused of trafficking illegal migrants for their own interests (CPI 2013c: 3).

In the protest arena, instead, migration becomes a primary concern of CPI from 2014 onwards. In concomitance with the European asylum policy crisis, in fact, the group organized a series of demonstrations to protest against the opening of shelters for migrants in Rome and the presence of Roma camps (*Il Corriere della Sera* 2014a, 2014b). In parallel it also promoted direct interventions to ensure security at the neighbourhood level, and various street blockades to prevent the settlement of migrants and Roma people (*Il Corriere della Sera* 2015, 2016).

CPI's mobilization further intensified in the following years, as the Italian government led by Matteo Renzi (Democratic Party) promoted two major laws related to migration issues. First, the so-called *ius soli* bill (which ultimately failed to pass) proposed a reform of Italy's citizenship law, facilitating citizenship for children of foreign parents who were born and schooled in the country. Second, the 'Minniti-Orlando' decree (approved via a vote of confidence vote) set out to simplify asylum procedures and curtail illegal immigration by means of bilateral agreements and an expanded network of administrative detention. While many pundits criticized the law for severely limiting the right to asylum and the protection of fundamental rights, and for reifying the idea that migration is a matter of emergency and criminality requiring state repression (Castelli Gattinara 2017), CPI judged it insufficient and useless (*Il Primato Nazionale* 2017a). To stop illegal migration, CPI proposed shutting down all Italian ports to foreign NGOs and 'rainbow smugglers' (*scafisti arcobaleno*). In the months preceding and following the approval of the Minniti decree, CPI took part – alongside several small far-right groups – in vocal public campaigns insinuating that NGOs involved in rescue operations in the Mediterranean acted in cooperation with human smugglers (*Il Primato Nazionale* 2017b). Whether or not in response to these campaigns, the Italian government eventually turned its attention to NGOs, threatening to shut the ports to the organizations who failed to sign up to a controversial code of conduct implying, among other things, that the Italian army will be allowed to accompany their rescue missions. Since then, CPI has openly endorsed Matteo Salvini's campaign *#chiudiamoiporti* (shut the harbours!).

FIGURE 6.6 Posters of CasaPound Italia's campaigns on immigration.

On the left, a poster for CasaPound's march against the introduction of *ius soli* in Italy's citizenship law, with the slogan 'Stop NGOs, cooperatives, speculators and slave drivers' (June 2017). In the middle and on the right, posters of CasaPound's protest vigils against reception centres in Calabria (2017), with the slogan 'Stop immigration, Italians first'.

In sum, as public debates on immigration grew in importance in the public sphere, CPI turned its attention to this issue. As shown earlier in this chapter, this seems to be a rewarding strategy, at least in terms of media visibility. One of the probable reasons why CasaPound leadership did not opt to address migration any sooner is related to the risks of handling similar issues publicly without being associated with racism. In this sense, it appears that CPI felt legitimate in dealing with migration only once it had begun its engagement in electoral politics where mainstream parties pay increasing attention to migration issues. At the same time, however, this strategy did not pay electorally: on the one hand, because CPI had to compete with stronger far-right parties in elections; on the other, because mainstream politics in Italy seems to have turned increasingly anti-immigration in recent years.

Conclusive remarks

The chapter discussed how CPI's high profile in the Italian public sphere relates to the group's hybrid strategy of external mobilization. As we have seen, even though CPI emerged as a grassroots group, it progressively also engaged in the electoral arena. Today, one of its defining features is precisely this hybrid approach to street politics and electoral competition. Our analysis shows that the group seeks to obtain media coverage in both the protest and electoral arenas through a careful mix of agitprop actions, campaigning and contentious demonstrations.

By involvement in grassroots politics as well as in local and national elections, CPI considers that conventional and contentious activism are not mutually exclusive. Yet we also show that protest tactics still prevail over conventional ones. While this mirrors the group's understanding of violence and contention as legitimate ways of doing politics, it also relates to the weak results obtained by CPI in the ballots. Beyond the election of a few local representatives, in fact, the group has not stood out among its many far-right competitors in the Italian party system. The choice to engage in elections mainly allowed the group to reshape its political supply and consolidate its visibility in the media. As an electoral competitor, CasaPound tried to take advantage of public debates on the European Union and the migration policy crisis. Electoral campaigning therefore allowed CPI to politicize issues on which it had long hesitated to take a clear-cut position in the protest arena.

Overall, rather than transitioning to electoral politics, CPI maintains a hybrid approach to mobilization combining conventional and protest actions. Through the mix of electoral competition tactics and the 'logic of damage' of social movements (Della Porta and Diani 2006), CPI seeks to maximize media coverage. This leads us to examine the way in which CPI interacts with the media and journalists, which will be the focus of the next chapter.

Notes

1 The 2019 European Parliament elections confirmed this trend, as CPI obtained just 0.3 per cent of the vote, corresponding to fewer than 90,000 preferences. At the local elections that took place on the same day, however, CPI elected 63 local council members, mainly in small towns in Lombardy and Piedmont.
2 CPI's electoral programme in fact kept the same title (*Una Nazione,* 'A Nation'), but the 2018 document is slightly longer than in 2013 (21 pages vs 17 pages; and 6,359 words vs 5,749 words, corresponding to 304 vs 252 quasi-sentences).
3 *Equitalia* is the Italian public agency in charge of tax collection.
4 Interview no. 3a of 01/06/2012.
5 This was further confirmed by Simone Di Stefano in a 2014 TV interview for the local broadcaster *Retesole*, available at: https://www.youtube.com/watch?v=S_BvGiNUSWc (accessed 20/12/2018).
6 Interview no. 1b of 19/04/2012.
7 Interview no. 2b of 27/04/2012.
8 This was recorded by the authors during CPI's national festival 'Direzione – Rivoluzione', Rome, 20–23 September 2012.
9 Statement by Simone Di Stefano during a TV interview for the local broadcaster *Retesole,* available at: https://www.youtube.com/watch?v=lQJ98YfPS2o (accessed 15/01/2019).

References

ADN Kronos. 2012. 'Primarie: La Provocazione Di Casapound: I Nostri Voteranno per Bersani', 10. *ADN Kronos.*

Bosi, L., and L. Zamponi. 2015. 'Direct Social Actions and Economic Crises: The Relationship between Forms of Action and Socio-Economic Context in Italy', *Partecipazione e Conflitto* 8(2): 367–91.

Castelli Gattinara, P. 2017. 'The "Refugee Crisis" in Italy as a Crisis of Legitimacy', *Contemporary Italian Politics* 9(3): 318–31.

———. 2018. 'Europeans, Shut the Borders! Anti-Refugee Mobilisation in Italy and France', in D. Della Porta (ed.), *Solidarity Mobilizations in the 'Refugee Crisis'*, London: Palgrave, pp. 271–97.

Castelli Gattinara, P., and C. Froio. 2018. 'Getting "Right" into the News: Grassroots Far-Right Mobilization and Media Coverage in Italy and France', *Comparative European Politics* 1–21.

CPI. 2013a. 'Viterbo, Da #casapound Nessuna Aggressione Ma Contestazione Pacifica Al Maleducato ruotolo', November 2. URL: http://radiobandieranera.org/?p=1194 (consulted February 2016).

———2013b. 'Roma: Aggredito Candidato Sindaco CasaPound Italia, Caschi e Manici Di Piccone Contro Auto Di Stefano', May 17. URL: www.casapounditalia.org/2013/05/roma-aggredito-candidato-sindaco.html (consulted February 2016).

———. 2013c. 'Una Nazione: Il Programma Politico Di CasaPound Italia'. URL: https://www.docdroid.net/Bg8qGdw/programma-casapound-2018.pdf#page=2 (consulted February 2016).

———. 2013d. 'CasaPound Italia Su Sciopero e Manifestazioni 9 Dicembre', December 5. URL: www.casapounditalia.org/2013/12/casapound-italia-su-sciopero-e.html (con sulted August 2018).

———. 2013e. '9 Dicembre, Blitz Pacifico Alla Sede Ue Di Roma per Mettere Tricolore, Fermato Simone Di Stefano'. URL: www.casapounditalia.org/2013/12/9-dicembre-blitz-pacifico-alla-sede-ue.html (consulted August 2018).

———. 2013f. 'Chi è Jean-Yves Le Gallou', September 8. URL: https://www.facebook.com/notes/casapound-italia/chi-%C3%A8-jean-yves-le-gallou/10151529465077924 (con sulted August 2018).

———. 2013g. 'Alba Dorata, Venerdì a CasaPound Confronto Con Esponenti Del Movimento Greco', November 26. URL: www.casapounditalia.org/2013/11/alba-dorata-venerdi-casapound-confronto.html (consulted August 2018).

———. 2014. 'CasaPound, 80000 Firme Raccolte Ma Una Legge Liberticida Impedirà Agli Italiani Di Votarci Alle Europee'. URL: www.casapounditalia.org/2014/04/europee-casapound-italia-80mila-firme.html (consulted August 2018).

———. 2016. 'Lamezia Terme, Azione Shock Di CasaPound Contro Olio Tunisino: "UE e PD Nemici Della Nazione Via La Bandiera Dai Palazzi Comunali"', April 4. URL: www.casapounditalia.org/2016/04/lamezia-terme-azione-shock-di-casapound.html (consulted February 2016).

———. 2018a. 'Elezioni, Di Stefano: Grazie Ai 300mila Italiani Che Hanno Scelto CasaPound, Voti Sestuplicati Dal 2013', March 5. URL: www.casapounditalia.org/2013/05/roma-casapound-protesta-sotto-gli-studi.html (consulted August 2018).

———. 2018b. 'Mutuo Sociale: Disegno Di Legge Regionale'. URL: www.mutuosociale.org/progetto.html (consulted August 2018).

———. 2018c. 'Ferma Equitalia – Il Sito Ufficiale'. URL:http://fermaequitalia.org/(con sulted August 2018).

———. 2018d. 'Tempo Di Essere Madri'. URL: www.tempodiesseremadri.org/(consulted August 2018).

———. 2018e. 'Una Nazione: Il Programma Politico Di CasaPound Italia'. URL: https://www.docdroid.net/Bg8qGdw/programma-casapound-2018.pdf#page=2 (consulted August 2018).

Della Porta, D., and M. Diani. 1999. 'Forms, Repertoires and Cycles of Protest', in D. della Porta and M. Diani (eds), *Social Movements: An Introduction*. Oxford: Blackwell, pp. 165–92.

———. 2006. *Social Movements: An Introduction*. Oxford: Blackwell.

Di Nunzio, D., and E. Toscano. 2011. *Dentro e Fuori CasaPound: Capire Il Fascismo Del Terzo Millennio*. Roma: Armando Editore.

Fanpage (2013) 'CasaPound (0,13% alle ultime elezioni): "Si parte da qui, ci vediamo nelle strade"', February 27, *Fanpage*. URL: https://www.fanpage.it/casapound-0-13-alle-ultime-elezioni-si-parte-da-qui-ci-vediamo-nelle-strade/(consulted May 2018).

Froio, C., and C.E. Little. 2015. 'Responsible Government and Representation in the Eurocrisis', in F. Muller-Rommel and F. Casal Bertoa (eds), *Party Politics and Democracy in Europe: Essays in Honor of Peter Mair*. Abingdon: Routledge, pp. 242–60.

Green-Pedersen, C., and P.B. Mortensen. 2010. 'Who Sets the Agenda and Who Responds to It in the Danish Parliament? A New Model of Issue Competition and Agenda-Setting', *European Journal of Political Research* 49(2): 257–81.

Huffington Post Italia. 2012, 10. 'Apologia Del Fascismo per Casa Pound Nelle Scuole', October 22. URL: https://www.huffingtonpost.it/daniele-m-regard/apologia-del-fascismo-per_b_2001445.html (consulted April 2019).

Ideodromo CasaPound. 2013. 'L'Europa Tra Albe e Tramonti'. URL: www.ideodromocasapound.org (consulted July 2014).

Il Corriere della Sera. 2014a. http://archiviostorico.corriere.it/2014/novembre/29/CasaPound_blocca_strada_rom_non_co_0_20141129_aa74da56-7793-11e4-9538-c4f4fffab8f3.shtml (accessed 10/03/2018).

———. 2014b. https://roma.corriere.it/notizie/cronaca/14_novembre_28/denuncia-militanti-destra-impediscono-rom-accesso-scuola-ee0ed120-7709-11e4-90d4-0eff89180b47.shtml (accessed 10/03/2018).

———. 2015. https://www.corriere.it/cronache/15_ottobre_11/gorizia-migranti-quel-bivacco-parco-caduti-be33ec74-6fe7-11e5-a08a-e76f18e62e8d.shtml (accessed 10/03/2018).

———. 2016. https://milano.corriere.it/notizie/cronaca/16_ottobre_27/migranti-manifestazione-lega-no-clandestini-montello-11b52b56-9c6a-11e6-aac3-b67f2733f2fe.shtml (accessed 10/03/2018).

———. 2017. 'CasaPound e Il Picco Di Ascolti in Tv «Ormai Noi Fascisti Siamo Sdoganati»', November 15. URL: www.corriere.it/politica/17_novembre_15/casapound-di-stefano-fascisti-picco-ascolti-tv-ad11f0d8-ca3c-11e7-bae0-69536c65a470.shtml (consulted April 2019).

Il Fatto Quotidiano, 2013. 'Forconi, Arrestato Vicepresidente di Casapound Mercoledì Presidio Nazionale', December 14. URL: www.ilfattoquotidiano.it/2013/12/14/forconi-arrestato-vicepresidente-di-casapound-scontri-a-torino-4-feriti/813659/(consulted April 2018).

Il Primato Nazionale. 2017a. 'Il Decreto Minniti? Non è Razzista, è Inutile Checché Ne Dica Saviano', March 19. URL: www.ilprimatonazionale.it/cronaca/decreto-minniti-razzismo-inutile-59572 (consulted April 2019).

———. 2017b. 'Torna La Tensione Nel Mediterraneo: Marina Libica Pronta a Sequestrale Le Navi Delle Ong', September 28. URL: https://www.ilprimatonazionale.it/politica/torna-la-tensione-nel-mediterraneo-marina-libica-pronta-sequestrale-le-navi-delle-ong-73440/(consulted April 2019).

Il Secolo d'Italia. 2018. 'Macerata, CasaPound Su Luca Traini: «Va Condannato Senza Esitazioni»', February 4. URL: www.secoloditalia.it/2018/02/macerata-casapound-su-luca-traini-va-condannato-senza-esitazioni/(consulted April 2019).

Kitschelt, H. 2006. 'Movement Parties', in R.S. Katz and W. Crotty (eds), *Handbook of Party Politics*. Thousand Oaks, CA: Sage, pp. 278–90.

Koopmans, R., and P. Statham. 1999. 'Political Claims Analysis: Integrating Protest Event and Political Discourse Approaches', *Mobilization: An International Quarterly* 4(2): 203–21.

Kriesi, H. et al.2008. *West European Politics in the Age of Globalization*. Cambridge: Cambridge University Press.

La Stampa. 2013. 'Grillo ai militanti di Casa Pound: "Se lo volete, benvenuti nei 5 Stelle"', January 11, URL: www.lastampa.it/2013/01/11/italia/grillo-ai-militanti-di-casapound-se-lo-volete-benvenuti-nei-stelle-QOhtlJXl8jg5qzKLGqErlN/pagina.html (consulted April 2019).

Mudde, C. 1999. 'The Single-issue Party Thesis: Extreme Right Parties and the Immigration Issue', *West European Politics* 22(3): 182–97.

Pirro, A.L. et al.2018. 'The Populist Politics of Euroscepticism in Times of Crisis: Comparative Conclusions', *Politics* 38(3): 378–90.

Rao, N. 2014. *Trilogia della celtica*. Milan: Sperling & Kupfer.

Reuters. 2017. 'Italy's Far-Right Makes Inroads Locally as Nation Frets about Fascism', November 20. URL: https://www.reuters.com/article/uk-italy-farright/italys-far-right-makes-inroads-locally-as-nation-frets-about-fascism-idUKKBN1DK1WQ (consulted April 2019).

Scianca, A. 2011. *Riprendersi tutto: le parole di CasaPound*. Rome: Società editrice Barbarossa.

Taggart, P., and A. Szczerbiak. 2008. 'Introduction: Opposing Europe? The Politics of Euroscepticism in Europe', in P. Taggart and A. Szczerbiak (eds), *Opposing Europe? The Comparative Party Politics of Euroscepticism, Volume 1: Case Studies and Country Surveys*. Oxford: Oxford University Press, pp. 1–15.

Tassinari, U.M. 2011. 'CasaPound Ha Eletto Cinque Consiglieri Comunali', *Fascinazione*, May 19. URL: www.fascinazione.info/2011/05/casapound-ha-eletto-cinque-consiglieri.htm (consulted September 2018).

The Guardian. 2018. 'The Fascist Movement That Has Brought Mussolini Back to the Mainstream', *The Guardian*, February 22. URL: www.theguardian.com/news/2018/feb/22/casapound-italy-mussolini-fascism-mainstream (consulted April 2019).

Tilly, C. 1978. *From Mobilization to Revolution*. Reading: Addison Wesley.

Vasilopoulou, S. 2017. *Far Right Parties and Euroscepticism*. Colchester: ECPR Press.

7
POLITICAL COMMUNICATION

The repertoire of communication defines the set of activist media practices that a group uses to reach social actors within and outside the movement milieu (Mattoni 2016). In this chapter, we show that CasaPound's communication involves a twofold hybrid dimension. On the one hand, it implies a variegated infrastructure and a set of media practices addressing a range of audiences. On the other, it combines the communication style of social movements and that of political parties. We will show that the coexistence of these different levels is aimed at satisfying the needs of composite audiences and is thus reminiscent of the 'marketing mix' approach adopted by professionals in highly competitive political communication environments (Kavanagh 1995; Vliegenthart 2012). Using data collected through interviews, participant observation, qualitative content analysis of online and offline material and online popularity indicators the chapter provides an overview of CPI's media infrastructure addressing internal and external publics (7.1). Subsequently, it outlines the main traits of CPI's communication style and traces the evolution of the group's strategy of media management (7.2). The concluding section discusses how CPI's hybrid repertoire of communication helped the group to attract media attention, while also accompanying its progressive engagement in the electoral arena.

7.1 Infrastructure: media outlets and targeted audiences

CasaPound's communication relies on various media outlets and practices used for sharing information internally, but also to disseminate CPI's campaigns and ideas externally. Three different channels stand out: first, CasaPound's newspaper, which is similar to the house organ papers of mass political parties and addresses primarily CPI members; second, a set of ad hoc online media aimed at reaching audiences both internal and external to CPI, including the website, web radio and web TV of the group; and finally, the social media profiles of CPI, notably the Facebook pages, which have a core role in external communication.

7.1.1 Internal communication and the house organ of CasaPound

A main platform for internal communication is CasaPound's newspaper *Il Primato Nazionale,* created in 2013 as an online news journal, with the running title *Quotidiano sovranista*: literally, 'The Daily Sovereigntist'. Since 2017, it is also available, monthly, in print version. While, as a newspaper, one might consider that *Il Primato Nazionale* also has external communication purposes, the paper addresses almost exclusively an internal audience. This is confirmed by the fact that the director, Adriano Scianca, is one of the prominent national leaders of the group, and by its very limited circulation outside the restricted circle of CPI. Moreover, when it was first launched to 7,500 newsstands in Italy (*Il Primato Nazionale* 2017a), the newspaper included the slogan *Non è un abbonamento, è un arruolamento* (This is not a subscription, this is recruitment). *Il Primato Nazionale* thus represents the semi-official press organ of CPI, reporting the group's positions on key issues, and hosting articles and opinion pieces by prominent political figures of the group, and by the intellectuals from whom CPI takes explicit inspiration.

Il Primato Nazionale is edited by *Altaforte*, an editorial group created in 2018 and closely linked to CPI.[1] In this respect, the outlet is part of CPI's broader investment in the ideological and cultural training of its activists, which we addressed in Chapter 4. *Altaforte*, in fact, also publishes political essays, investigations and comic novels targeting CPI members and sympathizers, and which are used by CPI as internal literature. Through these internal communication channels, CPI members and militants are expected to learn and comply with the official positions of the group on each political topic, and to learn specific ways to communicate these positions in public. The connection between CPI and *Altaforte* also serves the purposes of legitimation and propaganda, as shown by the controversy concerning the publisher's participation in the 2019 Turin international book fair. The inclusion of a publisher with close links to a neo-fascist party led many intellectuals and institutions – including the Auschwitz-Birkenau state museum – to boycott the event. *Altaforte* was ultimately banned from the book fair, but the controversy helped to focus attention on CPI's cultural engagement. The group could thus present itself as a victim of censorship at a time when it was under heavy pressure for preventing a Roma family access to a council flat it had been legally assigned in the Casal Bruciato district of Rome, and for the arrest of a town councillor belonging to the group for alleged gang rape. Interviews suggest that CasaPound's activists acquire familiarity with the group's beliefs through internal channels of communication, internal literature and official magazines. From this point of view, the circulation of books, articles and opinion pieces produced by CPI's thinkers represents a system that supports socialization. While being accessible to the wider public, most of the books used for the training of activists primarily address insiders. This includes the book by Gabriele Adinolfi, one of the founders of Italy's 'Third Position', the volumes written by Adriano Scianca, the official in charge of culture for CPI (notably *Riprendersi tutto* – Getting it all back) and the work on right-wing squats in Italy, written by the group's lawyer, Domenico Di Tullio. In addition, CPI promotes a monthly magazine (*L'Occidentale,* The Westerner) and a quarterly paper (*Fare Quadrato,* Closing Ranks).

Thanks to CPI's internal circuit of communication, these magazines and books, and notably *Il Primato Nazionale,* have become a source of information and political socialization for members and sympathizers. This is in line with Bowman-Grieve's (2009: 999) report on the circulation of 'internal literature' in the empirical study on the virtual online communities of the far right, notably the online forum *Stormfront.* The circulation of movement literature, and in particular information about the history and ideology of CPI, allows people to develop 'an understanding of specific issues and the importance of these issues to the movement and to the individual's own development of self-identity' (Bowman-Grieve 2009: 999).

7.1.2 Online platforms to communicate internally and externally

Similar to most contemporary political organizations, CPI also invests in the internet to communicate (Chadwick 2006; Dahlgren 2009). A second crucial dimension of CPI's communication thus rests on the galaxy of online media platforms created by CPI. These diversified media outlets allow CPI to network with its members and potential sympathizers, but also to disseminate its messages to broader audiences. The most notable online platforms are CPI's website, the radio channel *Radio Bandiera Nera* (Black Flag radio) and the group's web TV (*Tortuga Web Tv*). These digital platforms sustain both internal and external communication, and provide a video and audio archive of the main actions promoted by CasaPound.

Notably, Black Flag Radio broadcasts political and cultural news on a daily basis, and hosts interviews with local and national CPI officials, thus complementing *Il Primato Nazionale.* In addition however, CPI's radio also airs music and cultural debates, including singers and songwriters usually associated with the left, and far-right music such as identity rock (Dornbusch and Raabe 2004; see Chapter 5). CPI's president Gianluca Iannone defined it as 'a window on our world, on our lifestyle, on our way of thinking, having fun, fighting' (ADN Kronos 2007), confirming the double role of the radio as a means to spread information *among* CPI's members but also *about* CPI's activities. At the time of our fieldwork, the radio was supported by 15 offices in Italy and three abroad.

Black Flag Radio, the web TV, as well as *Il Primato Nazionale* and other online outlets created by the group can be accessed through the main website, which centralizes all information. CPI's web portal (updated in 2019) has a user-friendly structure, which facilitates access to sections containing information about the structure of the organization, its main activities and the manifesto for the 2018 general elections, as well as CPI's territorial chapters and its parallel associations. As regards the latter, each section provides links redirecting to a Facebook page or external website providing information about activities, beliefs and events. The website thus offers information to users interested in CPI's electoral activities, and to those who are more interested in CPI's engagement in a wider cultural, entertainment and sport environment. The user-friendly interface of CPI's website may be a response to the highly competitive galaxy of far-right activism which is very fragmented and extremely populated in Italy (Caiani et al. 2012). On the Web, a multitude of far-right groupuscules compete for the attention of a limited amount of sympathizers, by producing a dense, yet variegated, landscape of blogs, webpages and discussion forums. The possibility that potential sympathizers get lost among the myriad of competing products currently available is thus very high.

While the main function of the website is to report and give visibility to CPI's political and social activities, the portal also allows the group to perform additional communicative and outreach tasks. It provides an official description of CPI for external observers, including a subsection providing the English version of CPI's 2018 electoral manifesto. Furthermore, the website details the modalities by which sympathizers can become members. It therefore has a crucial organizational function, giving the possibility to users to become 'regular supporters' or 'web-supporters' by paying a regular or reduced membership fee (see Chapter 4). In addition, the website helps to strengthen the group identity, offering activists and militants an information repository, for popularization purposes, for merchandizing and fundraising (Toscano 2017: 84–5). Finally, the website also fulfils a media management function. The main page header includes – along with the classic navigation menu linkages – the necessary information to contact CPI's press office, which is 'organized in a network of regional press officers, responsible for local initiatives, and a national coordination office that must be contacted for interviews, articles and videos regarding the general aspects of the movement' (CPI 2019).

Hence, CPI's website serves multiple hybrid functions of communication. It hosts traditional party activities concerning membership and participation. It serves an external communication function, disseminating information about CPI's activities to the wider public. And it facilitates networking across the various channels of online participation offered by CPI and its affiliated organizations. Overall, it centralizes the galaxy of political, social and communicative practices of the group, increasing the recognizability of CPI and its activities. The popularity of CPI's website is confirmed by an analysis of its web traffic, which is higher than most other extreme-right organizations in Italy. Table 7.1 reports the number of monthly unique visitors on the website of CPI and of other political parties in Italy, providing a proxy of the online popularity of each

TABLE 7.1 Website traffic statistics of CasaPound and other political parties in Italy (2018)

Party	*No. of total visits (unique users)*
M5S	909,772
Partito Democratico	395,462
Lega	270,558
CasaPound	82,204
Forza Italia	54,151
Forza Nuova	28,396
Fiamma Tricolore	< 5,000

group. Notably, we included parties with which CPI usually competes, albeit for very different reasons. Forza Nuova (FzNv) and Movimento Sociale-Fiamma Tricolore (MS-FT) are the two main competitors of CPI on the extreme right of the political spectrum. The Partito Democratico (Democratic Party, PD) and Forza Italia (Go Italy, FI) are the two Italian political parties that have been in government the longest in the past two decades. Finally, Lega Nord (LN) and Movimento 5 Stelle (M5S) represent major populist parties in Italy, with which CPI inevitably has had to interact over the years.

The analysis of web traffic reveals that, while CPI's website is substantially less frequented than those of established political parties in Italy, the group has taken the lead across the Italian extreme-right scene. Indeed, its website is considerably more popular than those of both FzNv and MS-FT, displaying a figure of unique visitors almost three times higher than the main competitor, FzNv. Perhaps in response to this, the website of Forza Nuova was renovated in 2016, emulating some of the key features originally used by CPI on its web portal, such as the thematic display of content, and the visibility provided to parallel organizations engaged in volunteering and other non-political activities.

7.1.3 External communication and social media

Despite its multiple functions and the crucial role in centralizing information about CPI, however, the website is updated less frequently than the other digital platforms used by the group for outreach. These platforms allow the continuous advertisement of the national or international activities of far-right groups, including cultural, protest, solidarity or even violent events. As noted in previous studies, online activities also allow the legitimation of racial hate speech through the phenomenon of 'reasonable racism' (Meddaugh and Kay 2009). This stems from practices of 'information laundering' (Klein 2012: 445) consisting of the presentation of anti-immigrant discourses and 'hate appeals' that 'can take on the encoded and protected forms of public debates, or popular culture, subsequently affecting the mainstream dialogue'. As regards this particular aspect, CPI and some of its national leaders can also count on official and personal accounts on both Twitter and Instagram. Yet the most widely used social media is certainly Facebook.[2]

Created in 2009, CPI's official Facebook page has over 250,000 followers and is updated with new content several times a day. On Facebook CPI devotes special attention to the community activities of CasaPound and its militants. This represents a major means of image-management and self-legitimation, which includes the promotion of the volunteering actions of the association SOL.ID, and the diffusion of photos of *La Salamandra* activists (see Chapter 4) side by side with the victims of earthquakes and other natural disasters. In addition, CPI pays much attention to the coverage of its actions by Italian and international quality media, especially when the accounts reproduce the image of CPI that the group wishes to convey. The Facebook page of Gianluca Iannone links to the long read by *The Guardian* on 'The fascist movement that has brought Mussolini back to the mainstream' (*The Guardian* 2018). It also posted the *Vanity Fair* Italia article on 'Blocco Studentesco' entitled 'Quei bravi ragazzi' ('Those good guys'), which describes the group's 'demonstrative actions, cult of the fire, but also the problems these new fascists have with their mums' (*Vanity Fair* Italia 2018).

As can be seen in Figure 7.1, the official Facebook page of CPI has a higher number of followers than other extreme-right parties in Italy, such as FzNv (248,428 followers) and MS-FT (2,953). Similarly, CPI's leaders Simone Di Stefano (140,286) and Gianluca Iannone (31,113) are more followed than other extreme-right leaders such as Roberto Fiore (leader of Forza Nuova) and Attilio Carelli (leader of Fiamma Tricolore). However, CPI's official pages and leaders remain considerably less followed than the most popular M5S and LN. While

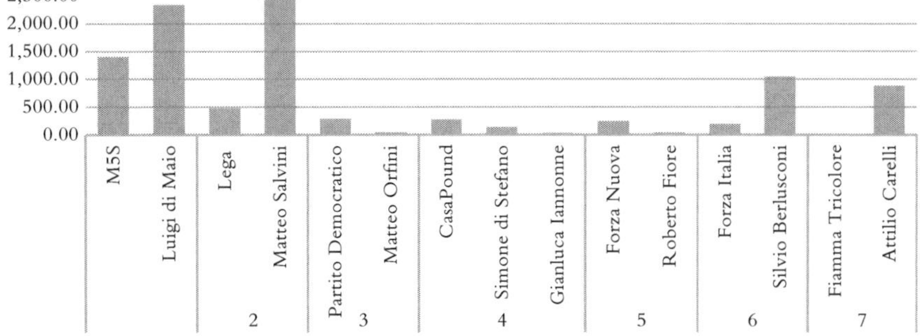

FIGURE 7.1 Facebook followers for CasaPound and other political organizations and leaders.

Source: Facebook. Note: Data to 1 January 2018.

the official pages of these two parties have many fewer followers than their respective leaders (Luigi Di Maio and Matteo Salvini), the opposite is true for CPI, as the group is more popular on social media than its prominent figures and leaders. In this respect, at least online, the personalization of communication seems to count less for CPI than for other parties, at least on Facebook.

Social media, and notably Facebook, thus serve a crucial function for building the community of sympathizers and supporters of CPI. Along with information diffusion, their main political function is to advertise CPI to potential sympathizers and members (Gerstenfeld et al. 2003). As noted above, social media offer an image of the group as a community of political activists sharing the same values and also work as a connection point with the local branches of CPI, and with other groups on the Italian far right. A recent analysis of the network of Italian far-right groups on Facebook shows that 935 pages out of 2,700 far-right pages belong to CasaPound (Patria Indipendente 2016). Put differently, CPI accounts – alone – for more than a third of Italy's far-right groups on Facebook. To illustrate this further, Table 7.2 reports information on CPI and FzNv, the two major aggregation points for the extreme right online. Next to the official pages of the two groups, the table reports the number of followers and interactions for their respective national leaders, and for a subsample of CPI's parallel organizations (presented in Chapter 4).

As can be seen in the column 'reciprocal likes', the organizations that 'like' the official page of CPI on Facebook roughly correspond to the group's parallel associations, or to other groups that closely follow its activities, such as the sports clubs, the bookstores and the thematic associations. This finding could reinforce the thesis of the existence of insular and homogeneous web users'

TABLE 7.2 Interactions among extreme-right organizations and their leaders on Facebook

Page	*Followers*	*Interactions*	*Interaction/ fan*	*Reciprocal likes*	*Ongoing likes*	*Outgoing likes*
CasaPound Italia	265987	15352	0.06	49	380	21
Simone Di Stefano (CPI)	131981	1341	0.01	7	169	15
Gianluca Iannone (CPI)	29860	205	0.01	6	156	7
Forza Nuova (FzNv)	249738	10127	0.04	28	436	17
Roberto Fiore (FzNv)	38541	3168	0.08	14	215	12
Blocco Studentesco	26009	258	0.01	43	146	15
La Salamandra	12592	219	0.02	16	105	19
Il Primato Nazionale	65711	18350	0.28	1	209	0

communities, aggregated along partisan lines (Adamic and Glance 2005). At the same time, it suggests that social media platforms work as much as means of internal communication than as tools for external propaganda.

7.2 Style: from protest to electoral politics

In addition to this variegated media infrastructure, hybridization in CPI's communication has much to do with the group's distinctive manner of disseminating information about itself to activists, sympathizers and external audiences. Over the years, external communication represented the 'hunting ground' used by CPI to recruit sympathizers and to diffuse its ideas and political proposals among the quality media. On the one hand, media activism became more professionalized, thanks to the creation of devoted channels of communication and entertainment allowing both the far-right milieu and external audiences to be addressed. On the other hand, the quality media crucially contributed to spreading CPI's image outside the smaller group of extreme-right sympathizers.

The 'marketing mix' adopted by CPI is the result of a strategic hybrid communication aiming at presenting CPI as a political party and as a social movement to mainstream media. We can distinguish two phases in CPI's media management towards mainstream television channels and the press. A first phase corresponds to the early years of the organization, when CPI needed to differentiate its image from the traditional parties of the Italian extreme right. Three key strategic choices help explain the strategy used by CPI to achieve its communication goals during this phase: *eclecticism*, *popularization* and *polarization*. As the group engaged in electoral politics, however, its political communication changed too, shifting the attention from the organization to its leaders. Thus, this second phase corresponds to CPI's increasing need to set up electoral campaigns, through three additional strategic choices: *sensationalization*, *presidentialization* and *centralization*.

7.2.1 Crafting a social movement profile

In the early years, the communication of CPI presented the group as a grassroots movement, in opposition to 'party models'. Recognizing the crucial role of the younger cohorts, which represent a traditional stronghold of extreme-right movements (Antonucci 2011; Roversi 1999), CPI intentionally opted for unconventional actions aimed at challenging the party-based hegemony of the Italian far right. In 2003, it advertised its first occupation with a minimalist black and white flyer: 'A cat has gone missing. Its name is Pound. If you find it, call this number.' In 2008, CPI distributed flyers and press releases reproducing the statement released after the occupation of the headquarters of MSI (see Chapter 2). The main goal of this communication strategy was to get visibility in the public sphere through quality media (mainstream press and television), but also – and perhaps more importantly – recognizability within the Italian extreme-right subculture.

The means of political communication selected for this purpose were adapted to this goal. They included tactics and symbols inspired by left-wing movements, as well as confrontational actions to attract the attention of the media (Castelli Gattinara and Froio 2018). This political communication mix also included the organization of spectacular events, which suggested a sort of ideal continuity with the creative and anti-establishment cultural movement of Italian Futurism (Koch 2013). In so doing, CPI promoted traditional extreme-right ideals, while also claiming to interpret a profound renewal of the far-right political culture. CPI thus presented itself as a group that is in continuity with historical Fascism, while at the same time rupturing with the 'sclerotic' and 'immobile' nature of political parties on the extreme right. This hybrid communication strategy granted CPI a certain degree of news prominence (Watt et al. 1993) in the far-right milieu and beyond.

Most notably, the main strategy that CPI put in place to achieve recognizability among the various actors of the Italian extreme right consisted of organizing public events that hosted political and cultural figures who did not share CPI's beliefs. We refer to this strategy as *eclecticism*, in that it expressed CPI's willingness to go beyond existing paradigms or sets of assumptions about the extreme right. These events aimed at conveying the idea that CPI draws upon different insights around a subject, or upon unconventional issues altogether (see Chapter 5). CPI explicitly sought to overcome the traditional division between the political right and left, contesting the symbolism that is usually associated with these political cultures.[3] In this sense, CPI's eclecticism consisted of using the codes of other political cultures and adapting them to the realm of their political communication (Miller-Idriss 2018; Schedler 2014). This strategy was mostly successful in attracting the attention of the mainstream media.

A second strategy rested on the adoption of pop-culture codes for the representation of extreme-right political content and messages. We refer to this strategy as *popularization*. A crucial element of this strategy was the branding of the communicative style of CasaPound, through a systematic choice of colours, fonts and styles. This ensured that any public claims by CPI and its affiliated organizations would be immediately associated with the group. Popularization was based on a multiplicity of iconic figures, including the hacktivist movement 'Anonymous', fictional characters like Captain Harlock and Corto Maltese, or the novel *Fight Club*. In this sense, CPI's communicative style targeted specifically adolescent cohorts, a tactic employed by other far-right and populist parties in Europe (Frigoli and Ivaldi 2017), based on the idea that younger people are more attracted by romantic ideals and powerful heroes than by the traditional fascist imagery. Combined with CPI's territorial structure, this communicative strategy was particularly successful for the recruitment of young people, facilitating the merging of different imageries and subcultures within the codes and routines of extreme-right politics (Koch 2017).

The third strategy we focus on consists of CPI's attempts to erode the legitimacy of their political opponents on key subjects. We refer to this strategy as *polarization,* which we understand in terms of Mouffe's notion of antagonism as opposed to agonism (Mouffe 1999). On the one hand, CPI campaigned on the inability of the progressive-left culture to protect the rights of underprivileged Italians against globalization and economic recession. The symbolic antagonism was thus based on the terrain of the classic left-wing issue of workers' rights. On the other, it stressed the illiberal nature of anti-fascist mobilization when it comes to the right to free speech of extreme-right groups. Hence, antagonism focused on liberal rights such as freedom of opinion and freedom of political organization. The communicative strategy implied antagonizing the left-wing and staging an opposition that stands between a decaying political culture and the emerging, challenging subculture, interpreted by CPI (Almagisti 2011). The success of this hybrid media management strategy over the past few years is confirmed by the intense coverage of events in which CasaPound demonstrated in front of factories or in support of blue-collar strikes (*La Repubblica* 2018).

7.2.2 Setting up an electoral profile

The second phase of CPI's communication strategy coincides with the choice of running for elections. In this new scenario, the group's main urgency was to present itself as a credible electoral competitor, even at the risk of losing grassroots support. To cope with this trade-off, CPI complemented the actions that had previously served as communication instruments (Bennett 1998), with more conventional ones belonging to the formal realm of political participation. Notably, these included formal electoral campaigning, legally authorized institutional rallies, meetings and festivals. On these occasions, CPI often sought the endorsement of established figures of the Italian cultural or intellectual scene, who were expected to increase the visibility of the events and the credibility of CPI candidates.[4] As a result, the communication repertoire became more like that of established political parties, shifting from a focus on the organization itself to highlight its leaders (Plasser and Lengauer 2008).

The progressive engagement in the electoral arena changed some, but not all, of the principles driving CPI's interaction with the media. Notably, the electoral shift further enhanced the group's propensity towards *sensationalization* of conflict. To justify its decision to run for elections, the communication style of CPI centred on dramatizing the political context in which the elections took place. The idea was to present CPI's electoral engagement not as a strategic choice, but as something made inevitable by extraordinary and urgent political circumstances.

The opening of new local chapters or the launching of electoral campaigns, for example, was often accompanied by confrontation with local opponents, resulting in increased media coverage by the press and television. In some cases, as in Parma,[5] physical confrontation was avoided only through the intervention of the police. CPI did nothing to avoid producing these provocative stunts, as confirmed by the choice of organizing the 2018 national festival in a city traditionally hostile to right-wing mobilization like Grosseto in Tuscany, and holding it on the symbolic date of 8 September, the anniversary of the Italian armistice during World War II.[6] Sensationalization therefore resulted from dramatic news, produced by the quality media, as a by-product of CPI's mobilization. Moreover, CPI was able to benefit not only from extensive exposure to the broader public, but also from a dual public image, since the news media presented the group alternatively as a legitimate political party and a confrontational street movement.

The electoral transition of CPI also triggered a radical change in the communication strategy, which shifted the focus from CPI as an organization to the figure of Simone Di Stefano as the leader and candidate. In line with existing literature on political communication, we refer to this strategy as *leaderization* (Mancini 2011). In fact, even though a hierarchical structure focusing strongly on the national leader existed prior to CPI's choice to run for elections (see Chapter 4), the decision to appoint Di Stefano as the party candidate in the 2013 and 2018 general elections triggered a concentration of all the group's political and media activities on this figure. Di Stefano became the official representative of CPI on television shows and radio programmes. While this choice responded to the need to present CPI as a classic political party, it was accompanied by sensationalizing claims in which Di Stefano evoked the 1948 slogan of MSI, according to which Fascism should 'neither be repudiated nor restored'.

Finally, electoral campaigning also led to a radical change in the issues at the core of CPI's agenda. We refer to this as *centralization,* because it stemmed from the progressive concentration of the media management around a restricted set of issues and themes. The video advertisement for the campaign circulated by CPI in 2018 illustrates clearly the transformation of the communication strategy, now only oriented at presenting the group as an anti-immigration and anti-establishment actor (see Chapter 6). The main message of the advert, pronounced by Di Stefano, summarizes the general, nationalistic undertones of CPI's campaign: 'As Italians, we have time and again been able to unite and fight to defend our borders and the accomplishments of previous generations' (CPI 2018). The advert builds upon the conspiracy theory of the 'Great Replacement', addresses negatively the main centre-right and centre-left parties in Italy, and refers to symbolic elements, notably the Redipuglia War Memorial (in north-eastern Italy) housing the remains of over 100,000 Italian soldiers who died during World War I. The symbolic aspects embedded in this choice produced a series of political reactions (especially by the presidency of the Friuli Venezia Giulia Region, where the memorial is located) and media debates, which further reinforced the visibility of the group and the symbolic relevance of the advert. References to historical Fascism therefore represent a crucial element in CPI's media management, as they provide an opportunity to link the internal and external sides of its communication strategy.

7.2.3 Appealing to quality media

The change in the strategy of CPI's communication described in the previous sections had only a moderate influence on the general coverage of the group's actions. Despite the electoral shift, in fact, the mass media remained mainly interested in the protest and extremist aspects of its politics (Castelli Gattinara and Froio 2018). However, the adoption of a more conventional repertoire is likely to have contributed to legitimizing CPI in the public debate. Until 2017, CPI's appearances on television had been limited to two specific occasions. In 2011, Gianluca Iannone intervened in a live show on public television to discuss CasaPound's involvement in the shooting of two Senegalese street-vendors by one of its sympathizers (see Chapter 2). In 2014, Simone Di Stefano was invited to a show on the private channel La7, to discuss the housing emergency and the alleged growth of the extreme right in Italy. During the interview, the journalist asked Di Stefano whether he was a fascist and he replied simply 'Yes, absolutely'.[7]

A few years later, the situation had changed both quantitatively and qualitatively. Quantitatively, the 'cordon sanitaire' in the quality media had been fully broken by CPI. As a candidate in the general elections, Simone Di Stefano was invited to several popular talk shows, and took part in traditional television and radio broadcasting as required by the Italian law on electoral communication.[8] Qualitatively, CPI's interactions with the media had changed too, as the group intensified its campaigns against quality media, while also growing increasingly aware that the relationship of the far right with the media is characterized by reciprocal advantage (Ellinas 2010). When Di Stefano was again invited to the La7 television show during the 2018 election campaign, his performance was celebrated by CPI's newspaper *Il Primato Nazionale*, which pointed out that during his intervention the talk show registered an increased audience share (*Il Primato* Nazionale 2017b). Furthermore, from 2017, CPI started inviting well-known television journalists to political debates that took place at its headquarters in Rome, and when a prominent journalist from La7 television accepted the invitation, Di Stefano commented on Facebook that: 'Television never invites CasaPound, but we are gentlemen and we have invited the TV to CasaPound' (*Huffington Post Italia* 2017).

These examples are illustrative of CPI's skill in traditional media management, and its capacity to gain visibility inside and outside its own ideological backyard. CPI's engagement in the electoral arena was accompanied by the development of a coherent strategy of media management. The main effort has been to avoid the mistakes of traditional extreme-right parties, by developing a professional communication style to best exploit the ambivalent relationship between the media and far-right organizations (De Jonge 2019). Political communication was therefore crafted to mirror CPI's hybridization strategy. On the one hand, it presented CPI as a movement in contrast to the apathy of far-right parties and striving to attract new members through unconventional political, social and communication activities. On the other, it presented the group as a party contesting elections, and interested

FIGURE 7.2 Posters of CasaPound's political debates with Italian journalists Enrico Mentana and Corrado Formigli (La7 TV).

The debate took place in the Rome headquarters of CasaPound in autumn 2017.

in gaining the highest level of attention not only through indirect coverage, but also through grassroots and conventional communication activities.

Conclusive remarks

Illustrating how CPI communicates is crucial to understand how the group achieved the high profile it currently enjoys. The results point at two major aspects of its communication repertoire: the infrastructure and the specific style by which the group approaches the media.

First, we find that CPI has caught the attention of the media thanks to its communication infrastructure. This rests on a complex set of media outlets and practices, which serve functions of internal communication, as well as diffusion towards the outside world. We observed that the newspaper of CPI addresses primarily group members similar to the house organs of political parties. Additional online media platforms, including the website, web radio and web TV, are located at an intermediate level and aim at both internal and external audiences, whereas the social media profiles are predominantly used for external communication and propaganda. We argue that this variegated infrastructure of media outlets and practices is closely connected with CPI's ambition to address audiences inside and beyond the restricted milieu of extreme-right supporters, extending into the political mainstream.

Second, we find that the high profile enjoyed by CPI in the media also relates to its particular communication style. This is based on a 'marketing mix' intended to satisfy the needs of composite audiences in the protest and electoral arenas. On the one hand, especially in the early years, CPI tried to differentiate its public profile from that of rival political parties, presenting itself as a protest movement and putting special emphasis on extreme-right political content and unconventional messages. On the other, and increasingly so over time, CPI aimed at consolidating its image as a legitimate political party, developing a more conventional communication style as well as a centralized electoral campaigning strategy.

Overall, CPI's visibility in the mass media owes much to this hybrid strategy and the combination of the professionalized media-oriented tactics of political parties and of social movements. The group's communication style, in fact, taps into commercial media demand for entertaining stories and simplified messages, exploiting the often-ambivalent relationship between the media and the far right (De Jonge 2019). CPI's communication infrastructure, furthermore, ensured the recognizability of the group not only among extreme-right sympathizers but also among mainstream audiences and journalists. This hybrid repertoire of communication consolidated the high profile of CPI in the media, facilitating the drift of its fringe messages into the political mainstream.

Notes

1 The website of the publisher is: https://altafortedizioni.it/chi-siamo/ (accessed 16/12/2018).
2 In April 2019, CPI could count on 39,000 Twitter followers, Simone Di Stefano had 28,000 followers, whereas Gianluca Iannone only 1,800.
3 Interestingly, CPI's motto on Twitter is still 'Destra, sinistra … oppure CasaPound' (Right, left … or CasaPound).
4 In particular, well-known figures of the intellectual far-right milieu like the philosopher Diego Fusaro (*Il Secolo d'Italia* 2014) or the art critic and politician Vittorio Sgarbi (*Il Secolo Nuovo* 2012).
5 See for example the case of the opening of the new seat in the city of Parma (*Gazzetta di Parma* 2016).
6 The event had extensive coverage by the local and the national press. The ANPI (National Association of Italian Partisans) called for a counter mobilization, with a march taking place during the opening day of the meeting.
7 The statement was made on the Italian TV show *Piazza Pulita*, aired on 4 November 2014 at the studios of La7. The video is available at: https://www.youtube.com/watch?v=WBIIRurWrG4 (accessed 20/05/2017).
8 On traditional media (TV and radio), candidates and parties are granted equal treatment under the *par condicio* law (Law no. 28 of 2000).

References

Adamic, L.A., and N. Glance. 2005. *The Political Blogosphere and the 2004 U.S. Election: Divided They Blog*, Proceedings of the 3rd International Workshop on Link Discovery. Chicago, Illinois.

ADN Kronos. 2007. 'Debutta Radio Bandiera Nera, La Web Radio Delle OSA', April 9. URL: www1.adnkronos.com/Archivio/AdnAgenzia/2007/09/04/Cronaca/INTER

NET-DEBUTTA-RADIO-BANDIERA-NERA-LA-WEB-RADIO-DELLE-OSA_140916.php (consulted April 2015).

Almagisti, M. 2011. *La Qualità Della Democrazia in Italia. Capitale Sociale e Politica*. Rome: Carocci.

Antonucci, M.C. 2011. *La Cultura Politica Dei Movimenti Giovanili Di Destra Nell'era Della Globalizzazione*. Milan: Franco Angeli.

Bennett, M. 1998. 'Intercultural Communication: A Current Perspective', *Basic Concepts of Intercultural Communication: Selected Readings*. London: Intercultural Press, pp. 1–34.

Bowman-Grieve, L. 2009. 'Exploring "Stormfront": A Virtual Community of the Radical Right', *Studies in Conflict & Terrorism* 32(11): 989–1007.

Caiani, M. et al.2012. *Mobilizing on the Extreme Right: Germany, Italy, and the United States*. Oxford: Oxford University Press.

Castelli Gattinara, P., and C. Froio. 2018. 'Getting "Right" into the News: Grassroots Far-Right Mobilization and Media Coverage in Italy and France', *Comparative European Politics* 1–21.

Chadwick, A. 2006. *Internet Politics: States, Citizens, and New Communication Technologies*. Oxford: Oxford University Press.

CPI. 2018. 'Vota Più Forte Che Puoi – Spot CasaPound Politiche 2018'. URL: https://www.youtube.com/watch?v=1DFrGmZbzVo (consulted December 2018).

———. 2019. 'Ufficio Stampa'. URL: https://www.casapounditalia.org/p/ufficio-stampa.html (consulted April 2019).

Dahlgren, P. 2009. *Media and Political Engagement: Citizens, Communication, and Democracy*. New York: Cambridge University Press.

De Jonge, L. 2019. 'The Populist Radical Right and the Media in the Benelux: Friend or Foe?', *International Journal of Press Politics* 24(2): 189–209.

Dornbusch, C., and J. Raabe. 2004. 'RechtsRock Das Modernisierungsmoment der extremen Rechten', in S. Braun and D. Hörsch (eds), *Rechte Netzwerke — eine Gefahr*. Wiesbaden: VS Verlag für Sozialwissenschaften, pp. 123–31.

Ellinas, A.A. 2010. *The Media and the Far Right in Western Europe: Playing the Nationalist Card*. Cambridge: Cambridge University Press.

Frigoli, G., and G. Ivaldi. 2017. 'L'extrême Droite et l'Islam : Fractures Idéologiques et Stratégies Électorales', *Hommes et Migrations* 1316(1).

Gazzetta di Parma. 2016. 'Apre Nuova Sede Casa Pound: Quartiere Cittadella Blindato'. URL: https://www.gazzettadiparma.it/video/24-ore-parma/347746/Apre-nuova-sede-Casa-Pound-.html (consulted January 2017).

Gerstenfeld, P.B. et al.2003. 'Hate Online: A Content Analysis of Extremist Internet Sites', *Analyses of Social Issues and Public Policy* 3(1): 29–44.

Huffington Post Italia. 2017. 'Mentana a Casapound per Un Dibattito'.URL: https://www.huffingtonpost.it/2017/09/14/mentana-a-casapound-per-un-dibattito_a_23209123/ (consulted October 2017).

Il Fatto Quotidiano. 2018. 'Casapound, Al via La Festa a Grosseto: L'Anpi Invita a Scendere in Piazza Iannone: "Sono Un Gruppo Di Emarginati"'. URL: https://www.ilfattoquotidiano.it/2018/09/07/casapound-al-via-la-festa-a-grosseto-lanpi-invita-a-scendere-in-piazza-iannone-sono-un-gruppo-di-emarginati/4610262/(consulted December 2018).

Il Primato Nazionale. 2017a. 'La Rivista de Il Primato Nazionale'. URL: https://www.facebook.com/ilprimatonatsionale/posts/1606522202737386 (consulted April 2019).

———. 2017b. 'La Tartaruga Frecciata Sfonda in Tv'. URL: https://www.ilprimatonazionale.it/politica/la-tartaruga-frecciata-sfonda-tv-record-ascolti-la-7-75359/(consulted November 2017).

Il Secolo d'Italia. 2014. 'Minacciato Il Filosofo Fusaro Che Doveva Parlare Di Marx a CasaPound: "Clima Intollerabile, Rinuncio Al Dibattito"'. URL: https://www.secoloditalia.it/2014/02/minacciato-il-filosofo-fusaro-che-doveva-parlare-di-marx-a-casapound-clima-intollerabile-rinuncio-al-dibattito/(consulted December 2014).

Il Secolo Nuovo. 2012. 'Roma Alla Festa Nazionale CasaPound, Sgarbi: "E' l'unica Speranza"'. URL: www.ilsecolonuovo.com/2012/09/24/roma-alla-festa-nazionale-casapound-sgarbi-%E2%80%98-e-l%E2%80%99unica-speranza%E2%80%99/(consulted December 2012).

Kavanagh, D. 1995. *Election Campaigning: The New Marketing of Politics*. Cambridge, MA: Blackwell.

Klein, A. 2012. 'Slipping Racism into the Mainstream: A Theory of Information Laundering', *Communication Theory* 22(4): 427–48.

Koch, H. 2013. *Casa Pound Italia: Mussolinis Erben*. Münster: Unrast.

———. 2017. 'CasaPound Italia: The Fascist Hybrid', in M. Fielitz and L.L. Laloire (eds), *Trouble on the Far Right: Contemporary Right-Wing Strategies and Practices in Europe*. Bielefeld: Transcript.

La Repubblica. 2018. 'Roma, Casapound e Movimenti Casa Manifestano All'ex Fabbrica Della Penicillina'.URL: https://roma.repubblica.it/cronaca/2018/11/08/news/roma_casapound_e_movimenti_casa_manifestano_all_ex_fabbrica_della_pennicillina-211128655/(consulted December 2018).

Mancini, P. 2011. 'Leader, President, Person: Lexical Ambiguities and Interpretive Implications – Paolo Mancini, 2011', *European Journal of Communication* 26(1): 48–63.

Mattoni, A. 2016. *Media Practices and Protest Politics: How Precarious Workers Mobilise*. London: Routledge.

Meddaugh, P.M., and J. Kay. 2009. 'Hate Speech or "Reasonable Racism?" The Other in Stormfront', *Journal of Mass Media Ethics* 24(4): 251–68.

Miller-Idriss, C. 2018. *The Extreme Gone Mainstream: Commercialisation and Far Right Youth Culture*. Princeton, NJ: Princeton University Press.

Mouffe, C. 1999. 'Deliberative Democracy or Agonistic Pluralism', *Social Research* 66(3): 745–758.

Patria Indipendente. 2016. 'La Galassia Nera Su Facebook'. URL: www.patriaindipendente.it/persone-e-luoghi/inchieste/la-galassia-nera-su-facebook/(consulted April 2019).

Plasser, F., and G. Lengauer. 2008. 'Television Campaigning Worldwide', *Routledge Handbook of Political Management*. London: Routledge, pp. 253–71.

Roversi, A. 1999. 'Giovani Di Destra e Giovani Di Estrema Destra', *Rassegna Italiana Di Sociologia* 40(4): 605–25.

Schedler, J. 2014. 'The Devil in Disguise: Action Repertoire, Visual Performance and Collective Identity of the Autonomous Nationalists', *Nations and Nationalism* 20(2): 239–58.

The Guardian. 2018. 'The Fascist Movement That Has Brought Mussolini Back to the Mainstream' URL: https://www.theguardian.com/news/2018/feb/22/casapound-italy-mussolini-fascism-mainstream (consulted February 2018).

Toscano, E. 2017. 'The Dark Side of Web-Activism: The Case of CasaPound Italia', in F. Antonelli (ed.), *Net-Activism. How Digital Technologies Have Been Changing Individual and Collective Actions*. Rome: RomaTrE Press.

Vanity Fair Italia. 2018. 'Quei Bravi Ragazzi'. URL: https://www.vanityfair.it/news/approfondimenti/2018/02/23/quei-bravi-ragazzi (consulted February 2018).

Vliegenthart, R. 2012. 'The Professionalization of Political Communication? A Longitudinal Analysis of Dutch Election Campaign Posters', *American Behavioral Scientist* 56(2): 135–50.

Watt, J. et al.1993. 'Agenda-Setting Effects of Television News Coverage and the Effects Decay Curve', *Communication Research* 20(3): 408–435.

8
CONCLUSIONS

Following the empirical analyses on each dimension of CPI's politics, this last chapter brings together the findings and discusses their implications. At the core of this volume, is the idea that hybridization has allowed this fringe extreme-right group to attract attention and visibility in the Italian public debate. Hybridization is the strategy by which CPI combines ideas and symbols inspired by different political cultures, as well as the organizational features, forms of mobilization and of communication of political parties and social movements. Throughout the empirical chapters, we have contended that hybrid aspects concerning the group's ideology, internal structure, activism, mobilization and communication help in understanding how CPI entered the Italian mainstream. It is these hybrid strategies, in fact, that allowed the group to build a recognizable profile within and outside the extreme-right milieu and to gather the resources necessary for organizational maintenance and mobilization. In this chapter, we discuss the double-edged outcomes of hybridization. We argue that this strategy may grant high-profile visibility in public debates for fringe groups and their ideas, but not electoral influence. We conclude by discussing the interest of this volume for specialists of the far right, and more broadly for scholars studying political parties and social movements.

8.1 Hybridization in the politics of CasaPound Italia

8.1.1 Drivers of hybridization

The volume examined how the internal workings and external mobilization choices of CPI help understand its high public profile. Our main argument has been that hybridization granted CPI leeway for the diffusion of its ideas and campaigns among a wider public than the (restricted) audience responding to right-wing extremist messages. This is explained by two main logics: the need to find the resources necessary to sustain the organization and activities of the group; and the need to achieve the recognizability necessary to capture wider support.

A first driver of hybridization is therefore the *need to find resources* to sustain collective action. In fact, one of the main challenges of CPI is that it crucially lacks resources that are conventionally associated with organizational strength, such as money, staff and members. Since its access to public office has been occasional and restricted to the local level (small towns, or suburban municipalities), CPI could not rely on state funding to sustain its activities. Hence, it formally organized as an NGO, and it invested in parallel associations with political, social and financial purposes. CPI's hybridization strategy thus results from a strategic differentiation of the venues addressed to gather financial resources and potential members, combining electoral politics with unionism, community engagement, environmental activism, sport training, tattooing and the organization of music events. Jointly, these political, subcultural and market-oriented activities maximize the group's efforts to find resources, both financial and in terms of recruitment and membership.

A second driver of hybridization is the *need for recognizability* beyond the extreme-right milieu. A main challenge for CPI, in fact, had to do with building a clearly identifiable profile in a political system already saturated with far-right and anti-immigrant actors. CPI had to compete not only with radical right political parties – the Lega Nord and Fratelli d'Italia – but also with smaller grassroots groups – such as Forza Nuova, Movimento Sociale-Fiamma Tricolore and a multiplicity of other groupuscules. Furthermore, it had to cope with the 'polyvalent nature' of the Movimento 5 Stelle, which was able to incorporate some of the anti-establishment and nativist features of the far right (Pirro and Castelli Gattinara 2018). In this setting, a hybridization strategy allowed CPI to construct a profile of its own, made of a few, clearly identifiable elements. The hybrid symbolism and communication style helped CPI to stand out among all other far-right organizations in Italy. Its unconventional way of doing politics helped it to appear more extremist than the radical right in the electoral arena, but more credible than old-fashioned extreme-right groups in the protest arena.

8.1.2 Dimensions of hybridization

To illustrate this argument, we observed empirically five dimensions of CPI's politics. In particular, the chapters have suggested that CPI's ideology, its internal structure, mobilization and communication strategies display features that are mediated from different political cultures, including, but not limited to, the tradition of the extreme right. In addition, the configuration of CPI as a political organization, its collective identity and its choice of repertoire of action and communication, display elements common to both political parties and to social movements.

On the one hand, CPI develops and diffuses its worldview by combining references to historical Fascism, post-war extremism, the progressive-left tradition and pop culture. On the other, the group invests both in the electoral and in the protest arenas, upholding the organizational features and mobilization activities of political parties and social movements. We referred to this unconventional combination of ideas, styles, configurations and tactics with the notion of hybridization. With this concept, we seek to explain the visibility that CPI came to acquire in the public debate, and the attention it currently enjoys in the protest and electoral arena despite open nostalgia for historical Fascism.

The book's first argument is that ideology needs to be considered in more detail when thinking about how extreme-right fringe groups gain prominence in public debates. Our analysis offers a call to move beyond simplistic interpretations of extreme-right ideologies as being either firmly entrenched in historical and post-war Fascism, or completely disconnected from the past. As Chapter 3 illustrates, in fact, hybridization brings nuance to this distinction. Rather than dismissing all references to inter-war and post-war worldviews, CPI uses the concept of *ethnopluralism* to attain ideological coherence. Ethnopluralism offers a consistent framing of core themes – like social welfare and globalization – as well as issues considered of secondary importance – like gender and the environment. Hybridization thus allowed CPI to emphasize its ideological roots in the tradition of the extreme right, while avoiding stigmatization as being outdated or openly racist.

The second argument concerns reconsidering the distinction between the organizational and strategic models of political parties and social movements to understand the visibility of a fringe extreme-right group in public debates. We showed that the internal structure, decision-making and recruitment of CPI does not fully conform to either the model usually followed by electoral actors, or that of grassroots organizations. Rather, it combines formal and informal features, hierarchic procedures and spaces of socialization, merging the organizational practices of social movements with those of formal political parties. We argue that the coexistence of these two organizational models crucially contributed to the high profile achieved by the group. CPI's hybrid configuration in fact allowed it to draw financial resources and personnel from different venues, and to offer both conventional and unconventional modes of political participation for militants and sympathizers.

Third, the volume suggests that the transition of fringe extreme-right groups into the mainstream has to do with factors pertaining to their collective identities. The analysis developed in Chapter 5 offered in-depth insights into the formation of solidarity bonds among CPI activists. We showed that CPI's collective identity is promoted through a composite mix of images, styles and practices originating from different political cultures. These include extreme-right identifiers (Mussolini, music in the form of 'identity rock' and violent narratives and practices), but also left-wing icons (e.g. Che Guevara and Karl Marx) and a set of aesthetic codes concerning activist clothing and the group's imagery. Our analysis shows that this hybrid stylistic repertoire is crucial to CPI's public profile: it contributes to reducing stigmatization by outsiders; it facilitates the recognizability of the group by potential sympathizers; and it actively sustains the identification of individuals within the group.

Fourth, the book suggests that external mobilization should be addressed more carefully when explaining the visibility of extreme-right fringe groups. We show that the repertoire of action of CPI combines activism inside and outside the institutional arena, including electoral campaigning, grassroots actions and agitprop operations. In this respect, the group does not consider protest tactics a suboptimal option compared to office-seeking strategies, but complementary to party competition. In this respect, CPI seeks to maximize media coverage by transposing the logics of damage into the electoral arena, and those of party competition into the grassroots extreme-right milieu.

Finally, the book contends that communication repertoires play a crucial role in driving the attention of quality media towards extreme-right fringe groups. The communication strategy of CPI combines the professionalized media-oriented tactics of both political parties and social movements and allows the group to get coverage for both protest and electoral activities. More specifically, CPI's variegated media infrastructure has enabled the group to become recognizable not only among far-right sympathizers but also among the broader public. Moreover, its particular communication style builds on simplified messages and agitprop campaigns, meeting the mass media demand for sensationalistic and entertaining stories. This hybrid communication repertoire allowed CPI's politics and fringe narratives to become part of mainstream public debates and media coverage.

8.1.3 The consequences of hybridization

Overall, these results suggest that hybridization allowed CPI to enter the mainstream by combining left-wing issues, extreme-right ideas and pop culture, and by juxtaposing the activities and communication repertoires of office-seeking parties and contentious movements. Despite CPI's minimal electoral support, its unusual forms of doing politics triggered increasing interest from external observers, the quality media and the public. They enabled extremist politics to become routine in mainstream public debates and facilitated the diffusion of fringe messages beyond the audience usually addressed by marginal political groups. The consequences of hybridization, thus, must be differentiated in terms of electoral and non-electoral impact. In this respect, the volume suggested distinguishing between CPI's electoral success, and the broader impact on the political and cultural domains resulting from its ability to achieve visibility in the public sphere (Giugni 2008).

Our findings suggest that CPI's hybridization strategy produced Janus-faced results. On the one hand, CPI was successful in cleaning up its public image, increasing the resources it could gather from different venues, and consolidating its credibility through a careful mix of election and protest campaigning. These resources facilitated organizational maintenance, the continuity of its mobilization and thus the diffusion of some of its themes into mainstream public debates, at least in the short term. On the other hand, over the medium and long term, CPI failed to achieve electoral breakthrough, the alliances it built with far-right parties proved short-lived, and its support in the polls and among the public remained minimal. So far, its electoral trajectory has been a remarkable failure if compared with the group's self-proclaimed ambitions, and despite the impressive amount of attention that it claimed during the latest election campaigns.

In this respect, hybrid ways of doing politics allow fringe groups recognizability in the short term: they imply the construction of new, unconventional profiles for extreme-right actors, which are often very attractive for the mass media, and thus may at first grant their promoters special visibility within the crowded market of nativist politics. At the same time, hybridization also implies that actors give up parts of their political and cultural legacy, preserving only the most iconic, provocative, and thus recognizable, symbols. This choice may ultimately isolate these groups both from the extreme-right milieu (that stigmatizes them as too moderate) and from the more moderate right (that see them as too extreme). Put differently: if hybridization allows extreme-right groups to capitalize on visibility and diffuse fringe ideas across the Italian mainstream, it still does not allow them to escape marginalization, since it runs the risk of alienating both radical and moderate audiences in the long run.

8.2 Future research

The central message of this book is that hybrid strategies of organization, mobilization and communication can explain the high-profile visibility of extreme-right actors, or the lack thereof. The themes that have guided the empirical analysis also have important implications for future research. Beyond specialists of the far right and experts of Italian politics, this volume offers insight into the study of political parties and social movements in general, and how to advance the methods employed in research on far-right politics.

To begin with, the results offer a plea for greater interdisciplinary dialogue between the study of political parties and social movements. In particular, our empirical analysis calls for a more nuanced reading of the distinction between movements and parties. Long appraised as separate entities in the respective literatures, the study of the interconnections between contentious and party politics can help understand the developments of the contemporary far right, and its impact on large-scale processes of social and political change (Hutter et al. 2018). We believe that the conceptualization of 'movement parties' (Kitschelt 2006), could help acknowledge the interconnections between far-right actors primarily seeking office positions, and grassroots groups accessing the public sphere mainly with informal means (Pirro and Castelli Gattinara 2018).

Our study of CasaPound also resonates with the increasing sociological interest over political parties, and with the growing demand for political science research on collective action and citizen protest (Hutter and Vliegenthart 2018). This seems rather compelling in the study of far-right politics at large, and with the rise of anti-austerity political actors stemming from grassroots activism and engaging in the institutional arena, such as the *Movimento 5 Stelle* in Italy and *Podemos* in Spain (Mosca and Quaranta 2017). Further research should highlight whether hybrid features and movement–party configurations may be transitory or be partly reconsidered if no longer rewarding in electoral terms. In this respect, the approach advanced in this enquiry can help understand the persistence of far-right parties and their 'normalization' in established democracies. The issue of 'restyling' of far-right ideologies and practices, in fact, has broad implications that go beyond the specific case of CasaPound, and which question the transformations of successful radical right parties in Europe.

This book has also made important contributions as regards research strategies and methodologies in studying far-right politics. The enquiry sought to reinstate the role of agency in determining far-right actors' own fortunes, by placing internal supply-side factors at the core of the analysis. In the vast research corpus on the populist radical right these elements have been deployed predominantly as independent variables explaining electoral performance (Betz and Immerfall 1998; Carter 2005), rather than as objects of enquiry in themselves. Through its internal supply-side approach, the book advanced a framework for the analysis of far-right ideology, leadership and internal structure, and illustrated how these factors crucially define the nature of CPI's mobilization in the streets, participation in elections and visibility in the public sphere.

The interactive analytical framework and the triangulation of different methods and data proved to be particularly helpful to analyse the electoral and non-electoral engagement of CasaPound. In this respect, this study can be listed as one of the first efforts to tackle the issues at the core of the ideology of non-party actors on the far right (Castelli Gattinara and Pirro 2018), and among the very few studies that look at the far right from the inside (see in particular Art 2011). By integrating official and unofficial data, semi-structured interviews and 'internalist' methods of data collection, as well as material produced for internal and external audiences, this study lay the ground for future research on the organization and strategies of right-wing parties and movements.

Overall, the theoretical, empirical and methodological insights of this volume might therefore advance avenues for future research, broadening the study of non-electoral far-right politics beyond the specific case of Italy and CasaPound, and extending the analysis of hybridization strategies comparatively.

8.3 Last thoughts

As political circumstances change, so do extreme-right politics. This simple, core statement of the book refutes simplistic understandings that still characterize most accounts of this phenomenon. With this study, we wished to advance knowledge on important continuities and changes in the contemporary extreme right.

In this respect, Cas Mudde has lately spoken of a widening chasm between far-right parties and politics (Mudde 2016), which is evidence of how nativist ideals have come to resonate across political arenas as much as across the wider public. Indeed, a variegated network of extreme- and radical right groups engaging in grassroots extra-parliamentary politics has been at the core of a new wave of xenophobic and social unrest, in the wake of the EU migration policy crisis (Benček and Strasheim 2016; Castelli Gattinara 2018). Even though far-right collective actors like PEGIDA, CasaPound, the Identitarians or the English Defence League have not enjoyed the electoral support that established political parties like the Front National (recently Rassemblement National) or Lega Nord have, they are nonetheless contributing to the ongoing redefinition of liberal democratic values through their unconventional practices.

The notion of hybridization can help make sense of these changes. At a time when the role of ideologies in politics and the related modes of participation are rapidly changing, it is all the more important to understand the balance between continuity and change in far-right politics. Acknowledging continuity means that the contemporary extreme right will not simply reiterate its inter-war manifestations and outmoded styles. Acknowledging change means recognizing that the extreme right has not renounced some of its original features.

The political, social and cultural impacts of these developments represent one of the most pressing challenges in contemporary politics, in Europe and beyond. We maintain that only an in-depth comprehension of the internal workings, organization and strategies of contemporary extreme-right collective actors can improve our understanding of the mechanisms of cultural and value change that they have triggered. The observations included in this volume about CasaPound will thus hopefully serve as a first step for further research into the multiple electoral and non-electoral manifestations of far-right politics that may follow. Through hybridization the far right may adapt to liberal democracy, with the goal of radicalizing mainstream ideas and audiences.

References

Art, D. 2011. *Inside the Radical Right: The Development of Anti-Immigrant Parties in Western Europe*. Cambridge: Cambridge University Press.

Benček, D., and J. Strasheim. 2016. 'Refugees Welcome? A Dataset on Anti-Refugee Violence in Germany', *Research and Politics* 3(4): 1–11.

Betz, H.-G., and S. Immerfall. (eds). 1998. *The New Politics of the Right: Neo-populist Parties and Movements in Established Democracies*. London: Palgrave Macmillan.

Carter, E.L. 2005. *The Extreme Right in Western Europe: Success or Failure?* Manchester: Manchester University Press.

Castelli Gattinara, P. 2018. 'Europeans, Shut the Borders! Anti-Refugee Mobilisation in Italy and France', in D. Della Porta (ed.), *Solidarity Mobilizations in the 'Refugee Crisis'*. London: Palgrave, pp. 271–97.

Castelli Gattinara, P., and A.L.P. Pirro. 2018. 'The Far Right as Social Movement', *European Societies* 0(0): 1–16.

Giugni, M. 2008. 'Political, Biographical, and Cultural Consequences of Social Movements', *Sociology Compass* 2(5): 1582–600.

Hutter, S., and R. Vliegenthart. 2018. 'Who Responds to Protest? Protest Politics and Party Responsiveness in Western Europe', *Party Politics* 24(4): 358–69.

Hutter, S. et al.2018. 'Social Movements in Interaction with Political Parties', in D. A. Snow, et al.(eds), *The Wiley Blackwell Companion to Social Movements*. Hoboken, NJ: John Wiley, pp. 322–37.

Kitschelt, H. 2006. 'Movement Parties', in R.S. Katz and W. Crotty (eds), *Handbook of Party Politics*. Thousand Oaks, CA: Sage, pp. 278–90.

Mosca, L., and M. Quaranta. 2017. 'Voting for Movement Parties in Southern Europe: The Role of Protest and Digital Information', *South European Society and Politics* 22(4): 427–46.

Mudde, C. 2016. *The Populist Radical Right: A Reader*. London: Routledge.

Pirro, A.L.P., and P. Castelli Gattinara. 2018. 'Movement Parties of the Far Right: Organization and Strategies of Nativist Collective Actors', *Mobilization* 23: 367–83.

APPENDICES

Appendix 1: List of interviews

30/3/2012

Interview no. 1a 30.03.2012, Central Italy.

19/4/2012

Interview no. 1b 19.04.2012, Central Italy.
Interview no. 1c 19.04.2012, Central Italy.

27/4/2012

Interview no. 2 27.04.2012, Central Italy.
Interview no. 2a 27.04.2012, Central Italy.
Interview no. 2b 27.04.2012, Central Italy.
Interview no. 2c 27.04.2012, Central Italy.
Interview no. 2d 27.04.2012, Central Italy.

1/6/2012

Interview no. 3a 01.06.2012, Northern Italy.

10/6/2012

Interview no. 3b 10.06.2012, Central Italy.

26/6/2012

Interview no. 5a 26.06.2012, Southern Italy.
Interview no. 5b 26.06.2012, Southern Italy.
Interview no. 5c 26.06.2012, Southern Italy.

28/6/2012

Interview no. 5b 28.06.2012, Southern Italy.
Interview no. 5c 28.06.2012, Southern Italy.

20/9/2012

Interview no. 6a 20.09.2012, Central Italy.
Interview no. 6b 20.09.2012, Central Italy.

Appendix 2: Documentary appendix: internal literature of CasaPound Italia

Borgonovo, F. 2016. *L'Impero dell'islam. Il Sistema che uccide l'Europa*. Milan: Bietti.

Centro Studi La Runa. 'Archivio di storia, tradizione, letteratura, filosofia. Online dal 1998'. URL: https://www.centrostudilaruna.it/(consulted May 2018).

CPI. 2013. 'Sul Fronte dell'essere. Le proposte di CasaPound sull'immigrazione'. URL: https://radiobandieranera.org/sitocasapound/sul-fronte-dellessere-le-proposte-di/(consulted May 2018).

CPI. 2018. 'Una Terribile Bellezza è Nata'. URL: www.casapounditalia.org/la-storia/(consulted April 2019).

CPI. *Fare Quadrato*, internal gazette published quarterly by CasaPound.

CPI. *L'Occidentale, rivista di Casa Pound Italia*, magazine published monthly by CasaPound.

De Benoist, A. 2017. *Minima Moralia. Per un'etica delle virtù*. Milan: Bietti.

De Benoist, A. 2016. *Il valore delle religioni*. Rome: Idrovolante Edizioni.

Di Tullio, D. 2010. *Nessun Dolore. Una Storia di CasaPound*. Milan: Rizzoli.

Di Tullio, D. 2005. *Centri sociali di destra. Occupazioni e culture non conformi*. Rome: Castelvecchi.

Donoso Cortèz, J. 2018. *Contro il Liberalismo*. Rome: Idrovolante Edizioni.

Dugin, A. 2018. *Putin Contro Putin*. Cusano Milanino: AGA Editrice.

Dugin, A. 2018. *L'ultima guerra dell'isola – mondo*. Cusano Milanino: AGA Editrice.

Faye, G. 2017. *Il Sistema per uccidere i popoli*. Cusano Milanino: AGA Editrice.

Francia, S. 1994. *Il pensiero tradizionale di Evola*. Milan: Società Editrice Barbarossa.

Galli, G. 2013. *L'impero antimoderno. La crisi della modernità americana da Clinton a Obama*. Milan: Bietti.

Gentile, G. 1925. *Manifesto degli intellettuali del fascismo*. URL: www.maat.it/livello2/fascismo-manifesto.htm (consulted August 2014).

Il Manifesto di Verona. 1943. Policy document for the government of the Italian Social Republic defining the political objectives of the Fascist Party.

Il Primato Nazionale, online newspaper of CasaPound, URL: www.ilprimatonazionale.it.

'Intervista con Simone Di Stefano', Interview with Simone Di Stefano. 2011. URL: https://www. youtube.com/watch?v=WbQUIQ5m-0Q (consulted February 2014).

La Carta del Lavoro. 1927. Document synthesizing the social principles of Fascism, the doctrine of corporatism, the ethics of Fascist trade unionism and Fascist economic policy.

Mussolini, B. 1933. 'The Political and Social Doctrine of Fascism', first authorized translation into English by Jane Soames. London: Hogarth Press.

Piazzesi, M. 2014. *Diario di Uno Squadrista Toscano*. Cusano Milanino: Aga Editrice.

Pound, E. 1954. *The Cantos*. New York: Columbia University Press.

Scianca, A. 2018. *La Nazione Fatidica. Elogio politico e metafisico dell'Italia*. Rome: Altaforte editore.

Scianca, A. 2017. *Contro l'Eroticamente corretto. Uomini e donne, padri e madri nell'epoca del gender*. Milan: Bietti.

Scianca, A. 2016. *L'identità Sacra. Dèi, popoli e luoghi al tempo della Grande Sostituzione*. Rome: La Testa di Ferro.

Scianca, A. 2013. *Ezra Fa Surf. Come e perché il pensiero di Pound salverà il mondo*. Milan: Zero91 Editore.

Scianca, A. 2011. *Riprendersi tutto. Le parole di CasaPound: 40 concetti per una rivoluzione in atto*. Rome: La Testa di Ferro.

Scianca, A. 2011. 'Braccia sottratte ai Campi … Hobbit', review of G. Tarantini *Da Giovane Europa ai Campi Hobbit* (Controcorrente Editore, 2011). URL: http://robertoalfattiappetiti.blogspot.fr/2011/11/braccia-sottratteai-campi-hobbit-di.html (consulted April 2014).

Tassinari, U.M. 2004. 'I colori del Nero', URL: www.youtube.com/watch?v=KE8VV46_0f0 (consulted February 2013).

Venner, D. 2018. *Per una critica positiva. Scritti di lotta per i militanti*. Florence: Passaggio Al Bosco Edizioni.

VivaMafarka. 2008. 'CasaPound occupa la sede di Fiamma Tricolore'. URL: www.vivamafarka.com/forum/index. php?topic=29274.0 (consulted July 2013).

ZetaZeroAlfa. 2019. 'ZetaZeroAlfa: Testi', song lyrics. URL: http://zetazeroalfa.org/testi/(consulted May 2019).

Appendix 3: The coding of political claims

We assess the nature and forms of CPI's external mobilization using Political Claims Analysis (Hutter 2014), a form of quantitative content analysis.[1] We assess CPI's modes of activism based on media coverage, quantifying the reports of CasaPound's activities in a national quality newspaper, *Il Corriere della Sera* (2004–2015).[2] The units of analysis are instances of 'claims-making', defined as the expression of political opinion by physical or verbal action in the public sphere, thus including both verbal acts, conventional forms and intervention, as well as protests (Koopmans and Statham 1999).[3] We coded data in order to measure the date, location and main topic of each political claim. Given our interest on external mobilization, the codebook distinguishes forms of action in terms of conventional and protest tactics. Conventional activism includes all types of verbal actions (e.g. public statements, interviews and public speeches), as well as lobbying, voting, petitioning and electoral campaigning. Protest action encompasses demonstrative events (such as legal actions and authorized demonstrations), confrontational actions (illegal demonstrations and blockades) and violent action (symbolic or physical violence). In terms of issue content, we use an existing codebook developed by Castelli and Froio 2017 (Castelli Gattinara and Froio 2018b). We distinguish six issue areas (Civil rights, (Commemorations of) Fascism, Immigration, Economy, Europe, and Law & Order). Data have been used in previous publications and are available for duplication upon request to the authors.

Appendix 4: The coding of election manifestos

We examine the content of CPI's electoral supply by using content analysis of party manifestos at general elections (Laver et al. 2003). CPI ran for general elections only in 2013 and 2018. As we are interested in policy emphasis rather than issue positions, we rely on the coding scheme of the Comparative Agendas Project available here: https://www.comparativeagendas.net/. This coding scheme is specifically designed to capture policy attention (Baumgartner et al. 2019). Data are available for duplication upon request to the authors.

Notes

1 For a similar approach see Hänggli and Kriesi's work on input–output strategies of agenda building (2010).

2 Newspaper data were gathered using the *Factiva* database. Mainstream quality papers report more extensively on political matters than other outlets (Druckman and Parkin 2005). While the tone and the logics of information production may change according to the political orientation of a newspaper, there is no significant difference in the likelihood of coverage (Koopmans 2004) as demonstrated in other publications using both centre-right and centre-left oriented quality newspapers (Bouron and Froio 2016; Castelli Gattinara and Froio 2018a).

3 Claims-making as a form of political behaviour implies 'the purposive and public articulation of political demands, calls to action, proposals, criticisms, or physical attacks, which, actually or potentially, affect the interests or integrity of the claimants and/or other collective actors' (Koopmans et al. 2005).

References

Baumgartner, F.R. et al.(eds). 2019. *Comparative Policy Agendas: Theory, Tools, Data.* Oxford: Oxford University Press.

Bouron, S., and C. Froio. 2016. 'Entrer En Politique Par La Bande Médiatique'. Presented at the Global Moral Spectatorship.

Castelli Gattinara, P., and C. Froio. 2018a. 'Quand les identitaires font la une', *Revue française de science politique* 68(1): 103–119.

———. 2018b. 'Getting "Right" into the News: Grassroots Far-Right Mobilization and Media Coverage in Italy and France', *Comparative European Politics* 1–21.

Druckman, J.N., and M. Parkin. 2005. 'The Impact of Media Bias: How Editorial Slant Affects Voters', *Journal of Politics* 67(4): 1030–1049.

Hänggli, R., and H. Kriesi. 2010. 'Political Framing Strategies and Their Impact on Media Framing in a Swiss Direct-Democratic Campaign', *Political Communication* 27(2): 141–157.

Hutter, S. 2014. 'Protest Event Analysis and Its Offspring', *Methodological Practices in Social Movement Research.* Oxford: Oxford University Press, pp. 335–67.

Koopmans, R. 2004. 'Movements and Media: Selection Processes and Evolutionary Dynamics in the Public Sphere', *Theory and Society* 33(3–4): 367–391.

Koopmans, R., and P. Statham. 1999. 'Political Claims Analysis: Integrating Protest Event and Political Discourse Approaches', *Mobilization: An International Quarterly* 4(2): 203–221.

Koopmans, R. et al.2005. *Contested Citizenship: Immigration and Cultural Diversity in Europe.* Minneapolis: University of Minnesota Press.

Laver, M. et al.2003. 'Extracting Policy Positions from Political Texts Using Words as Data', *American Political Science Review* 97(2): 311–331.

INDEX

Printed in Great Britain
by Amazon

16539770R00099